Genes

A New Start with God

Harold J Booth

'Genesis' A new start with God

ISBN 978-1-910693-00-1

First Published 2009 by
Berforts Group Limited

Printed and bound in Great Britain by
Print2Demand Ltd
Westoning

CONTENTS

FOREWORD TO THE FIRST EDITION

BY DR DEREK STRINGER

Do you ever feel like your life is sort of spinning out of control in some kind of chaos? Maybe it's financial, career, relational or health chaos. Or, maybe it's not chaos you're dealing with but almost the opposite, there's emptiness in your life. Maybe it's a marriage that feels dead, or you long for a good friend but you don't have one, or maybe you're a little bored with life. Or, maybe you're just down on yourself, and you feel, "I'm just a mistake," and you keep trying to fill your life with activities, entertainment, or buying things for the temporary thrill of it.

Whether it is chaos in your life, or a void in your life, either way Genesis has good news for you. God is the God who both orders the chaos in our lives, and fills the void. God doesn't just create. God creates with redemption in mind. If God can do that with the universe, well then, what can He do with the chaos or void in our life? Is there darkness in our life? He can fill it with light. God can fill that void with meaning, joy, more than enough, with plenty left over, so that we can thrive. Real strength comes from the security of knowing I am not a mistake. I am a child of God and redeemed in Jesus Christ. He made me. He died for me. He loves me. I have worth. No one can change that.

Harold Booth does a good job at getting the message of Genesis from head to heart. The truths of his book will inform and transform. There is no darkness in our life so dark that God can't bring light to it, no void so empty that He can't fill it, no suffering so great that He can't comfort it, no pit so deep that He can't raise us out of it, no burden so heavy He can't lift it, and no sorrow so sharp He can't give us joy.

We were born not just to exist, not just to survive. God made us to thrive, with purpose, abundance, and joy, more than enough with plenty left over, until we say, "Do it again, God.

Do it again." And God will say, "It is good. And you, my daughter, you my son, you are very good."

Derek Stringer
National Director

Good News Broadcasting Association (GB)
Ranskill, Retford,
Nottinghamshire.
DN22 8NN, England, UK.

FOREWORD TO THE SECOND EDITION

Some ten years have passed since the First Edition was published. Copies are no longer available.

In this Second Edition, we have quoted the chapters from the NIV before commenting on them.

To keep this book within some two hundred and fifty pages, we have omitted the Notes and Appendicies included in the First Edition. Feedback was conflicting. Some said that they were of assistance to them. Others considered they were not needed to explain the text.

We have also changed the format to make this Second Edition easier to read, and revised the text to make it applicable to believers and those who are not yet believers.

There is little doubt that a good knowledge of Genesis greatly assists Bible Study, as this first book of The Bible introduces us to the essential subject of sin, and God's desire to forgive those who sin against Him and restore them to fellowship with Him. Genesis helps us to understand why Jesus had to die and be raised from the dead so that our sins could be forgiven, and God could offer His Salvation to those who repented of their sins and accepted Jesus as their personal Saviour.

The author wishes to thank his sister and brother-in-law, Joan and John Pickbourne, retired missionaries who worked in France for many years, for their helpful suggestions and for proof reading the First Edition. Errors in this Second Edition remain my responsibility.

This Second Edition is published with our prayer that it will be of spiritual value to those who read it.

Harold J Booth,
Greater Manchester,
United Kingdom.

NOTICES AND COPYRIGHT NOTICE

The views and opinions expressed in this book are those of the author.

INTENTION, NOTES AND SUGGESTIONS

This book contains comments that should provoke all who read it to consider the events recorded and their own personal relationship to the God who created the world and yet wishes to be involved in and bless the daily lives of His creatures.

Chapters of this book may be published separately. Hence some matters may be mentioned in more than one chapter. This is particularly so where incidents in the chapter illustrate God's Salvation or give warning about the consequences that ensue when God's Offer of Salvation is rejected.

We have used a capital letter for every reference to God. As you will read in the Introduction, in Genesis, there are different Names used by God to refer to Himself. To simplify our text, we only use the Name 'God.' Also, important words, such as Salvation have a capital letter to show that they are vital to an understanding of the message that God has for us today.

The text of this book is written in English (UK) but where we have quoted from The Bible, we have used various translations that we mention in the text. For copyright reasons, we use the capitalisations, spellings and punctuation of The Bibles we quote from. Hence, there will be a difference in the capitalisations, the spellings of words and the grammar used in the text of this book and in The Bibles we quote from. The main difference is that in the text we have:

- capitalised words referring to God.
- included 'u' in words like 'colour.'
- used 's' instead of 'z' in words like 'realise.'

In Genesis there are fifty chapters and some chapters contain lists of family histories known as genealogies. While these are important for experienced Bible students, a study of them will take a considerable number of weeks, if not years. It is suggested that you do not study the genealogies so that you will be able to read Genesis in hours. Spiritually, it will be more profitable to study the remainder of The Bible before specialising in a study of genealogies.

Do not assume that the chapters or the stories in Genesis are in historical or chronological order.

Where there is repetition, it could be that God wants to highlight a truth or tell the story from a different perspective or viewpoint.

INTRODUCTION TO GENESIS

Genesis means 'beginnings.' In the fifty chapters of this first book of The Bible we can read:

- about the creation of the Earth and life.
- where sin on the Earth originated.
- how sin changed what God had planned for man.

We can discover the history of the first man and woman and their immediate family and descendants, and the history of God's ancient people, known today as 'the Jews.'

We can find out why:

- we die when God made us to live forever.
- man, and many animals are no longer vegetarians.
- man lives in different parts of the world and speaks different languages.

Most importantly, we can see the beginnings of God's Plan of Salvation and how that although man sinned and continues to sin against God, God has always desired that man should repent and return to Him, so that his sins may be forgiven.

In Genesis we read the histories of real people. We read how they behaved and how God dealt with them. Remember that:

- when Jesus was preaching and teaching, He referred to and confirmed that Adam and Noah were real people. He accepted Genesis as being accurate.
- Jesus came to Earth to die to save man from sin and God's judgment and restore him to the fellowship that Adam enjoyed with God before Adam sinned.
- the histories of Adam and Noah and their families show that although God hates sin, God is willing to forgive sinners and provide a way of Salvation from His judgment.
- repenting sinners can have 'A New Start with God.'

The writers of The Old and New Testaments also accepted Genesis as historically true. However, there are many who consider that Genesis is a book of myths. It suits them to believe this because they can, but only for the time being, ignore sin's consequences.

In Genesis we read about:

- The sinful nature of the first man, Adam.
- The consequences of Adam's sin against God.

Adam's sinful nature has been passed from generation to generation. Hence, no one needs to be taught how to sin. But despite this evidence that proves we are all born with a sinful nature, those who reject what Genesis teaches us, also reject what The Bible teaches. It is only by knowing the truth and believing it that we can escape God's eternal punishment for our sin and live eternally in Heaven.

What do we learn about God from Genesis? In Chapter 1 He is referred to as 'God.' In Chapter 2 He is referred to as 'the Lord God.' There are more than ten thousand references to God in The Bible. The most frequent Name used for God is 'Lord.' It means 'The Eternal One.' Although we cannot in the space available in this book explain the different meanings of God's Names, you should be aware that God uses His Names as a way of revealing Himself. As you read Genesis you will realise that it is God's desire that everyone should come to know Him, not only as their Creator, but as their Saviour. Despite our sin, God is loving and gracious. He desires only our blessing both now and for eternity.

A PERSONAL WORD TO READERS

As you read Genesis, keep in mind that the eternal all-powerful God of creation loves you. If you are a believer, you belong to Him and all His blessings are available to you. If you are not yet a believer, God loves you and wants to save and bless you. But we must state that when God made man, He gave him freedom of choice. We can choose:

- what to do and what we do not want to do.
- our own eternal destiny.

We are not robots. We can choose to accept or reject God's Offer of Salvation. If we reject it, we forfeit the eternal bliss of Heaven and, as there is no alternative, we choose Hell and The Lake of Fire as our eternal destiny.

WHAT WILL YOU LEARN IN GENESIS?

You will not read all you might want to know about the beginnings of the Universe, Earth or man. You will read what God wants you to know. God has hinted elsewhere in The Bible that there were periods of time before the Earth was created, but we cannot comment on these in this book.

We concentrate on what God has told us in Genesis and ignore speculation on what He has chosen not to tell us. This avoids us mentioning less important matters. We can then give our attention to considering why our sin has either to be forgiven or punished, and why God has left that decision to us.

GENESIS CHAPTER 1

In the beginning God created the heavens and the earth. (2) Now the earth was formless and empty, darkness was over the surface of the deep, and the Spirit of God was hovering over the waters. (3) And God said, "Let there be light," and there was light. (4) God saw that the light was good, and he separated the light from the darkness. (5) God called the light "day," and the darkness he called "night." And there was evening, and there was morning—the first day. (6) And God said, "Let there be a vault between the waters to separate water from water." (7) So God made the vault and separated the water under the vault from the water above it. And it was so. (8) God called the vault "sky." And there was evening, and there was morning—the second day. (9) And God said, "Let the water under the sky be gathered to one place, and let dry ground appear." And it was so. (10) God called the dry ground "land," and the gathered waters he called "seas." And God saw that it was good. (11) Then God said, "Let the land produce vegetation: seed-bearing plants and trees on the land that bear fruit with seed in it, according to their various kinds." And it was so. (12) The land produced vegetation: plants bearing seed according to their kinds and trees bearing fruit with seed in it according to their kinds. And God saw that it was good. (13) And there was evening, and there was morning—the third day. (14) And God said, "Let there be lights in the vault of the sky to separate the day from the night, and let them serve as signs to mark sacred times, and days and years, (15) and let them be lights in the vault of the sky to give light on the earth." And it was so. (16) God made two great lights—the greater light to govern the day and the lesser light to govern the night. He also made the stars. (17) God set them in the vault of the sky to give light on the earth, (18) to govern the day and the night, and to separate light from darkness. And God saw that it was good. (19) And there was evening, and there was morning—the fourth day. (20) And

God said, "Let the water teem with living creatures, and let birds fly above the earth across the vault of the sky." (21) So God created the great creatures of the sea and every living thing with which the water teems and that moves about in it, according to their kinds, and every winged bird according to its kind. And God saw that it was good. (22) God blessed them and said, "Be fruitful and increase in number and fill the water in the seas, and let the birds increase on the earth." (23) And there was evening, and there was morning—the fifth day. (24) And God said, "Let the land produce living creatures according to their kinds: the livestock, the creatures that move along the ground, and the wild animals, each according to its kind." And it was so. (25) God made the wild animals according to their kinds, the livestock according to their kinds, and all the creatures that move along the ground according to their kinds. And God saw that it was good. (26) Then God said, "Let us make mankind in our image, in our likeness, so that they may rule over the fish in the sea and the birds in the sky, over the livestock and all the wild animals, and over all the creatures that move along the ground." (27) So God created mankind in his own image, in the image of God he created them; male and female he created them. (28) God blessed them and said to them, "Be fruitful and increase in number; fill the earth and subdue it. Rule over the fish in the sea and the birds in the sky and over every living creature that moves on the ground." (29) Then God said, "I give you every seed-bearing plant on the face of the whole earth and every tree that has fruit with seed in it. They will be yours for food. (30) And to all the beasts of the earth and all the birds in the sky and all the creatures that move along the ground—everything that has the breath of life in it—I give every green plant for food." And it was so. (31) God saw all that he had made, and it was very good. And there was evening, and there was morning—the sixth day.

COMMENTARY. GENESIS CHAPTER 1

It is important to note that Genesis 1 begins and ends with the clear and emphatic statement that God was the Creator of the heavens and the Earth.

- Genesis 1:1. '... God created the heavens and the earth.'
- Genesis 1:31. 'God saw all that he had made …'

God has chosen to tell us about the creation in simple words that we can understand. The word 'create' means to make something out of nothing. Man can only make something out of existing materials, but God made the heavens and the Earth out of nothing. The vast majority of us are not scientific geniuses. If God had disclosed how He made something out of nothing, how many of us, if any, would understand what God actually did? Could it be we have all that God intends to disclose to us? The answer is "Yes." In Hebrews, one of The New Testament letters, it states that we require faith to understand how the universe was formed. We read:

'By faith we understand that the universe was formed at God's command, so that what is seen was not made out of what was visible.' Hebrews 11:3. NIV.

The word 'we' in Hebrews 11:3 refers to believers. Thus, readers are in two categories. Those who:

- have faith and believe what God says.
- do not have faith and do not believe what God says.

There is no third category made up of those who are not sure. Never minimise how important our faith is to God.

The brevity and simplicity of the creation narrative prepares us for reading The Bible. In The Bible, in simple words, is all that we need to know. Consider God's 'Offer of Salvation' that we read, variously worded, many times in The Bible. Many in the world are not educated and cannot read. So, The Gospel is presented in The Bible in simple terms that can be passed on by word-of-mouth anywhere and everywhere to everyone. No academic or other ability is required to pass on the message of The Gospel or to believe it.

We can all understand that although we have sinned against God, He has made His Salvation available to us through the death, burial and resurrection of Jesus.

Jesus accepted God's punishment for our sins when He was crucified.

As we read Genesis, we realise that we do not need to be geniuses to understand it. Hence, in Genesis1:1 we read that there was a point in time when God created the heavens and the Earth. We are not told when it was. We only know that it was the beginning of God's work of creation.

We are told what God did over a period of six 'days' or 'periods of time.' For the sake of simplicity, we refer to 'days.' We are not told, so we must not assume, that the events of Genesis 1:2-31 followed immediately after the events in Genesis 1:1, or if an unknown period elapsed between them. The same applies to Genesis 1:2 and Genesis 1:3.

DAY 1: From the empty waste, the darkness, and the waters over which The Spirit of God was hovering, God's first command was for light to shine. God divided the light from the darkness and this resulted in the first day and night:

- God did His work in the light.
- We read in The Bible that there is no darkness in God. We refer to this again in connection with truth and error.

DAY 2: Having created the materials, God formed them to make the sky. Various words are used to describe what God did during this period. We must distinguish between:

- God creating something out of nothing.
- God forming or making something out of materials He had previously created.

DAY 3: God made the land, oceans and seas. On the land God put plants and trees with the ability to propagate. Everything God made was intended to last.

DAY 4: God made the Sun, Moon and stars to rule the day and night and to distinguish seasons, days and years. There was light and darkness before Day 4, but thereafter the Sun, Moon and stars gave light to the Earth. The Sun and Moon ruled the day and night, dividing the light from the darkness.

DAY 5: God created fish and birds that had the ability to breed.

DAY 6: God made animals, both domestic and wild, reptiles, and finally man. There is more information in Genesis 2 as to how God made man. God put man in charge of the things that He had created or made during Days 5 and 6 and specified what man could eat. Note the change of language as to what God did on Day 6:

- Prior to God making man we read that God said, "Let ..." and what He commanded happened.
- When God made man, He added the word "Us." He said, "Let Us ..."
- God also mentioned creating man in "Our image or likeness." We would say today "like ourselves."

So, we know that God is not a singular God. We read in:

- Genesis 1:2 of 'The Spirit of God.'
- Genesis 1:26 the words 'Us' and 'Our.'

In The Bible, God chooses to refer to Himself in the singular and so in this chapter, as in The Bible, we read 'God' and not 'Gods.' We learn more about this truth in The Bible as God introduces us to 'The Trinity.'

As we come to the end of our study of Day 6, note that God reviewed His work and He approved it. God's verdict was that "it was good." Note also God's final comment after He had made man and concluded His work of creation. God said, "it was very good." We will discover in Genesis 3 why things went from being 'very good' to the awful condition we see worldwide today.

GENESIS CHAPTER 2

Thus the heavens and the earth were completed in all their vast array. (2) By the seventh day God had finished the work he had been doing; so on the seventh day he rested from all his work. (3) Then God blessed the seventh day and made it holy, because on it he rested from all the work of creating that he had done. (4) This is the account of the heavens and the earth when they were created, when the LORD God made the earth and the heavens. (5) Now no shrub had yet appeared on the earth and no plant had yet sprung up, for the LORD God had not sent rain on the earth and there was no one to work the ground, (6) but streams came up from the earth and watered the whole surface of the ground. (7) Then the LORD God formed a man from the dust of the ground and breathed into his nostrils the breath of life, and the man became a living being. (8) Now the LORD God had planted a garden in the east, in Eden; and there he put the man he had formed. 9) The LORD God made all kinds of trees grow out of the ground—trees that were pleasing to the eye and good for food. In the middle of the garden were the tree of life and the tree of the knowledge of good and evil. (10) A river watering the garden flowed from Eden; from there it was separated into four headwaters. (11) The name of the first is the Pishon; it winds through the entire land of Havilah, where there is gold. (12) (The gold of that land is good; aromatic resin and onyx are also there.) (13) The name of the second river is the Gihon; it winds through the entire land of Cush. (14) The name of the third river is the Tigris; it runs along the east side of Ashur. And the fourth river is the Euphrates. (15) The LORD God took the man and put him in the Garden of Eden to work it and take care of it. (16) And the LORD God commanded the man, "You are free to eat from any tree in the garden; (17) but you must not eat from the tree of the knowledge of good and evil, for when you eat from it you will certainly die."(18) The LORD God said, "It is not good for the man to be alone. I will make a helper suitable for him." (19) Now the LORD God had formed out of the ground all the wild animals and all the birds in the sky. He brought them to the man to see what he would name them; and whatever the man called each living creature, that was its name. (20) So the man gave names to all the livestock, the birds in the sky and all the wild animals. But for Adam no suitable helper was found. (21) So the LORD God caused the man to fall into a deep sleep; and while he was sleeping, he took one of the man's ribs and then closed up the place with flesh. (22) Then the LORD God made a woman from the rib he had taken out of the man, and he brought her to the man. (23) The man said, "This is now bone of my bones and flesh of my flesh; she shall be called 'woman,' for she was taken out of man." (24) That is why a man leaves his father and mother and is united to his wife, and they become one flesh. (25) Adam and his wife were both naked, and they felt no shame.

COMMENTARY. GENESIS CHAPTER 2

The fact that God rested or ceased working on Day 7, and declared it to be a special day, is often referred to in The Bible. God was not tired. God never tires but we do when we work. So, God made one day of the week 'work-free' so that we could rest from physical toil and use the day for spiritual purposes. The Law of Moses, often called 'The Ten Commandments,' Jesus, and some New Testament writers all refer to one day of the week being of special significance to God and to us.

In Genesis 2 we read more details of creation. God is now referred to as 'Lord God.' Bible names have significant meaning whether applied to God or man. A number of Names, e.g., Creator, Almighty One and Redeemer, refer to God. They describe different aspects of His Person:

- God made man and God is entitled to our reverence.
- God loves us individually and He is interested in our lives.

The truth that God loves us becomes even more wonderful when we realise that God knows all about us. Who would claim to be worthy of God's love?

We might have wondered how the plants and trees were watered before Day 6 and we now read about the mist.

We are told how God made Adam and Eve, the first man and woman, and placed them in The Garden of Eden. What do we read about Adam and Eve and this garden?

- It was their home and workplace. God intended that Adam should work in the garden and not live an idle existence.
- Note the geographical references to the garden. It was a real garden for a real man and woman. It was also a perfect garden made by a perfect God.
- We read about the trees later.
- Adam and Eve were not told they could do as they pleased in the garden. Adam was expected to work for his food. He was told what he could and could not eat.

God told Adam that he could eat the fruit of all the trees in the garden except one. Adam was also told what would happen if he was disobedient. Note Adam's knowledge:

- He knew which tree produced 'the forbidden fruit.'
- He knew that eating this fruit would teach him the difference between good and evil.
- Although Adam did not know what evil was, he knew that if he disobeyed what God had said, he would die. In Genesis 3 we will read about the disastrous events that took place when Adam chose to disobey God.

Adam was made from the soil, as were the animals and the birds. Once God had formed his body and God had breathed life into him, Adam began to live. If Adam had not sinned, he would be alive today. The breath of life from God was not given to the animals, fish and birds. That is what has always distinguished man from the rest of creation. We read how a woman was made from Adam's rib. She was not called Eve until sin came into the world. For the sake of simplicity, we call her Eve from the day that she was made.

- God wanted Adam to rule the animals and the birds and God gave him the task of naming them. When God formed man from the dust, man was wonderfully made.
- We will never know how much man has lost of his original God-given dignity and ability because Adam disobeyed God and sinned.

It was only when God made a woman for him that Adam recognised how suitable she was to be his wife. God was teaching Adam and Eve then, and us today, that marriage is part of God's plan for mankind and that the sexual differences between men and women are part of a marriage relationship.

GENESIS CHAPTER 3

Now the serpent was more crafty than any of the wild animals the LORD God had made. He said to the woman, "Did God really say, 'You must not eat from any tree in the garden'?" (2) The woman said to the serpent, "We may eat fruit from the trees in the garden, (3) but God did say, 'You must not eat fruit from the tree that is in the middle of the garden, and you must not touch it, or you will die.'" (4) "You will not certainly die," the serpent said to the woman. (5) "For God knows that when you eat from it your eyes will be opened, and you will be like God, knowing good and evil." (6) When the woman saw that the fruit of the tree was good for food and pleasing to the eye, and also desirable for gaining wisdom, she took some and ate it. She also gave some to her husband, who was with her, and he ate it. (7) Then the eyes of both of them were opened, and they realized they were naked; so they sewed fig leaves together and made coverings for themselves. (8) Then the man and his wife heard the sound of the LORD God as he was walking in the garden in the cool of the day, and they hid from the LORD God among the trees of the garden. 9) But the LORD God called to the man, "Where are you?" (10) He answered, "I heard you in the garden, and I was afraid because I was naked; so I hid." (11) And he said, "Who told you that you were naked? Have you eaten from the tree that I commanded you not to eat from?" (12) The man said, "The woman you put here with me—she gave me some fruit from the tree, and I ate it."(13) Then the LORD God said to the woman, "What is this you have done?" The woman said, "The serpent deceived me, and I ate." (14) So the LORD God said to the serpent, "Because you have done this, "Cursed are you above all livestock and all wild animals! You will crawl on your belly and you will eat dust all the days of your life. (15) And I will put enmity between you and the woman, and between your offspring and hers; he will crush your head, and you will strike his heel." (16) To the woman he said, "I will make your pains in childbearing very severe; with painful labor you will give birth to children. Your desire will be for your husband, and he will rule over you." (17) To Adam he said, "Because you listened to your wife and ate fruit from the tree about which I commanded you, 'You must not eat from it,' "Cursed is the ground because of you; through painful toil you will eat food from it all the days of your life. (18) It will produce thorns and thistles for you, and you will eat the plants of the field. (19) By the sweat of your brow you will eat your food until you return to the ground, since from it you were taken; for dust you are and to dust you will return." (20) Adam named his wife Eve, because she would become the mother of all the living. (21) The LORD God made garments of skin for Adam and his wife and clothed them. (22) And the LORD God said, "The man has now become like one of us, knowing good and evil. He must not be allowed to reach out his hand and take also from the tree of life and eat, and live forever." (23) So the LORD God banished him from the Garden of Eden to work the ground from which he had been taken. (24) After he drove the man out, he placed on the east side of the Garden of Eden cherubim and a flaming sword flashing back and forth to guard the way to the tree of life.

COMMENTARY. GENESIS CHAPTER 3

We have read in Genesis of wonderful events and things that we find very difficult to visualise when we look at the world today. What happened to bring about such a dramatic change? The answer is found in Genesis 3. God does not give us every detail, but He has told us sufficient for us to know how sin entered into this world.

We read about the person and work of Satan, also called 'the Devil.' We read other names for him in The Bible. We learn:

- who he is.
- where he came from.
- what he has done in the past and what he does now.
- his final act of rebellion and his eternal punishment.

Satan used a serpent, a snake that lives by being cunning, to pass a message to Eve. Consider the events:

- The serpent spoke Satan's words to Eve. She knew God's command about the trees and their fruit and what could and could not be eaten. Satan wanted Eve to doubt what God had said. He asked her a question and told the first lie. Eve had never heard a lie before.
- Eve told the serpent what God said, but she added words that God did not say. God said, "Do not eat ..." Eve added, "or touch." God never mentioned touching the fruit.

Satan challenged what God said about dying and accused God of lying. Satan promised Eve that if she ate the fruit, she would become as wise as God and know good and evil. It is important that we understand what Satan did because we mention in Genesis 49 what Satan is doing now. You will not be surprised to learn that he still deceives men and women into believing error and lies.

Eve made three serious mistakes. She should have:

1. rejected the serpent's lies and believed God.
2. recalled that God loved and blessed her and Adam.
3. told Adam what the serpent said and sought his guidance.

What did Eve do that enabled Satan to deceive her? She:

- relied on her own opinion.
- wanted to be wise.
- wanted to know about good and evil.

What Eve and Adam did discover was that:

- the serpent was correct. They could recognise good and evil. However, they both found it:
  - impossible to do good and impossible not to sin.
  - easy to sin and hard to do good.

Although made by God perfect, they became sinners.

Satan did not discuss the matter with Adam. Adam was not deceived. What did he do wrong? He:

- chose to disobey God.
- knew Eve should not have eaten the fruit, but he decided to do the same.
- chose allegiance to Eve rather than obedience to God.

Question: What were the consequences for Adam and Eve?

Answer: They immediately knew that they were naked. They were afraid. We know that this was no gradual realisation of guilt because they chose a quick and temporary solution. They made clothes out of fig leaves.

In The Bible we discover that there is a gulf between:

- man's ingenuity to solve his sin problem.
- God's answer to man's sin problem.

What do we read?

- They were afraid. They had the problem of meeting a holy God and explaining why they had been disobedient.
- They decided to avoid the problem by hiding. Their solution failed. They had to come out of hiding and face God.

Read the excuses that Adam and Eve made to God in a futile attempt to explain away their sin:

- Adam blamed Eve and He even thought of blaming God because God had given Eve to him.
- Eve blamed the serpent.

Adam and Eve did not blame themselves. Little has changed over the years. We make excuses for our sin. We fail to admit our sin to God, and do not seek God's forgiveness. We choose to blame someone or something else.

Consider the punishments and the curses. God punished the serpent, Eve and Adam. They had brought sin into God's perfect creation. The order in which God dealt with them was the same as their involvement:

- The serpent and the ground were cursed. The serpent would have to grovel and eat dirt. There would be enmity between serpents and man. We read God's reference to 'the serpent's head' and 'mans' heel.'
- Adam and Eve were not cursed. However, woman would have severe pain in childbirth and be subject to man's authority.
- The Bible mentions the sins that Satan had committed before Creation, and the eternal punishment that God had already reserved for him.
- Man would work hard to produce food from the ground.

- Men and women would now die and return to the ground from which they had been made.

Adam and Eve were expelled from their perfect home in the garden where they had enjoyed God's fellowship. They could never return to the garden. They now knew good and evil and were in the process of dying. They were now barred from the tree of life that was in the garden. This tree was now securely guarded. They had lost both their fellowship with God and eternal life. They were now sinners.

Because God is loving and merciful, He did not leave them without ensuring that they were properly clothed. God made animal skin coats. To provide cover and protection for these two sinners, the blood of animals had to be shed.

The 'shedding of blood' is a subject of great importance that we read in Genesis and throughout The Bible.

Consider what Adam and Eve learned the day they sinned:

1. They were answerable to God for their sin. They could not hide from Him.
2. They became aware of good and evil.
3. They became afraid of God because they had sinned.
4. Satan was a deceiving liar. He wanted them to sin. He wanted them to lose the blessings that a loving and gracious God had planned for them for eternity.
5. God did not lie. Hence, what God said He would do He did. This applied to both His blessings and His punishment.

IMPORTANT NOTES TO READERS

- Blood had to be shed to provide the coats that hid Adam's and Eve's nakedness and shame.
- Adam and Eve lost their eternal life by sinning and they would never get it back from the tree of life.

- God told Adam and Eve that the day would come when a Man would bruise the serpent's head. We now know from The Bible that God was referring to Jesus because He was victorious over Satan when He died and rose again. It became possible for sinners to receive God's Salvation, and in particular, eternal Life.

Because we do not want to mislead readers, we must be blunt and state that only a minority will regain the eternal life that man lost by sinning against God.

To support what we have written, we quote what Jesus said. Those who read The Gospels will probably know these words. Sadly, few will have heard a preacher mention them.

The AV was first printed in 1611. Hence, English speaking readers should have been fully aware of Jesus' words for centuries. If they are not familiar to you, we ask that you read them carefully. Space limitations preclude us from referring to Jesus' other teaching on this subject, but these words, that we quote from the AV, are crystal clear:

Jesus said: '"Enter ye in at the strait gate: for wide is the gate, and broad is the way, that leadeth to destruction, and many there be which go in thereat: Because strait is the gate, and narrow is the way, which leadeth unto life, and few there be that find it."' Matthew 7:13-14. AV.

Jesus said that many are on the broad way that leads to destruction. Only a few have found and are on the narrow way that leads to life. We ask and answer two questions that we trust you will find helpful:

Question 1: Is the narrow way reserved for a select few?

Question 2: Is it possible for those on the broad way to transfer to the narrow way?

Answers: We do not need to use our own words to answer these two questions. We only need quote John 3:16. We ask you to study John's words before you continue reading:

'For God so loved the world, that he gave his only begotten Son, that whosoever believeth in him should not perish, but have everlasting life.' John 3:16. AV.

We have once again quoted from the AV. Like Jesus' words printed above from Matthew 7:13-14, the words in John 3:16 were printed over 400 years ago, but experience proves that:

- few have read them.
- few have heard a preacher mention them.

We know why the truths in Matthew 7:13-14 and John 3:16 are not preached. Consider what they have in common:

- Jesus mentioned the word 'destruction' and contrasted it with the word 'life.'
- John mentioned the word 'perish' and contrasted it with the words 'everlasting life.'

People do not want to hear that they are perishing and on the way to 'destruction.' They rightly associate the words with Hell and judgment. So, even if they do not use The Bible to support what they say, churchgoers and non-churchgoers want preachers to say that everyone will be in Heaven.

We repeat our two questions and explain our answers:

Question 1: Is the narrow way reserved for a select few? Answer 1: "No."

Question 2: Is it possible for those on the broad way to transfer to the narrow way? Answer 2: "Yes."

Those on the narrow way leading to life were not born on it. They were born on the broad way leading to destruction but, they believed The Gospel. Many showed no interest in it and rejected it because they enjoyed their sin and sinning.

Only those on the broad road who wanted to have their sins forgiven believed The Gospel. They repented of their sins and changed their lifestyle because they believed that Jesus had suffered for their sins when He was crucified, and He had risen from the dead. They accepted Jesus as their Saviour. They received God's eternal Salvation. Their repentance and belief has enabled God to forgive them and regard them as justified, that is, God regards them as if they had never sinned. They now travel on the narrow way that leads to life.

Few respond to The Gospel but John 3:16 states, 'whosoever believeth in him.' Those on the narrow way leading to life have done what anyone and everyone can do. But, we have to be frank and state that experience over 60 years teaches that few are prepared to do it. The vast majority want to remain on the broad way. We repeat that 'they love their sin and sinning.' The broad way has to be 'broad' because there are so many on their way to destruction. By way of contrast, the 'narrow way' accommodates the few travelling to everlasting life.

We revert to the history of Adam and Eve. It was only when they were expelled from the garden that Adam gave his wife the name 'Eve.' God had said that Eve would bring children into the world. Eve means 'the mother of all mankind.'

The Bible tells us that one day there will be a new Heaven and a new Earth. Then God's curse on the ground will cease.

GENESIS CHAPTER 4

Adam made love to his wife Eve, and she became pregnant and gave birth to Cain. She said, "With the help of the LORD I have brought forth a man."(2) Later she gave birth to his brother Abel. Now Abel kept flocks, and Cain worked the soil.(3) In the course of time Cain brought some of the fruits of the soil as an offering to the LORD.(4) And Abel also brought an offering—fat portions from some of the firstborn of his flock. The LORD looked with favor on Abel and his offering, (5) but on Cain and his offering he did not look with favor. So Cain was very angry, and his face was downcast. (6) Then the LORD said to Cain, "Why are you angry? Why is your face downcast? (7) If you do what is right, will you not be accepted? But if you do not do what is right, sin is crouching at your door;

it desires to have you, but you must rule over it." (8) Now Cain said to his brother Abel, "Let's go out to the field." While they were in the field, Cain attacked his brother Abel and killed him. (9) Then the LORD said to Cain, "Where is your brother Abel?" "I don't know," he replied. "Am I my brother's keeper?" (10) The LORD said, "What have you done? Listen! Your brother's blood cries out to me from the ground. (11) Now you are under a curse and driven from the ground, which opened its mouth to receive your brother's blood from your hand. (12) When you work the ground, it will no longer yield its crops for you. You will be a restless wanderer on the earth." (13) Cain said to the LORD, "My punishment is more than I can bear. (14) Today you are driving me from the land, and I will be hidden from your presence; I will be a restless wanderer on the earth, and whoever finds me will kill me." (15) But the LORD said to him, "Not so; anyone who kills Cain will suffer vengeance seven times over." Then the LORD put a mark on Cain so that no one who found him would kill him. (16) So Cain went out from the LORD's presence and lived in the land of Nod, east of Eden. (17) Cain made love to his wife, and she became pregnant and gave birth to Enoch. Cain was then building a city, and he named it after his son Enoch. (18) To Enoch was born Irad, and Irad was the father of Mehujael, and Mehujael was the father of Methushael, and Methushael was the father of Lamech. (19) Lamech married two women, one named Adah and the other Zillah. (20) Adah gave birth to Jabal; he was the father of those who live in tents and raise livestock. (21) His brother's name was Jubal; he was the father of all who play stringed instruments and pipes. (22) Zillah also had a son, Tubal-Cain, who forged all kinds of tools out of bronze and iron. Tubal-Cain's sister was Naamah. (23) Lamech said to his wives, "Adah and Zillah, listen to me; wives of Lamech, hear my words. I have killed a man for wounding me, a young man for injuring me. (24) If Cain is avenged seven times, then Lamech seventy-seven times." (25) Adam made love to his wife again, and she gave birth to a son and named him Seth, saying, "God has granted me another child in place of Abel, since Cain killed him." (26) Seth also had a son, and he named him Enosh. At that time people began to call on the name of the LORD.

COMMENTARY. GENESIS CHAPTER 4

This chapter records some of the events that occurred in the lifetime of Adam and Eve, after the birth of their first son, Cain and it covers some events that occurred during the lifetime of Seth, the third son of Adam and Eve. As mentioned earlier, we only know what God has chosen to tell us. When Cain was born, although he was only a baby, Eve called him a man. Was she thinking that Cain was the Man, the Saviour, that God had promised would be born and one day bruise the serpent's head? We do not know, but in view of Cain's subsequent sinful behaviour, it must have become obvious to Eve that Cain was not the Saviour that God had promised. We now know that God referred to Jesus.

As we read this chapter, we soon realise that sin had quickly shown its ability to cause havoc and misery. The first child born grew up to become the first murderer. He killed Abel his brother. Let us ask questions that might assist us to understand why this heinous crime occurred:

- Did the arrogant Cain murder Abel because Abel humbled himself and brought a sacrifice to God that acknowledged he was a sinner seeking forgiveness from a loving and gracious God?
- Did the sacrifice of Abel's lambs signify that he knew he deserved only death for his sin, but that innocent blood had been shed that enabled God to forgive him?

Had Adam and Eve told their sons that innocent blood had been shed so that God could clothe them when, because of their sin, they hid from Him in the garden and realised for the first time that they were naked? We do not know but, we do know that what Abel did was acceptable to God.

Note the contrast between the attitudes of Abel and Cain. Cain brought to God the fruit of the ground that God had cursed when Adam and Eve sinned. What was Cain's objective?

Question 1: Did Cain want God to see how good he was at farming the ground that God had cursed?

Answer: Probably.

Question 2: What did Cain do about his sin and sinful ways?

Answer: Nothing, absolutely nothing.

Question 3: Why would God not accept Cain's offering?

Answer: It was based on Cain's own good works.

Even though Cain was proud and arrogant, note how a loving and a gracious God dealt with him. In The Bible you will discover these truths about God:

- God hates sin but He loves sinners.
- God is merciful to those who are willing to repent.
- God delights in forgiving repentant sinners.

Experience teaches that God is more willing to forgive than sinners are to be forgiven. Cain is an example of this truth. God told Cain how he, like Abel, could be accepted:

- God told Cain what he must do.
- Cain refused the offer of forgiveness.
- God warned Cain that his sin would increase.
- Cain ignored the warning.
- Secretly, so Cain thought, he murdered his brother Abel.
- Cain's response to God showed his contempt for God.

Cain discovered four important truths about God:

1. God sees and knows everything.
2. God knows our open and our secret sins.

3. God knows when blood is shed.

4. God must punish unforgiven sin.

Many think that God ignores sin. Genesis and The Bible teach that this is a false and foolish notion. We shall learn in Genesis that God is holy. The truth is that:

- God does not overlook sin.
- God either forgives or punishes sin.

Hence, we read that God punished Cain. God cursed him. Abel's blood had defiled the ground. Cain would never again farm it. He became a restless wanderer. He complained about his punishment. But even at this stage he did not repent and ask God for forgiveness. He was only concerned about his own safety and security. Note Cain's response to God's love:

- God reassured him that anyone punishing him would receive seven times the punishment they inflicted on him.
- To ensure that Cain was recognised, God put a mark on him as a warning that he was not to be killed.
- Cain knew what God required, but he did not repent.

Cain may have been the first, but he will not be the last of those who know 'God's Way of Salvation' but do not do what God requires them to do. We ask a question.

Question: Have you accepted 'God's Gift of Salvation' that He offers to everyone?

Read again the words of Genesis 4:16. Cain left the presence of God. Cain was a proud, foolish, and arrogant man. But, experience teaches that many who do not behave like Cain, know about God's Gift of Salvation but never accept it.

Adam and Eve had unnamed sons and daughters. Cain must have married one of his sisters. She gave birth to Enoch. They lived in a city of the same name. We read about Lamech who had two wives, and about the skills the people acquired and their daily work. Note that when Lamech spoke about the assault on him and the dead youth, he did not name him. Maybe, he did not know him. This could be an indication that the number of people on Earth at that time was substantial, even though we only read about the lives of a few families. The Bible concentrates on 'Salvation History' that is, the history of the ancestors of Joseph and Mary, Jesus' mother.

In the first eight chapters of Genesis, there is no reference to laws relating to murder and manslaughter, incest or bigamy, crimes in general or punishments.

Genesis 4 ends with the birth of Adam and Eve's third son, Seth and the life of Seth's son, Enos. Seth's name means 'granted.' Eve thought that God had granted her a son to replace the murdered Abel.

Despite the disappointing history that we have read so far in Genesis, it is pleasing to note that when Seth's son, Enos, was born, there was a period when men 'called upon the Name of the Lord.' Translations of these words vary. It might be that 'they called themselves The Lord's people.'

Even today, when the world is populated with so many who have no time or inclination for God and spiritual matters, there are a small number who willingly acknowledge that 'Jesus Christ is Lord.' They have discovered that Jesus is not only 'the Saviour of the world.' He wanted to be and He is their personal Saviour. They belong to Him now and for eternity.

GENESIS CHAPTER 5

This is the written account of Adam's family line. When God created mankind, he made them in the likeness of God. (2) He created them male and female and blessed them. And he named them "Mankind" when they were created. (3) When Adam had lived 130 years, he had a son in his own likeness, in his own image; and he named him Seth. (4) After Seth was born, Adam lived 800 years and had other sons and daughters. (5) Altogether, Adam lived a total of 930 years, and then he died. (6) When Seth had lived 105 years, he became the father of Enosh. (7) After he became the father of Enosh, Seth lived 807 years and had other sons and daughters. (8) Altogether, Seth lived a total of 912 years, and then he died. (9) When Enosh had lived 90 years, he became the father of Kenan. (10) After he became the father of Kenan, Enosh lived 815 years and had other sons and daughters. (11) Altogether, Enosh lived a total of 905 years, and then he died. (12) When Kenan had lived 70 years, he became the father of Mahalalel. (13) After he became the father of Mahalalel, Kenan lived 840 years and had other sons and daughters. (14) Altogether, Kenan lived a total of 910 years, and then he died. (15) When Mahalalel had lived 65 years, he became the father of Jared. (16) After he became the father of Jared, Mahalalel lived 830 years and had other sons and daughters. (17) Altogether, Mahalalel lived a total of 895 years, and then he died. (18) When Jared had lived 162 years, he became the father of Enoch. (19) After he became the father of Enoch, Jared lived 800 years and had other sons and daughters. (20) Altogether, Jared lived a total of 962 years, and then he died. (21) When Enoch had lived 65 years, he became the father of Methuselah. (22) After he became the father of Methuselah, Enoch walked faithfully with God 300 years and had other sons and daughters. (23) Altogether, Enoch lived a total of 365 years. (24) Enoch walked faithfully with God; then he was no more, because God took him away. (25) When Methuselah had lived 187 years, he became the father of Lamech. (26) After he became the father of Lamech, Methuselah lived 782 years and had other sons and daughters. (27) Altogether, Methuselah lived a total of 969 years, and then he died. (28) When Lamech had lived 182 years, he had a son. (29) He named him Noah and said, "He will comfort us in the labor and painful toil of our hands caused by the ground the LORD has cursed." (30) After Noah was born, Lamech lived 595 years and had other sons and daughters. (31) Altogether, Lamech lived a total of 777 years, and then he died. (32) After Noah was 500 years old, he became the father of Shem, Ham and Japheth.

COMMENTARY. GENESIS CHAPTER 5

Only Bible historians need to spend time studying verses of historical information, such as those in Genesis 5, but there are truths in Genesis 5 that we cannot ignore. We list them:

1. Note the words that begin Genesis 5:

   'This is the written account of Adam's family line.'

   We ask an important question:

   If the story of Adam and Eve was a myth, why would anyone go to the trouble of writing Adam's family history?

2. Note that three time the word 'created' is used:

   1) Genesis 5:1. 'when God created mankind ...'

   2) Genesis 5:2. 'He created them male and female ...'

   3) Genesis 5:2. 'He named them "Mankind" when they were created.'

   It seems to us that these words stress God's involvement in the creation of mankind. It is as though the author of Genesis knew that a time would come when The Bible story as to the origin of mankind would be disputed.

3. If you compare the number of verses relating to man with those relating to animals, birds, and fish in The Bible story of creation, it come as no surprise that we read:

   1) Genesis 5:1. 'When God created mankind, he made them in the likeness of God.'

   2) Genesis 5:2. 'He created them male and female and blessed them.'

   Consider the above two statements carefully. We have no difficulty understanding Genesis 5:2, but what about the statement in Genesis 5:1?

Genesis 5:1. 'When God created mankind, he made them in the likeness of God.'

These words are so important that they are written following the words 'This is the written account of Adam's family line.' Hence, they are first words we read about 'Adam's family line.' They cannot be ignored because we humans cannot understand them. Like the record of creation that we have read in Genesis, you either believe what The Bible teaches, or you do not. But, the statement in Genesis 5:1 explains why we also read at the end of Genesis 5:2 these very important three words:

'... and blessed them.'

Man is special to God. We do not have the space to develop this subject, but we mention one matter in Genesis 9. We abridged five verses:

' ... the animals, birds, and fish .... are all placed under your power .... I give them all to you for food .... I will punish with death any animal that takes a human life .... Human beings were made like God, so whoever murders one of them will be killed ...' Genesis 9:2-6. GNB. (abridged)

These five verses state God's instructions to Noah after the flood. Human beings could kill animals, birds, and fish for food. Any animal or human being that killed a human being had to be killed. We are told why 'The Death Penalty' was introduced by God. Human beings were 'made like God.'

3. We learn that God chose the name Adam, or man.

4. Although we are not told how Adam was like God, when Seth, Adam's third son was born, Adam recognised that Seth was like himself. The NIV states:

   '... he had a son in his own likeness, in his own image; and he named him Seth.' Genesis 5:3. NIV.

   We do not know why Adam only noticed this similarity when his third son was born, or if he knew that mankind had been created in God's likeness. We do not know if sin has diminished man's likeness to God as sin has passed from generation to generation. We know that some teach this, but that teaching does not explain the meaning of:

'He made them in the likeness of God.' Genesis 5:1. NIV.

We are content to believe these important words, and to keep them in mind as we read The Bible. The truths we learn in Genesis are vital to Bible study.

5. Of the many who are named or referred to in Genesis 5, only Enoch is mentioned as living in fellowship with God. When Enoch was three hundred and sixty-five years old, God removed him from the world.

   You will recall that before Adam and Eve sinned, God talked with them in The Garden of Eden. When God came to speak with them after they sinned they hid. Disobedience changed their former privileged status. Fellowship with God changed to fear of Him. Their sin was an obstacle to fellowship with God. It still is.

6. Once again we read of Lamech. You recall that He found that the curse God had put on the ground when Cain killed Abel made farming hard work. When he was one hundred and eighty-two years old and his son was born, he named him Noah meaning 'relief.'

   Lamech wanted respite from hard work. We do not read that his wish was granted. He was like Cain. He knew why the curse had been imposed, but he never sought God's forgiveness for his sins although he lived another five hundred and ninety-five years.

   Although wisdom should come with advancing years, in spiritual things, The Bible teaches, and experience proves, that hearts harden and there is increasing deafness to God's voice. An exception was Noah, one of Bible History's most famous men. Noah's three sons were born when he was five hundred years old.

GENESIS CHAPTER 6

When human beings began to increase in number on the earth and daughters were born to them, (2) the sons of God saw that the daughters of humans were beautiful, and they married any of them they chose. (3) Then the LORD said, "My Spirit will not contend with humans forever, for they are mortal; their days will be a hundred and twenty years." (4) The Nephilim were on the earth in those days—and also afterward—when the sons of God went to the daughters of humans and had children by them. They were the heroes of old, men of renown. (5) The LORD saw how great the wickedness of the human race had become on the earth, and that every inclination of the thoughts of the human heart was only evil all the time. (6) The LORD regretted that he had made human beings on the earth, and his heart was deeply troubled. (7) So the LORD said, "I will wipe from the face of the earth the human race I have created—and with them the animals, the birds and the creatures that move along the ground—for I regret that I have made them." (8) But Noah found favor in the eyes of the LORD. (9) This is the account of Noah and his family. Noah was a righteous man, blameless among the people of his time, and he walked faithfully with God. (10) Noah had three sons: Shem, Ham and Japheth. (11) Now the earth was corrupt in God's sight and was full of violence. (12) God saw how corrupt the earth had become, for all the people on earth had corrupted their ways. (13) So God said to Noah, "I am going to put an end to all people, for the earth is filled with violence because of them. I am surely going to destroy both them and the earth. (14) So make yourself an ark of cypress wood; make rooms in it and coat it with pitch inside and out. (15) This is how you are to build it: The ark is to be three hundred cubits long, fifty cubits wide and thirty cubits high. (16) Make a roof for it, leaving below the roof an opening one cubit high all around. Put a door in the side of the ark and make lower, middle and upper decks. (17) I am going to bring floodwaters on the earth to destroy all life under the heavens, every creature that has the breath of life in it. Everything on earth will perish. (18) But I will establish my covenant with you, and you will enter the ark—you and your sons and your wife and your sons' wives with you. (19) You are to bring into the ark two of all living creatures, male and female, to keep them alive with you. (20) Two of every kind of bird, of every kind of animal and of every kind of creature that moves along the ground will come to you to be kept alive. (21) You are to take every kind of food that is to be eaten and store it away as food for you and for them." (22) Noah did everything just as God commanded him.

COMMENTARY. GENESIS CHAPTER 6

In Genesis 5, we read that Enoch had fellowship with God and God removed him from this Earth. We are given a hint of what Enoch was saved from and the evil God saw.

We read that God was sorry He had created man. Their thoughts and actions were only evil and got worse as each day passed. But we have unanswered questions:

- How had man become so evil and what was happening?
- What was the cause of so much wickedness?

We know from Genesis 5 that longevity resulted in many children being born. What moral education did they receive? We know that:

- Cain was a murderer and a proud, arrogant, liar.
- Lamech was a bigamist who wanted an easier life.

What sort of home life, discipline and example did children have? There was widespread sexual intercourse. It was based on desire rather than on God's principle of marriage that is written at the end of Genesis 2.

There are two specific evils identified in Genesis 6. They are separated by God's denunciation and warning:

1. Genesis 6:2. The sons of God married any of the daughters of men that they desired.
2. Genesis 6:4. Evil male giants had sexual intercourse with women who were not their wives. This may refer to rape.

These evil liaisons produced children who became violent and giant fighters. They were full of wickedness. Stories of their sins existed for many years. Genesis 6:11 describes the Earth as being filled with corruption, depravity and violence.

We revert to Genesis 6:2 where we read about 'the sons of God.' This expression is contrasted with 'the daughters of men.' We are not told who the sons of God were.

There was some good news despite all the bad news. We find it many times in The Bible. Despite man's dreadful sin, The Holy Spirit willingly spoke to them. He wanted them to know that repentance would result in their forgiveness. Sadly, experience teaches that God is more willing to forgive than sinners are to accept God's offer and be forgiven. We examine this good news more before reading on. We must not overlook a divine warning. These verses teach two truths:

1. No matter how evil repentant sinners have been, God's forgiveness and Salvation are always totally effective.
2. No one should assume that God's blessings will always be available. We read in Genesis 6:3 that God's warning had a 'time limit.' Thereafter, there would be judgment.

Men had one hundred and twenty years to repent of their evil or face the disastrous consequences of the flood that occurred during Noah's lifetime. We read about a contrast between Noah's life, that brought pleasure to God, and the evil lives of others. Only Noah was seeking to live as God required. We know very little about Noah or the five hundred years he lived before his three sons were born. We do know that his background and environment were not good because one of his forefathers was the murderer Cain and his father was Lamech, the lazy bigamist.

Noah was not like the people of today. He did not live a sinful life and blame his background or the circumstances in which he lived. Noah lived to please God.

One day Noah received instructions from God to build an ark. God told him why it was required and gave him the details he needed to build it. You can read the size of the ark, how it was constructed and details of the fixtures and fittings. Noah only had to follow God's instructions.

- God trusted Noah with this massive project that kept Noah busy for one hundred and twenty years. The ark:
    - had three decks but only one window that was half a metre deep at roof level.
    - only had one door in its side.

What was so amazing about Noah's trust in God was that the ark was built in a desert. Prior to the flood, it had never rained. We read where the water came from that floated the ark and drowned those who were not in it.

- Noah knew that whether God promised His blessing or warned about His judgment, He would keep His word.
- As Noah believed that what God had told him about the coming judgment was true, we read in 2Peter 2:5 that Noah preached righteousness while building the ark.
- Noah took on board the ark, animals, reptiles and birds, two of each species, male and female with food to feed them. Noah also needed food for his own family.
- Fish are not mentioned. They would survive the flood.

We do not know how much detail God gave Noah, but Noah must have known that food was required for a long period. Even though the rain and the subterranean waters lasted for forty days, the ship floated for one hundred and fifty days before it rested in the mountain range of Ararat. It would take some time for the water to recede.

GENESIS CHAPTER 7

The LORD then said to Noah, "Go into the ark, you and your whole family, because I have found you righteous in this generation. (2) Take with you seven pairs of every kind of clean animal, a male and its mate, and one pair of every kind of unclean animal, a male and its mate, (3) and also seven pairs of every kind of bird, male and female, to keep their various kinds alive throughout the earth. (4) Seven days from now I will send rain on the earth for forty days and forty nights, and I will wipe from the face of the earth every living creature I have made." (5) And Noah did all that the LORD commanded him. (6) Noah was six hundred years old when the floodwaters came on the earth. (7) And Noah and his sons and his wife and his sons' wives entered the ark to escape the waters of the flood. (8) Pairs of clean and unclean animals, of birds and of all creatures that move along the ground, (9) male and female, came to Noah and entered the ark, as God had commanded Noah. (10) And after the seven days the floodwaters came on the earth. (11) In the six hundredth year of Noah's life, on the seventeenth day of the second month—on that day all the springs of the great deep burst forth, and the floodgates of the heavens were opened. (12) And rain fell on the earth forty days and forty nights. (13) On that very day Noah and his sons, Shem, Ham and Japheth, together with his wife and the wives of his three sons, entered the ark. (14) They had with them every wild animal according to its kind, all livestock according to their kinds, every creature that moves along the ground according to its kind and every bird according to its kind, everything with wings. (15) Pairs of all creatures that have the breath of life in them came to Noah and entered the ark. (16) The animals going in were male and female of every living thing, as God had commanded Noah. Then the LORD shut him in. (17) For forty days the flood kept coming on the earth, and as the waters increased they lifted the ark high above the earth. (18) The waters rose and increased greatly on the earth, and the ark floated on the surface of the water. (19) They rose greatly on the earth, and all the high mountains under the entire heavens were covered. (20) The waters rose and covered the mountains to a depth of more than fifteen cubits. (21) Every living thing that moved on land perished—birds, livestock, wild animals, all the creatures that swarm over the earth, and all mankind. (22) Everything on dry land that had the breath of life in its nostrils died. (23) Every living thing on the face of the earth was wiped out; people and animals and the creatures that move along the ground and the birds were wiped from the earth. Only Noah was left, and those with him in the ark. (24) The waters flooded the earth for a hundred and fifty days.

COMMENTARY. GENESIS CHAPTER 7

It is important to consider the detailed account given of the flood. Many people today assume that this event did not occur and the story of Noah and the flood is a myth. It is probably no coincidence that those who dismiss this story will also suffer God's judgment because, like the people of Noah's day, they love their sin and sinning, and will not repent. They reject 'God's Offer of Salvation.'

God specified the number of animals, reptiles and birds that Noah had to have onboard the ark, and Noah took additional ones to sacrifice. Noah had sufficient food onboard for the animals, reptiles and birds and for his own family. God told Noah when to take his family onboard. The animals, reptiles and birds, obviously motivated by God, followed.

Seven days later, God closed the door. After one hundred and twenty years of giving the people an opportunity to repent, you might think that a further seven days was unnecessary. But God has always been loving, gracious and merciful, and God would have saved those who boarded the ark to join Noah and his family. No one did. Did they think that:

- what Noah had been doing for one-hundred and twenty years was ridiculous?
- Noah's preaching about righteousness and judgment was foolish nonsense?
- their lifestyles were too enjoyable to give up, and any suggestion of repentance was unacceptable to them?

Experience teaches that many today would have ignored Noah's preaching. The vast majority ignore God's invitation to repent, accept Jesus as their Saviour and be forgiven.

There came a time when God shut the door. God, not Noah, decided the time of judgment. Noah was God's servant for the purpose of warning the people that the flood was coming. It was God's involvement that ensured the safety of those inside the ark and the judgment of those on the outside. Note that:

- in blessing and in judgment, God keeps His word.
- those thinking about repenting were drowned.

People were either:

- inside the ark and saved from drowning.
- outside the ship and drowned.

Those who were drowned could have boarded the ark and been saved from the flood. Instead:

- they refused God's offer to repent and be saved.
- they chose God's punishment for their sins.

Those who were drowned, not God who closed the door, chose between blessing or judgment. The same applies today to The Gospel and God's Salvation. We choose either:

- an eternal future in Heaven.
- an eternal future in The Lake of Fire.

We are told Noah's exact age when the flood started. It is detailed to year, month and day. This is no myth. It is a true story of a real man and his family. We have read that man became so evil that God regretted He had made man. God brought a flood to drown those who did not repent. Only eight people were saved from God's judgment.

We are not told what the people's reaction was during the forty days that it rained and gushing water came out of the ground. The people had never experienced these things before but no one outside the ark survived. There was no escape. The water covered the mountains and lasted for one hundred and fifty days. The only place of safety from God's judgment was inside the ark and God had closed the only door.

GENESIS CHAPTER 8

But God remembered Noah and all the wild animals and the livestock that were with him in the ark, and he sent a wind over the earth, and the waters receded. (2) Now the springs of the deep and the floodgates of the heavens had been closed, and the rain had stopped falling from the sky. (3) The water receded steadily from the earth. At the end of the hundred and fifty days the water had gone down, (4) and on the seventeenth day of the seventh month the ark came to rest on the mountains of Ararat. (5) The waters continued to recede until the tenth month, and on the first day of the tenth month the tops of the mountains became visible. (6) After forty days Noah opened a window he had made in the ark (7) and sent out a raven, and it kept flying back and forth until the water had dried up from the earth. (8) Then he sent out a dove to see if the water had receded from the surface of the ground. (9) But the dove could find nowhere to perch because there was water over all the surface of the earth; so it returned to Noah in the ark. He reached out his hand and took the dove and brought it back to himself in the ark. (10) He waited seven more days and again sent out the dove from the ark. (11) When the dove returned to him in the evening, there in its beak was a freshly plucked olive leaf! Then Noah knew that the water had receded from the earth. (12) He waited seven more days and sent the dove out again, but this time it did not return to him. (13) By the first day of the first month of Noah's six hundred and first year, the water had dried up from the earth. Noah then removed the covering from the ark and saw that the surface of the ground was dry. (14) By the twenty-seventh day of the second month the earth was completely dry. (15) Then God said to Noah, (16) "Come out of the ark, you and your wife and your sons and their wives. (17) Bring out every kind of living creature that is with you—the birds, the animals, and all the creatures that move along the ground—so they can multiply on the earth and be fruitful and increase in number on it." (18) So Noah came out, together with his sons and his wife and his sons' wives. (19) All the animals and all the creatures that move along the ground and all the birds—everything that moves on land—came out of the ark, one kind after another. (20) Then Noah built an altar to the LORD and, taking some of all the clean animals and clean birds, he sacrificed burnt offerings on it. (21) The LORD smelled the pleasing aroma and said in his heart: "Never again will I curse the ground because of humans, even though every inclination of the human heart is evil from childhood. And never again will I destroy all living creatures, as I have done. (22) "As long as the earth endures, seedtime and harvest, cold and heat, summer and winter, day and night will never cease."

COMMENTARY. GENESIS CHAPTER 8

Obedience to God brings His security because despite the awful judgment of the forty days of rain and the subterranean gushing waters, God did not forget those the ark. God sent a wind and the waters started to recede.

There was only one window at the top of the ship so those in the ship did not see God's judgment on the unbelievers. Although they could see that the rain had stopped, they did not know if the flood was still covering the ground. You can read the method Noah used to investigate the problem. He must have known from his discussions with God that a long period of time was involved because as we have read, he had sufficient food in the ship to feed all the occupants.

Although Noah satisfied himself that the floodwaters were receding, he did not need to do this because when the ground was dry, God told him that it was time to leave the ship. In The Bible, we read of other incidents where men do what they think is logical rather than wait to hear from God.

The Bible states the geographical location where the ship came to rest. Such detail is not usually part of a myth. The animals disembarked in an orderly manner. This comes as no surprise because the God of Creation works in an orderly way. Disorder is associated with human effort.

Noah made a sacrifice to God using the extra animals and birds that God had designated for that purpose before Noah entered the ship. Noah's sacrifice was an acknowledgement that God had saved him and his family from judgment. From beginning to end, it was God who had planned the Salvation of eight people, the animals, reptiles and birds. Noah was only required to obey God and to follow His instructions. No ingenuity or inventiveness of his own would have saved them.

If we want God's Salvation, obedience is as necessary as it was in Noah's day. We must do exactly what God has said we must do. If we disobey, we will not receive God's Salvation. We either obey or we will be judged. We decide whether to be 'saved or lost.' These are the only alternatives.

God was pleased with Noah's sacrifice and agreed never to curse or destroy the ground again. In Genesis 8:21 you will read the promise that God made even though God knew that sin would continue. We see evil within us, all around us and throughout the world, but God has kept His promise.

GENESIS CHAPTER 9

Then God blessed Noah and his sons, saying to them, "Be fruitful and increase in number and fill the earth. (2) The fear and dread of you will fall on all the beasts of the earth, and on all the birds in the sky, on every creature that moves along the ground, and on all the fish in the sea; they are given into your hands. (3) Everything that lives and moves about will be food for you. Just as I gave you the green plants, I now give you everything. (4) "But you must not eat meat that has its lifeblood still in it. (5) And for your lifeblood I will surely demand an accounting. I will demand an accounting from every animal. And from each human being, too, I will demand an accounting for the life of another human being. (6) "Whoever sheds human blood, by humans shall their blood be shed; for in the image of God has God made mankind. (7) As for you, be fruitful and increase in number; multiply on the earth and increase upon it." (8) Then God said to Noah and to his sons with him: (9) "I now establish my covenant with you and with your descendants after you (10) and with every living creature that was with you—the birds, the livestock and all the wild animals, all those that came out of the ark with you—every living creature on earth. (11) I establish my covenant with you: Never again will all life be destroyed by the waters of a flood; never again will there be a flood to destroy the earth." (12) And God said, "This is the sign of the covenant I am making between me and you and every living creature with you, a covenant for all generations to come: (13) I have set my rainbow in the clouds, and it will be the sign of the covenant between me and the earth. (14) Whenever I bring clouds over the earth and the rainbow appears in the clouds, (15) I will remember my covenant between me and you and all living creatures of every kind. Never again will the waters become a flood to destroy all life. (16) Whenever the rainbow appears in the clouds, I will see it and remember the everlasting covenant between God and all living creatures of every kind on the earth." (17) So God said to Noah, "This is the sign of the covenant I have established between me and all life on the earth." 18) The sons of Noah who came out of the ark were Shem, Ham and Japheth. (Ham was the father of Canaan.) (19) These were the three sons of Noah, and from them came the people who were scattered over the whole earth. (20) Noah, a man of the soil, proceeded to plant a vineyard. (21) When he drank some of its wine, he became drunk and lay uncovered inside his tent. (22) Ham, the father of Canaan, saw his father naked and told his two brothers outside. (23) But Shem and Japheth took a garment and laid it across their shoulders; then they walked in backward and covered their father's naked body. Their faces were turned the other way so that they would not see their father naked. (24) When Noah awoke from his wine and found out what his youngest son had done to him, (25) he said, "Cursed be Canaan! The lowest of slaves will he be to his brothers." (26) He also said, "Praise be to the LORD, the God of Shem! May Canaan be the slave of Shem. (27) May God extend Japheth's territory; may Japheth live in the tents of Shem, and may Canaan be the slave of Japheth." (28) After the flood Noah lived 350 years. (29) Noah lived a total of 950 years, and then he died.

COMMENTARY. GENESIS CHAPTER 9

As we begin to read this chapter, we see that man had a new start. The evil that displeased God had been judged. God blessed Noah and his sons and instructed them to populate the Earth. There were to be changes that applied to both man and to the animals. Man was no longer a vegetarian and he could kill animals for food provided their blood was shed. Murder was punishable by death and animals that killed men had to die.

GOD'S FIRST LESSON FOR NOAH

God regards blood, which gives life to man and animals, to be of special significance. Therefore, when a man sheds an animal's blood that is killed for food, it reminds him that blood is life-giving. You will recall that Cain brought a bloodless sacrifice to God. God did not accept it.

Question: Why is the blood so important to God?

Answer: When blood flowed from a sacrificed animal, it was a picture of the sacrifice that Jesus would one day make when His blood was shed on a Cross. Jesus died that we might be forgiven. The sacrificed animals had not sinned. They died on behalf of those who had:

- Jesus was sinless. He died for the ungodly.
- Jesus' shed blood guarantees forgiveness for those who repent and accept Him as their Saviour.

GOD'S SECOND LESSON FOR NOAH

Man was created in the image of God and is special to God:

- God loves us even though we sin against Him.
- God gave us life on Earth. God wants to give us eternal life so that we can live with Him for eternity in Heaven.

Only God has the right to take away human life:

- The fact that we cannot kill human beings should remind us that man was created in the image of God.
- God instituted the judicial execution of murderers as the penalty for taking another's life. It was God, not Noah, who required that a murderer's blood be shed.

We have learnt in Genesis that:

- man was created in the image of God. Animals were not. God breathed into man, but not animals, the breath of life.
- killing animals, initially for sacrifice, but since the flood for food, was God ordained.
- the penalty for killing a human being, referred to in Genesis as 'shedding their blood' was execution. In Genesis, execution is referred to as 'their blood being shed.'

To receive forgiveness for their sins, sinners needed to repent and shed an animal's blood. Remember as you read Genesis that God gives us many pictures of Calvary:

- God was preparing us for the time when Jesus would shed His blood. His sacrifice was the final sacrifice for sin forever.
- We see a wonderful example of God's love in His promise that He would not curse the ground again or destroy all living creatures. The rainbow is the sign of God's promise. Read the extent of this promise in Genesis 9.
- For blessing or for judgment, God keeps His promises.

God loves you and He wants to bless you for eternity. Because of what Jesus did on the Cross for you, God offers you His Salvation. If you repent and accept it, God's Holy Spirit will indwell you. Unlike Noah and his family, you will not need a rainbow as evidence of God's Salvation. Your desire to change your lifestyle and please God will be the evidence.

Remember that although what you are reading is historical, God has not changed. As mentioned before, God hates sin, but God loves sinners. This is a vitally important truth. Although there are many people on Earth, God desires to be your personal God and to save and bless you.

We are introduced to Noah's sons and to Ham in particular as he was the father of the Canaanites. We read the curse that Noah put upon Ham and his descendants. Ham:

- did not cover Noah when he found him naked.
- left Noah exposed and told Noah's two other sons.

As we are given no details, we must not assume that Noah was at fault for being drunk. Whether Noah knew the strength of the wine he made we do not know. This incident is but one example of the problems we will experience if we read Genesis with our present-day knowledge, and condemn people who did not have our education. Unlike Ham, Shem and Japheth showed respect for Noah in a difficult situation.

Remember Noah's curse and blessings. You will be able to assess the effect of the curse in those books of The Bible that refer to the Canaanites.

We know little of Noah's life after the flood. We only know that he lived for another three hundred and fifty years.

GENESIS CHAPTER 10

This is the account of Shem, Ham and Japheth, Noah's sons, who themselves had sons after the flood. (2) The sons of Japheth: Gomer, Magog, Madai, Javan, Tubal, Meshek and Tiras. (3) The sons of Gomer: Ashkenaz, Riphath and Togarmah. (4) The sons of Javan: Elishah, Tarshish, the Kittites and the Rodanites. (5) (From these the maritime peoples spread out into their territories by their clans within their nations, each with its own language.) (6) The sons of Ham: Cush, Egypt, Put and Canaan. (7) The sons of Cush: Seba, Havilah, Sabtah, Raamah and Sabteka. The sons of Raamah: Sheba and Dedan. (8) Cush was the father of Nimrod, who became a mighty warrior on the earth. (9) He was a mighty hunter before the LORD; that is why it is said, "Like Nimrod, a mighty hunter before the LORD." (10) The first centers of his kingdom were Babylon, Uruk, Akkad and Kalneh, in Shinar. (11) From that land he went to Assyria, where he built Nineveh, Rehoboth Ir, Calah (12) and Resen, which is between Nineveh and Calah—which is the great city. (13) Egypt was the father of the Ludites, Anamites, Lehabites, Naphtuhites, (14) Pathrusites, Kasluhites (from whom the Philistines came) and Caphtorites. (15) Canaan was the father of Sidon his firstborn, and of the Hittites, (16) Jebusites, Amorites, Girgashites, (17) Hivites, Arkites, Sinites, (18) Arvadites, Zemarites and Hamathites. Later the Canaanite clans scattered (19) and the borders of Canaan reached from Sidon toward Gerar as far as Gaza, and then toward Sodom, Gomorrah, Admah and Zeboyim, as far as Lasha. (20) These are the sons of Ham by their clans and languages, in their territories and nations. (21) Sons were also born to Shem, whose older brother was Japheth; Shem was the ancestor of all the sons of Eber. (22) The sons of Shem: Elam, Ashur, Arphaxad, Lud and Aram. (23) The sons of Aram: Uz, Hul, Gether and Meshek. (24) Arphaxad was the father of Shelah, and Shelah the father of Eber. (25) Two sons were born to Eber: One was named Peleg, because in his time the earth was divided; his brother was named Joktan. (26) Joktan was the father of Almodad, Sheleph, Hazarmaveth, Jerah, (27) Hadoram, Uzal, Diklah, (28) Obal, Abimael, Sheba, (29) Ophir, Havilah and Jobab. All these were sons of Joktan. (30) The region where they lived stretched from Mesha toward Sephar, in the eastern hill country. (31) These are the sons of Shem by their clans and languages, in their territories and nations. (32) These are the clans of Noah's sons, according to their lines of descent, within their nations. From these the nations spread out over the earth after the flood.

COMMENTARY. GENESIS CHAPTER 10

There are unbelievers who doubt the truth of Genesis. We have in this chapter a list of the descendants of Noah, just as we had a list of the descendants of Adam in Genesis 5. Why would anyone go to the trouble of writing detailed genealogies of imaginary people? We read the names of the descendants of Noah's sons. We are told what they did, where they lived, and that they:

- formed tribes and spoke different languages.
- spread out to various geographical locations.

Nimrod is the only one who is chosen for special mention. He lived on Earth as in the presence of God. So, God blessed him, and people spoke respectfully of him and his exploits.

You will also read about a man named Peleg. All we know about him is that during his lifetime the population was dispersed. This is the story that begins the next chapter. As though to emphasise that what is written about the flood is true, this chapter concludes with a very positive statement that identifies two truths.

1. If those named all descended from Noah, only Noah and his family could have survived the flood.
2. Nations only developed after the flood. The flood did occur in the locality where Noah lived. It was vast enough to destroy all mankind except those in the ark.

GENESIS CHAPTER 11

Now the whole world had one language and a common speech. (2) As people moved eastward, they found a plain in Shinar and settled there. (3) They said to each other, "Come, let's make bricks and bake them thoroughly." They used brick instead of stone, and tar for mortar. (4) Then they said, "Come, let us build ourselves a city, with a tower that reaches to the heavens, so that we may make a name for ourselves; otherwise we will be scattered over the face of the whole earth." (5) But the LORD came down to see the city and the tower the people were building. (6) The LORD said, "If as one people speaking the same language they have begun to do this, then nothing they plan to do will be impossible for them. (7) Come, let us go down and confuse their language so they will not understand each other." (8) So the LORD scattered them from there over all the earth, and they stopped building the city. (9) That is why it was called Babel—because there the LORD confused the language of the whole world. From there the LORD scattered them over the face of the whole earth. (10) This is the account of Shem's family line. Two years after the flood, when Shem was 100 years old, he became the father of Arphaxad. (11) And after he became the father of Arphaxad, Shem lived 500 years and had other sons and daughters. (2) When Arphaxad had lived 35 years, he became the father of Shelah. (13) And after he became the father of Shelah, Arphaxad lived 403 years and had other sons and daughters. (14) When Shelah had lived 30 years, he became the father of Eber. (15) And after he became the father of Eber, Shelah lived 403 years and had other sons and daughters. (16) When Eber had lived 34 years, he became the father of Peleg. (17) And after he became the father of Peleg, Eber lived 430 years and had other sons and daughters. (18) When Peleg had lived 30 years, he became the father of Reu. (19) And after he became the father of Reu, Peleg lived 209 years and had other sons and daughters. (20) When Reu had lived 32 years, he became the father of Serug. (21) And after he became the father of Serug, Reu lived 207 years and had other sons and daughters. (22) When Serug had lived 30 years, he became the father of Nahor. (23) And after he became the father of Nahor, Serug lived 200 years and had other sons and daughters. (Genesis 11:24) When Nahor had lived 29 years, he became the father of Terah. (25) And after he became the father of Terah, Nahor lived 119 years and had other sons and daughters. (26) After Terah had lived 70 years, he became the father of Abram, Nahor and Haran. (27) This is the account of Terah's family line. Terah became the father of Abram, Nahor and Haran. And Haran became the father of Lot. (28) While his father Terah was still alive, Haran died in Ur of the Chaldeans, in the land of his birth. (29) Abram and Nahor both married. The name of Abram's wife was Sarai, and the name of Nahor's wife was Milkah; she was the daughter of Haran, the father of both Milkah and Iskah. (30) Now Sarai was childless because she was not able to conceive. (31) Terah took his son Abram, his grandson Lot son of Haran, and his daughter-in-law Sarai, the wife of his son Abram, and together they set out from Ur of the Chaldeans to go to Canaan. But when they came to Harran, they settled there. (32) Terah lived 205 years, and he died in Harran.

COMMENTARY. GENESIS CHAPTER 11

The population lived as one community with a common language. We now read why the people were dispersed and why there are many languages today. God asked Noah and his sons to repopulate the earth and after a few generations the population had grown to a size where the people needed new places to live.

We read about the people who settled in Shinar, also called Babylon. It would be strange if they had not heard of the flood that God sent in judgment, but there is no reference in the verses to anyone worshipping God. We read that they wanted:

- a city with a huge tower reaching to the sky to make a name for themselves.
- to be united to save themselves from being scattered.

In their arrogance they wanted to become a superpower. Nothing suggests that they openly rebelled against God:

- They made their decisions ignoring God.
- They were only concerned with themselves.
- God's ways and demands were not part of their thinking.

We read what God said when He saw the partly built city and the tower. The simplicity of the wording is wonderful. Just as in Genesis 1 in relation to Creation, God used the pronoun "Us" and not "I" when speaking of Himself.

From time to time we read in The Bible that man has planned this or that. In his conceit, he forgets that God exists and knows everything. God knew that the city and tower at Babylon had started a new period of wickedness. God knew their hearts and motives and intervened in their plans by giving them different languages. They could not communicate with each other. Confusion resulted, building work ceased and the people went to live elsewhere. The genealogy that follows introduces us to the ancestors of Abraham.

Abraham is the subject of Genesis 11-25. Hence, fifteen chapters are written about him and his relationship with God. So, it is important that believers consider his life in detail for lessons that will assist them in their relationship with God.

Abraham and his wife Sarah were originally called Abram and Sarai. We read about their marriage. We read later why their names were changed by God. For the sake of simplicity, we refer to them as Abraham and Sarah. The end of Genesis 11 introduces us to Abraham's family. Abraham's:

- father was Terah. Terah died in Haran.
- brother, also called Haran, died leaving a son named Lot. Lot features extensively in the story of Abraham.

We do not know why Terah left Ur accompanied by his family. All we read is that he intended to travel to Canaan but settled with his family in Haran.

GENESIS CHAPTER 12

The LORD had said to Abram, "Go from your country, your people and your father's household to the land I will show you. (2) "I will make you into a great nation, and I will bless you; I will make your name great, and you will be a blessing. (3) I will bless those who bless you, and whoever curses you I will curse; and all peoples on earth will be blessed through you." (4) So Abram went, as the LORD had told him; and Lot went with him. Abram was seventy-five years old when he set out from Harran. (5) He took his wife Sarai, his nephew Lot, all the possessions they had accumulated and the people they had acquired in Harran, and they set out for the land of Canaan, and they arrived there. (6) Abram traveled through the land as far as the site of the great tree of Moreh at Shechem. At that time the Canaanites were in the land. (7) The LORD appeared to Abram and said, "To your offspring I will give this land." So he built an altar there to the LORD, who had appeared to him. (8) From there he went on toward the hills east of Bethel and pitched his tent, with Bethel on the west and Ai on the east. There he built an altar to the LORD and called on the name of the LORD. (9) Then Abram set out and continued toward the Negev. (10) Now there was a famine in the land, and Abram went down to Egypt to live there for a while because the famine was severe. (11) As he was about to enter Egypt, he said to his wife Sarai, "I know what a beautiful woman you are. (12) When the Egyptians see you, they will say, 'This is his wife.' Then they will kill me but will let you live. (13) Say you are my sister, so that I will be treated well for your sake and my life will be spared because of you." (14) When Abram came to Egypt, the Egyptians saw that Sarai was a very beautiful woman. (15) And when Pharaoh's officials saw her, they praised her to Pharaoh, and she was taken into his palace. (16) He treated Abram well for her sake, and Abram acquired sheep and cattle, male and female donkeys, male and female servants, and camels. (17) But the LORD inflicted serious diseases on Pharaoh and his household because of Abram's wife Sarai. (18) So Pharaoh summoned Abram. "What have you done to me?" he said. "Why didn't you tell me she was your wife? (19) Why did you say, 'She is my sister,' so that I took her to be my wife? Now then, here is your wife. Take her and go!" (20) Then Pharaoh gave orders about Abram to his men, and they sent him on his way, with his wife and everything he had.

COMMENTARY. GENESIS CHAPTER 12

We read an amazing instruction from God. To be told to leave our country, people, and family, and begin a new life in a place we know to be satisfactory, would cause most of us to think about the advantages and the disadvantages of the move.

Abraham was told to leave, but not told the destination.

A single man might have taken the risk. Abraham was married. God's amazing instruction was followed by His amazing promises. As you read them, you realise that God had a unique plan for Abraham. God promised that He would:

- guide him to an undisclosed destination.
- make him the father of a great nation.
- bless him and make his name famous.
- use him to bless others.

God guaranteed His plans would not be thwarted, and to bless Abraham's friends and curse his enemies. God also said that Abraham would bring blessing to the entire world.

Abraham believed that God would keep His promises and he did as instructed, except that he took his nephew Lot. If Abraham had done exactly what God said, Abraham would not have had the problems we read about in later chapters, although Lot was not his only problem. In Genesis 13 we detail God's conversation with him and the involvement of his family.

Abraham, Sarah and Lot arrived in Canaan. As they travelled south through that country, God told Abraham at Shechem that he was in the land that now belonged to his offspring. Abraham built an altar at Moreh to indicate that God had visited him there.

Abraham, Sarah and Lot continued south and near Bethel Abraham built another altar. He prayed to God before travelling to the desert area of Negebiza, Southern Judah.

Remember as you read about Abraham that he was an ordinary person who trusted the God who makes ordinary people into people who He can use in His divine service. Abraham was not sinless. His sinful deeds are recorded in Genesis so that we may learn how to avoid them:

- Abraham was instructed by God to leave his family in Haran. He disobeyed and took Lot with him.
- There are times when Abraham was afraid, told lies, and put his wife in danger to save himself.

We mention Abraham's sins when Genesis records them. Things only went wrong for him when he stopped relying on God. The lesson for us could not be clearer. God knows what is best for us. And if, like Abraham, we disobey God or stop relying on His love for us, He will forgive us if we repent and restore us to the fellowship He desires to have with us.

There is more than adequate evidence in Genesis that when Abraham sinned, he was not discarded by God. Some think that God is a merciless tyrant, but that was not Abraham's experience. We ask two question. Readers will answer the first question. We answer the second one.

1. Have you realised that Genesis records true events in the lives of real people?
2. What have we learnt about sin in the first twelve chapters of Genesis?

Answer:

Sin came into the world through Adam. As a result:

1) We are all are born with a sinful nature.
2) No one has to be taught how to sin.
3) We all sin because we are all sinners.

We have noted in Genesis that God does not overlook sin. Sin cannot be covered up or hidden. We learn the consequences of sinning in the lives of real people. Hence, we read about the time when Abraham's faith in God failed and he relied upon his own initiative for survival.

Although at Shechem, God promised Abraham that He would give Canaan to his offspring, at a time of famine, Abraham ceased to trust that God would never desert him and leave him and his family to starve. He left Canaan with Sarah and Lot and went to live in Egypt. Abraham had no reason to fear for his life. God had promised to make him the father of a great nation. He had no children. His premature death would have made God's promise impossible. That could never happen.

GENESIS CHAPTER 13

So Abram went up from Egypt to the Negev, with his wife and everything he had, and Lot went with him. (2) Abram had become very wealthy in livestock and in silver and gold. (3) From the Negev he went from place to place until he came to Bethel, to the place between Bethel and Ai where his tent had been earlier (4) and where he had first built an altar. There Abram called on the name of the LORD. (5) Now Lot, who was moving about with Abram, also had flocks and herds and tents. (6) But the land could not support them while they stayed together, for their possessions were so great that they were not able to stay together. (7) And quarreling arose between Abram's herders and Lot's. The Canaanites and Perizzites were also living in the land at that time. (8) So Abram said to Lot, "Let's not have any quarreling between you and me, or between your herders and mine, for we are close relatives. (9) Is not the whole land before you? Let's part company. If you go to the left, I'll go to the right; if you go to the right, I'll go to the left."(10) Lot looked around and saw that the whole plain of the Jordan toward Zoar was well watered, like the garden of the LORD, like the land of Egypt. (This was before the LORD destroyed Sodom and Gomorrah.) (11) So Lot chose for himself the whole plain of the Jordan and set out toward the east. The two men parted company: (12) Abram lived in the land of Canaan, while Lot lived among the cities of the plain and pitched his tents near Sodom. (13) Now the people of Sodom were wicked and were sinning greatly against the LORD. (14) The LORD said to Abram after Lot had parted from him, "Look around from where you are, to the north and south, to the east and west. (15) All the land that you see I will give to you and your offspring forever. (16) I will make your offspring like the dust of the earth, so that if anyone could count the dust, then your offspring could be counted. (17) Go, walk through the length and breadth of the land, for I am giving it to you." (18) So Abram went to live near the great trees of Mamre at Hebron, where he pitched his tents. There he built an altar to the LORD.

COMMENTARY. GENESIS CHAPTER 13

Abraham was expelled from Egypt in disgrace. He returned to Bethel in Canaan, where he had built his second altar. He worshipped God. He had learnt an important spiritual lesson. We must trust God. He knows what is best for us.

We read the dispute between Abraham's and Lot's servants. Lot was not entitled to any land. Only Abraham's children were entitled to it. We are not told why Abraham gave some land to Lot. Maybe Lot had the use, but not the ownership of the land. His ignoble choice to go east had disastrous consequences.

Readers may have sympathy for Abraham and regard Lot as an ungrateful villain, but we need to consider how and why Abraham's problem arose. Genesis informs us of two events that resulted in Abraham's problems with Lot. Abraham's:

1. disobedience in both Ur and Haran.

2. lack of faith in Canaan.

We are not looking at Abraham's disobedience or his lack of faith with a critical attitude. There is no spiritual advantage to be gained in doing that. Believers need to avoid his problems. We consider his disobedience first. Note the contrast between the words of Genesis 11:31 and Genesis 12:1:

- Genesis 11:31. 'Terah took his son Abraham ...'
- Genesis 12:1. 'The Lord had said to Abraham, "Go ..."

It seems from Genesis 12:1 that God spoke to Abraham when his family lived in Ur. God told him to leave them and travel to an unknown destination.

Terah's decision to move his family to Canaan had nothing to do with God's instruction to Abraham:

- Terah's destination was Canaan. Abraham's destination was not disclosed to him.
- Terah left with Ur with all his family. Abraham was instructed to leave his family.
- Terah was content to settle in Haran.

Only after Terah's death did Abraham leave Haran. But, Abraham did not leave all his family. He took Lot with him. Some teach that God did not permit Abraham to leave Haran until Terah died but Genesis does not teach this. Abraham did not receive new instructions when Terah died. If we look at the tenses, a past event is mentioned:

- Genesis 12:1. 'The LORD had said ...'
- Genesis 12:4. '... as the LORD had told him ...'

Stephen referred to this period in Abraham's life when he defended himself before The Sanhedrin. We read what he said in Acts 6-7. Maybe his words have been misunderstood.

"... After the death of his father, God sent him to this land where you are now living." Acts 7:4. NIV.

We now consider Abraham's lack of faith. We read in Genesis 12 that a famine occurred in Canaan. Abraham took his family to Egypt. He did what he thought was best when he should have trusted that God would have looked after him and his family in Canaan. He left the land that God had identified to him was the land that He had given to his descendants.

Abraham and Lot had spent many years living in tents in deserts and barren places. What would they see in Egypt and what impression would it have on Lot, a wealthy bachelor? We can only imagine what he saw during his time in Egypt. He never forgot the Egyptian houses and the beautiful countryside at Zoar in Egypt. The land to the east that Lot chose when Abraham suggested they separate was similar to Zoar. Like Egypt, it had cities. Do not forget that God made no promises to Lot. He would not inherit Canaan.

We are not excusing Lot, but Abraham should never have taken him to Egypt where there were many sinful pleasures to impress him. Was it in Egypt that Lot decided that city life was better than a nomadic existence? He chose to go east:

- It gave Lot the opportunity of living near the city of Sodom. Like its neighbour, Gomorrah, it was a place of wickedness, but we do not know whether Lot was aware of this.
- Abraham's decision that he and Lot separate resulted in Lot leaving the righteous influence of Abraham's home to live near the ungodly Sodomites.

At the beginning of Genesis 12 we read about God's instruction to Abraham to leave his country, people and family. Once Lot had gone east, Abraham had broken the earthly ties that God had instructed him to do. Abraham was close enough to Lot to assist him should he ever be in danger.

When Lot departed, God spoke to Abraham about the land. Read what God said. It is as though God confirmed to Abraham that the land was not only for his descendants, who would be so numerous that they could not be counted, it was also for him. God invited Abraham to explore the land to see how vast an area he had been given. Abraham decided to live near Hebron and he built his third altar there.

GENESIS CHAPTER 14

At the time when Amraphel was king of Shinar, Arioch king of Ellasar, Kedorlaomer king of Elam and Tidal king of Goyim, (2) these kings went to war against Bera king of Sodom, Birsha king of Gomorrah, Shinab king of Admah, Shemeber king of Zeboyim, and the king of Bela (that is, Zoar). (3) All these latter kings joined forces in the Valley of Siddim (that is, the Dead Sea Valley). (4) For twelve years they had been subject to Kedorlaomer, but in the thirteenth year they rebelled. (5) In the fourteenth year, Kedorlaomer and the kings allied with him went out and defeated the Rephaites in

Ashteroth Karnaim, the Zuzites in Ham, the Emites in Shaveh Kiriathaim (6) and the Horites in the hill country of Seir, as far as El Paran near the desert. (7) Then they turned back and went to En Mishpat (that is, Kadesh), and they conquered the whole territory of the Amalekites, as well as the Amorites who were living in Hazezon Tamar. (8) Then the king of Sodom, the king of Gomorrah, the king of Admah, the king of Zeboyim and the king of Bela (that is, Zoar) marched out and drew up their battle lines in the Valley of Siddim (9) against Kedorlaomer king of Elam, Tidal king of Goyim, Amraphel king of Shinar and Arioch king of Ellasar—four kings against five. (10) Now the Valley of Siddim was full of tar pits, and when the kings of Sodom and Gomorrah fled, some of the men fell into them and the rest fled to the hills. (11) The four kings seized all the goods of Sodom and Gomorrah and all their food; then they went away. (12) They also carried off Abram's nephew Lot and his possessions, since he was living in Sodom. (13) A man who had escaped came and reported this to Abram the Hebrew. Now Abram was living near the great trees of Mamre the Amorite, a brother of Eshkol and Aner, all of whom were allied with Abram. (14) When Abram heard that his relative had been taken captive, he called out the 318 trained men born in his household and went in pursuit as far as Dan. (15) During the night Abram divided his men to attack them and he routed them, pursuing them as far as Hobah, north of Damascus.(16) He recovered all the goods and brought back his relative Lot and his possessions, together with the women and the other people. (17) After Abram returned from defeating Kedorlaomer and the kings allied with him, the king of Sodom came out to meet him in the Valley of Shaveh (that is, the King's Valley). (18) Then Melchizedek king of Salem brought out bread and wine. He was priest of God Most High, (19) and he blessed Abram, saying, "Blessed be Abram by God Most High, Creator of heaven and earth. (20) And praise be to God Most High, who delivered your enemies into your hand." Then Abram gave him a tenth of everything. (21) The king of Sodom said to Abram, "Give me the people and keep the goods for yourself." (22) But Abram said to the king of Sodom, "With raised hand I have sworn an oath to the LORD, God Most High, Creator of heaven and earth, (23) that I will accept nothing belonging to you, not even a thread or the strap of a sandal, so that you will never be able to say, 'I made Abram rich.' (24) I will accept nothing but what my men have eaten and the share that belongs to the men who went with me—to Aner, Eshkol and Mamre. Let them have their share."

COMMENTARY. GENESIS CHAPTER 14

Lot had to be rescued by Abraham and his allies when the King of Sodom waged war in vain. We might have thought that Lot would have left Sodom at a time of war and returned to Abraham. He must have known that God protected Abraham. Whatever the risks, Lot chose to stay with the ungodly.

In 2Peter 2:6-8, Peter stated that Lot was 'righteous.' This surprises some Bible readers. They assumed from reading Genesis that Lot was ungodly. Hence, we again emphasise that assumptions and conjecture have no place in Bible study.

In Genesis 13 we read that Lot left Abraham to dwell near Sodom. When Lot was captured and carried away during the war, we read that he was living in Sodom. Abraham and his allies rescued Lot, the other captives and the stolen booty. On his return, Abraham met the Kings of Sodom and Salem.

The King of Salem, later called Jerusalem, was Melchizedek. He was a King and God's priest. He brought bread and wine and blessed Abraham, and then departed.

We are only given limited information in Genesis, but God wants us to remember this occasion as Psalm 110:4 and The New Testament Letter to the Hebrews mentions a priest who lived long before the Jewish priests from the Tribe of Levi.

Read Melchizedek's blessing. It is good to know that believers are in the care of the God who created everything. Abraham responded by giving Melchizedek one-tenth of the booty.

The King of Sodom was only interested in recovering the captives. Abraham declined his offer of the booty. He promised God he would not give the King opportunity to take the glory that Abraham owed to God for all that God had provided for him. So, Abraham accepted only the cost of the food eaten and said that his allies should receive the booty.

GENESIS CHAPTER 15

After this, the word of the LORD came to Abram in a vision: "Do not be afraid, Abram. I am your shield, your very great reward." (2) But Abram said, "Sovereign LORD, what can you give me since I remain childless and the one who will inherit my estate is Eliezer of Damascus?" (3) And Abram said, "You have given me no children; so a servant in my household will be my heir." (4) Then the word of the LORD came to him: "This man will not be your heir, but a son who is your own flesh and blood will be your heir." (5) He took him outside and said, "Look up at the sky and count the stars—if indeed you can count them." Then he said to him, "So shall your offspring be." (6) Abram believed the LORD, and he credited it to him as righteousness. (7) He also said to him, "I am the LORD, who brought you out of Ur of the Chaldeans to give you this land to take possession of it." (8) But Abram said, "Sovereign LORD, how can I know that I will gain possession of it?" (9) So the LORD said to him, "Bring me a heifer, a goat and a ram, each three years old, along with a dove and a young pigeon." (10) Abram brought all these to him, cut them in two and arranged the halves opposite each other; the birds, however, he did not cut in half. (11) Then birds of prey came down on the carcasses, but Abram drove them away. (12) As the sun was setting, Abram fell into a deep sleep, and a thick and dreadful darkness came over him. (13) Then the LORD said to him, "Know for certain that for four hundred years your descendants will be strangers in a country not their own and that they will be enslaved and mistreated there. (14) But I will punish the nation they serve as slaves, and afterward they will come out with great possessions. (15) You, however, will go to your ancestors in peace and be buried at a good old age. (16) In the fourth generation your descendants will come back here, for the sin of the Amorites has not yet reached its full measure." (17) When the sun had set and darkness had fallen, a smoking firepot with a blazing torch appeared and passed between the pieces. (18) On that day the LORD made a covenant with Abram and said, "To your descendants I give this land, from the Wadi of Egypt to the great river, the Euphrates— (19) the land of the Kenites, Kenizzites, Kadmonites, (20) Hittites, Perizzites, Rephaites, (21) Amorites, Canaanites, Girgashites and Jebusites."

COMMENTARY. GENESIS CHAPTER 15

Recall as you read this chapter, these words in Genesis 12:

'The LORD had said to Abram, "Go from your country, your people and your father's household to the land I will show you. I will make you into a great nation ..."

In Chapter 15 we read about four events when the Lord and Abraham spoke about future events. We do not know the precise details of where Abraham was, but it seems that:

1. during the day he had a vision in his tent.
2. after the vision, the Lord spoke to him outside his tent.
3. as the sun was setting Abraham had a special dream.
4. after the sun had set and darkness had fallen, the Lord spoke to Abraham again.

We do know what was said as Abraham asked two questions and received clarification of God's various promises. It seems that within a few hours, he was reassured about the blessings God had chosen to bestow on him and his descendants:

- he would be safe and have an heir, a son, and descendants too numerous to count.
- his descendants would possess the land from the River Nile to the River Euphrates, even though there were ten nations living there at the time when God made His promise.

As Abraham believed God, God counted him among those who, although they are sinners by nature and behaviour, He regards as righteous, meaning right with God.

If you are not yet a believer, the good news is that your sin can be forgiven. You, like Abraham, can be regarded by God as righteous, but this cannot happen until you repent and accept Jesus as your personal Saviour.

Genesis 11:31 stated that Abraham's father, Terah, left Ur with his family to travel to Canaan. But Genesis 15:7 informs us that God only planned the journey to Canaan for Abraham as He wanted to give Canaan to Abraham. It seems to us that because Abraham believed what God said to him, he had that special dream about future events. Abraham learnt that:

- God would allow His people to suffer, but after four hundred years they would have great wealth and those who ill-treated them would be punished.
- he would live a long life and die in peace.
- Canaan would not be possessed before the fourth generation of his descendants and the Amorites, who lived in Canaan, would be punished by his descendants when they possessed Canaan.

The fire, and the lamp confirmed to Abraham that he had spoken to God. We are not given further details about the Amorites' sins, but as God knows what sins will be committed in the future, He can plan future punishment. The Amorites are mentioned in seventy-seven Old Testament verses. Only four of them are in Genesis. As God had said, the Amorites were dispossessed of their land by Abraham's descendants.

Abraham had previously asked God for clarification of His promise regarding Canaan. So, as we have read, God specified the geographical area He referred to.

GENESIS CHAPTER 16

Now Sarai, Abram's wife, had borne him no children. But she had an Egyptian slave named Hagar; (2) so she said to Abram, "The LORD has kept me from having children. Go, sleep with my slave; perhaps I can build a family through her." Abram agreed to what Sarai said. (3) So after Abram had been living in Canaan ten years, Sarai his wife took her Egyptian slave Hagar and gave her to her husband to be his wife. (4) He slept with Hagar, and she conceived. When she knew she was pregnant, she began to despise her mistress. (5) Then Sarai said to Abram, "You are responsible for the wrong I am suffering. I put my slave in your arms, and now that she knows she is pregnant, she despises me. May the LORD judge between you and me." (6) "Your slave is in your hands," Abram said. "Do with her whatever you think best." Then Sarai mistreated Hagar; so she fled from her. (7) The angel of the LORD found Hagar near a spring in the desert; it was the spring that is beside the road to Shur. (8) And he said, "Hagar, slave of Sarai, where have you come from, and where are you going?" "I'm running away from my mistress Sarai," she answered. (9) Then the angel of the LORD told her, "Go back to your mistress and submit to her."(10) The angel added, "I will increase your descendants so much that they will be too numerous to count." (11) The angel of the LORD also said to her: "You are now pregnant and you will give birth to a son. You shall name him Ishmael, for the LORD has heard of your misery. (12) He will be a wild donkey of a man; his hand will be against everyone and everyone's hand against him, and he will live in hostility toward all his brothers." (13) She gave this name to the LORD who spoke to her: "You are the God who sees me," for she said, "I have now seen the One who sees me." (14) That is why the well was called Beer Lahai Roi; it is still there, between Kadesh and Bered. (15) So Hagar bore Abram a son, and Abram gave the name Ishmael to the son she had borne. (16) Abram was eighty-six years old when Hagar bore him Ishmael.

COMMENTARY. GENESIS CHAPTER 16

Sarah wanted a child. What she said appears to doubt God's promises. God had not specifically mentioned Sarah in his promises, but God had promised Abraham that He would make him into a great nation on three occasions:

1. In Haran.
2. After Lot left Abraham to live near Sodom.
3. We are not told when God's third promise was made.

We are not told Sarah's concerns that made her devise a plan involving her Egyptian maid, Hagar. We know from Genesis 17 that Sarah was ten years younger than Abraham and from Genesis that they had many servants of their own race.

Abraham agreed to Sarah's suggestion. For a second time in Genesis we read about men who agreed to their wives' requests and tragic consequences resulted:

1. Adam ate what Eve gave him rather than refuse it and obey God. Adam's misplaced loyalty brought sin into the world.
2. Abraham did as Sarah suggested. Nothing suggests that he asked God if Sarah's plan had His approval. We have read the consequences.

Sarah and Abraham were unhappy. Hagar was pregnant and ran away after Sarah beat her. Was this tragedy the result of God's plan going wrong? "No." It was Sarah's plan that went wrong. Like Adam, Abraham had to learn that whatever advice or pressure he received from his wife, it must not stop him putting God first in his life. If these men had listened to God, and not their wives, both wives would have avoided the consequences of their own folly.

We read about others in The Bible who also discovered the hard way that God knows what is best. Two of them, Jacob and his mother Rebekah are mentioned later in Genesis. God does not need our ingenuity to assist Him. Even though many years had passed since God's first promise to Abraham, God knows the best time to fulfil His promises.

Fortunately for Hagar and us, God knows where we are, and He wants us to return to a place of blessing. Hagar received a visitor, who asked her to return. Read the conversation and the promises made to Hagar. Very few mothers mentioned in The Bible were informed by God that they would give birth to a son and told his name.

'Ishmael,' means 'God hears.' God still hears today. Hagar also discovered that God cares. God still cares today. Hagar was obedient. She did as instructed and returned to Abraham, who, when his son was born, called him Ishmael.

GENESIS CHAPTER 17

When Abram was ninety-nine years old, the LORD appeared to him and said, "I am God Almighty; walk before me faithfully and be blameless. (2) Then I will make my covenant between me and you and will greatly increase your numbers." (3) Abram fell facedown, and God said to him, (4) "As for me, this is my covenant with you: You will be the father of many nations. (5) No longer will you be called Abram; your name will be Abraham, for I have made you a father of many nations. (6) I will make you very fruitful; I will make nations of you, and kings will come from you. (7) I will establish my covenant as an everlasting covenant between me and you and your descendants after you for the generations to come, to be your God and the God of your descendants after you. (8) The whole land of Canaan, where you now reside as a foreigner, I will give as an everlasting possession to you and your descendants after you; and I will be their God." (9) Then God said to Abraham, "As for you, you must keep my covenant, you and your descendants after you for the generations to come. (10) This is my covenant with you and your descendants after you, the covenant you are to keep: Every male among you shall be circumcised. (11) You are to undergo circumcision, and it will be the sign of the covenant between me and you. (12) For the generations to come every male among you who is eight days old must be circumcised, including those born in your household or bought with money from a foreigner—those who are not your offspring. (13) Whether born in your household or bought with your money, they must be circumcised. My covenant in your flesh is to be an everlasting covenant. (14) Any uncircumcised male, who has not been circumcised in the flesh, will be cut off from his people; he has broken my covenant." (15) God also said to Abraham, "As for Sarai your wife, you are no longer to call her Sarai; her name will be Sarah. (16) I will bless her and will surely give you a son by her. I will bless her so that she will be the mother of nations; kings of peoples will come from her." (17) Abraham fell facedown; he laughed and said to himself, "Will a son be born to a man a hundred years old? Will Sarah bear a child at the age of ninety?" (18) And Abraham said to God, "If only Ishmael might live under your blessing!" (19) Then God said, "Yes, but your wife Sarah will bear you a son, and you will call him Isaac. I will establish my covenant with him as an everlasting covenant for his descendants after him. (20) And as for Ishmael, I have heard you: I will surely bless him; I will make him fruitful and will greatly increase his numbers. He will be the father of twelve rulers, and I will make him into a great nation. (21) But my covenant I will establish with Isaac, whom Sarah will bear to you by this time next year." (22) When he had finished speaking with Abraham, God went up from him. (23) On that very day Abraham took his son Ishmael and all those born in his household or bought with his money, every male in his household, and circumcised them, as God told him. (24) Abraham was ninety-nine years old when he was circumcised, (25) and his son Ishmael was thirteen; (26) Abraham and his son Ishmael were both circumcised on that very day. (27) And every male in Abraham's household, including those born in his household or bought from a foreigner, was circumcised with him.

COMMENTARY. GENESIS CHAPTER 17

Abraham was now ninety-nine years old. It was thirteen years since Ishmael was born and we know nothing about this period. God only wants us to learn 'The History of Salvation' and we only read about events that are part of that history.

In the last chapter we read that Abraham and Sarah did not wait for God to keep His promises but arranged for Hagar to have a child instead of Sarah. It was the wrong time. Abraham could have fathered a child at the age of eighty-five as the birth of Ishmael proved. God's plan was for:

- Abraham to father a son at a time when, on account of his age, it would have been humanly impossible.
- Sarah to give birth to a son long after she had passed her childbearing years.
- the birth of Isaac to be a miracle.

God was gradually teaching Abraham about His eternal plan. For instance, on the third occasion that God spoke to him, Abraham discovered that he would be the father of not just one, but a multitude of nations. We ask three questions:

1. Had it taken Abraham twenty-four years to appreciate the magnitude of God's promises to him?
2. Did Abraham finally realise that because of his age, it would take a miracle for him to father a son, and so, there was a very special reason in God's Plan for this child to be born?

3. After twenty-four years, did Abraham think that because he agreed to Sarah's plan God had decided not to use him?

We are not given the answers, but we know that when Abraham heard God repeat His promise, and add that he would be the father of not just one but many nations, Abraham fell down with his face in the dust.

The Bible teaches that God hates pride. Abraham's act of humility meant that he was now ready for God's Plan to commence. God disclosed more facts about His future and changed his name. It confirmed the change in Abraham.

Abram became Abraham. You can read God's promise to him. It was a contract. He knew that if he and his descendants obeyed God, then God would be their God and they would be God's people. Canaan, 'the promised land,' would be theirs forever. Note that God required every male to be circumcised. It was visible proof of their agreement to God's terms.

Question: What happened to any male who refused to be circumcised?

Answer: They were separated from their own people.

When we have read God's instructions in Genesis, we have noted that there are only two responses. They are obedience or disobedience. There is no third option.

Delay for any reason is disobedience. Those who are not sure or want time to consider God's instructions are disobedient.

God spoke to Abraham about the changes involving Sarai. Her new name was Sarah as she would now be the mother of nations. When God referred to Sarah and a son, Abraham assumed that God must have been referring to Ishmael. So Abraham asked God to bless the thirteen-year-old Ishmael.

God repeated His promise of a boy born to Sarah. God also blessed Ishmael and outlined his great future. But note that God did not make a contract with Ishmael.

Abraham was informed that God's contract related only to his unborn child. Abraham laughed. So, God told him to call Sarah's baby boy, Isaac. Isaac means laughter. Abraham would always be reminded that he laughed at God's promise of a son to a couple with a combined age of one hundred and ninety years. It is not for us to judge Abraham. To his credit, he did what God required immediately.

GENESIS CHAPTER 18

The LORD appeared to Abraham near the great trees of Mamre while he was sitting at the entrance to his tent in the heat of the day. (2) Abraham looked up and saw three men standing nearby. When he saw them, he hurried from the entrance of his tent to meet them and bowed low to the ground. (3) He said, "If I have found favor in your eyes, my lord, do not pass your servant by. (4) Let a little water be brought, and then you may all wash your feet and rest under this tree. (5) Let me get you something to eat, so you can be refreshed and then go on your way—now that you have come to your servant." "Very well," they answered, "do as you say." (6) So Abraham hurried into the tent to Sarah. "Quick," he said, "get three seahs of the finest flour and knead it and bake some bread." (7) Then he ran to the herd and selected a choice, tender calf and gave it to a servant, who hurried to prepare it. (8) He then brought some curds and milk and the calf that had been prepared, and set these before them. While they ate, he stood near them under a tree. (9) "Where is your wife Sarah?" they asked him. "There, in the tent," he said. (10) Then one of them said, "I will surely return to you about this time next year, and Sarah your wife will have a son." Now Sarah was listening at the entrance to the tent, which was behind him. (11) Abraham and Sarah were already very old, and Sarah was past the age of childbearing. (12) So Sarah laughed to herself as she thought, "After I am worn out and my lord is old, will I now have this pleasure?" (13) Then the

LORD said to Abraham, "Why did Sarah laugh and say, 'Will I really have a child, now that I am old?' (14) Is anything too hard for the LORD? I will return to you at the appointed time next year, and Sarah will have a son." (15) Sarah was afraid, so she lied and said, "I did not laugh." But he said, "Yes, you did laugh." (16) When the men got up to leave, they looked down toward Sodom, and Abraham walked along with them to see them on their way. (17) Then the LORD said, "Shall I hide from Abraham what I am about to do? (18) Abraham will surely become a great and powerful nation, and all nations on earth will be blessed through him. (19) For I have chosen him, so that he will direct his children and his household after him to keep the way of the LORD by doing what is right and just, so that the LORD will bring about for Abraham what he has promised him." (20) Then the LORD said, "The outcry against Sodom and Gomorrah is so great and their sin so grievous (21) that I will go down and see if what they have done is as bad as the outcry that has reached me. If not, I will know." (22) The men turned away and went toward Sodom, but Abraham remained standing before the LORD. (23) Then Abraham approached him and said: "Will you sweep away the righteous with the wicked? (24) What if there are fifty righteous people in the city? Will you really sweep it away and not spare the place for the sake of the fifty righteous people in it? (25) Far be it from you to do such a thing—to kill the righteous with the wicked, treating the righteous and the wicked alike. Far be it from you! Will not the Judge of all the earth do right?" (26) The LORD said, "If I find fifty righteous people in the city of Sodom, I will spare the whole place for their sake." (27) Then Abraham spoke up again: "Now that I have been so bold as to speak to the Lord, though I am nothing but dust and ashes, (28) what if the number of the righteous is five less than fifty? Will you destroy the whole city for lack of five people?" "If I find forty-five there," he said, "I will not destroy it." (29) Once again he spoke to him, "What if only forty are found there?" He said, "For the sake of forty, I will not do it." (30) Then he said, "May the Lord not be angry, but let me speak. What if only thirty can be found there?" He answered, "I will not do it if I find thirty there." (31) Abraham said, "Now that I have been so bold as to speak to the Lord, what if only twenty can be found there?" He said, "For the sake of twenty, I will not destroy it." (32) Then he said, "May the Lord not be angry, but let me speak just once more. What if only ten can be found there?" He answered, "For the sake of ten, I will not destroy it." (33) When the LORD had finished speaking with Abraham, he left, and Abraham returned home.

COMMENTARY. GENESIS CHAPTER 18

We know little about this event other than the time and place. We read that God appeared, but we do not know what was said. We are then told about three visitors. Read Abraham's conversation with them. One of the visitors was God and the other two were angels. As they approached, Abraham ran to meet them and bowed to the ground. His actions, words and hospitality were customary. The word 'lord' was a polite customary greeting at that time.

There was a change in the conversation during the meal. The visitors referred to Sarah. We read that God spoke. This was the fifth time that God had spoken to Abraham.

- God again promised that he would have descendants.
- The promise of a son for Sarah was repeated and the birth was in the next year.

Previously, we read that Abraham laughed when hearing that he and Sarah could have a baby. On overhearing God's promise, Sarah laughed for the same reason as Abraham. But she laughed silently. God knows everything and Sarah's laughter was discussed with Abraham. Memorise God's wonderful question that did not require an answer:

"Is anything too hard for the Lord?"

God's question will always be answered "No." Believers will always be able to rely on God to provide all that is needed for His eternal plans to come to fruition. His promises never fail.

If you are not a believer, you are not part of God's Plan of Salvation. You, unlike believers, do not possess God's Salvation. Your eternal future is bleak, but it does not have to stay bleak. If you decide to become a believer, you will also possess God's Salvation.

Sarah was afraid and denied laughing. Abraham and Sarah had both laughed at the news that Sarah would give birth to a son. However, as humanly impossible as it seemed to them, they obeyed God. Sarah did not suggest that Abraham sleep with a younger woman as she had done previously. Although beyond childbearing age, Sarah conceived Abraham's son. Sarah's trust that God would make the humanly impossible possible was rewarded when she gave birth to Isaac.

The three visitors left Abraham's home for their journey to Sodom. Abraham joined them for part of their journey. Read how God disclosed to him the purpose of His visit. The narrative records God's mercy towards sinners. Note that God delayed punishing the evil people of Sodom and Gomorrah:

- God visited Abraham to announce the birth of Isaac.
- God listened to Abraham's appeal.

Abraham's appeal ceased when the number he pleaded for was only ten and he heard God's reply. Did Abraham then realise that the Sodomites deserved God's punishment for their wickedness? When we read what Abraham mentioned to God, we note his maturity in his knowledge of God and the things that matter to God. He appears to have grasped the truth that however many differences there might be between people, as far as God is concerned, mankind can be divided into two. Those who have repented, and God has forgiven and those who have not repented, and God has not forgiven.

We know Abraham's spiritual assessment was correct by the way God spoke to him. Nothing has changed. This division still divides mankind. God taught Abraham that He wants to spare rather than punish, but He must punish those who of their own free choose not to repent, not to be forgiven, and who want to live sinful lives.

What a contrast there is between the lives of the unrighteous who love their sin and sinning and the small minority who have repented, are righteous, and live righteously to please God.

We note that God wants to be merciful rather than punish in the gradual reduction in number that Abraham pleaded for and God agreed to. Once ten was agreed, they separated. We read later that Abraham also pleaded for the safety of Lot.

What a momentous day it was for Abraham and Sarah. They entertained God and two angels and received confirmation that Sarah would give birth to a son the next year.

GENESIS CHAPTER 19

The two angels arrived at Sodom in the evening, and Lot was sitting in the gateway of the city. When he saw them, he got up to meet them and bowed down with his face to the ground. (2) "My lords," he said, "please turn aside to your servant's house. You can wash your feet and spend the night and then go on your way early in the morning." "No," they answered, "we will spend the night in the square." (3) But he insisted so strongly that they did go with him and entered his house. He prepared a meal for them, baking bread without yeast, and they ate. (4) Before they had gone to bed, all the men from every part of the city of Sodom—both young and old—surrounded the house. (5) They called to Lot, "Where are the men who came to you tonight? Bring them out to us so that we can have sex with them." (6) Lot went outside to meet them and shut the door behind him (7) and said, "No, my friends. Don't do this wicked thing. (8) Look, I have two daughters who have never slept with a man. Let me bring them out to you, and you can do what you like with them. But don't do anything to these men, for they have come under the protection of my roof." (9) "Get out of our way," they replied. "This fellow came here as a foreigner, and now he wants to play the judge! We'll treat you worse than them." They kept bringing pressure on Lot and moved forward to break down the door. (10) But the men inside reached out and pulled Lot back into the house and shut the door. (11) Then they struck the men who were at the door of the house, young and old, with blindness so that they could not find the door. (12) The two men said to Lot, "Do you have anyone else here—sons-in-law, sons or daughters, or anyone else in the city who belongs to you? Get them out of here, (13) because we are going to destroy this place. The outcry to the LORD against its people is so great that he has sent us to destroy it." (14) So Lot went out and spoke to his sons-in-law, who were pledged to marry his daughters. He said, "Hurry and get out of this place, because the LORD is about to destroy the city!" But his sons-in-law thought he was joking. (15) With the coming of dawn, the angels urged Lot, saying, "Hurry! Take your wife and your two daughters who are here, or you will be swept away when the city is punished." (16) When he hesitated, the men grasped his hand and the hands of his wife and of his two daughters and led them safely out of the city, for the LORD was merciful to them. (17) As soon as they had brought them out, one of them said, "Flee for your lives! Don't look back, and don't stop anywhere in the plain! Flee to the mountains or you will be swept away!" (18) But Lot said to them, "No, my lords, please! (19) Your servant has found favor in your eyes, and you have shown great kindness to me in sparing my life. But I can't flee to the mountains; this disaster will overtake me, and I'll die. (20) Look, here is a town near enough to run to, and it is small. Let me flee to it—it is very small, isn't it? Then my life will be spared." (21) He said to him, "Very well, I will grant this request too; I will not overthrow the town you speak of. (22)

But flee there quickly, because I cannot do anything until you reach it." (That is why the town was called Zoar.) (23) By the time Lot reached Zoar, the sun had risen over the land. (24) Then the LORD rained down burning sulfur on Sodom and Gomorrah—from the LORD out of the heavens. (25) Thus he overthrew those cities and the entire plain, destroying all those living in the cities—and also the vegetation in the land. (26) But Lot's wife looked back, and she became a pillar of salt. (27) Early the next morning Abraham got up and returned to the place where he had stood before the LORD. (28) He looked down toward Sodom and Gomorrah, toward all the land of the plain, and he saw dense smoke rising from the land, like smoke from a furnace. (29) So when God destroyed the cities of the plain, he remembered Abraham, and he brought Lot out of the catastrophe that overthrew the cities where Lot had lived. (30) Lot and his two daughters left Zoar and settled in the mountains, for he was afraid to stay in Zoar. He and his two daughters lived in a cave. (31) One day the older daughter said to the younger, "Our father is old, and there is no man around here to give us children—as is the custom all over the earth. (32) Let's get our father to drink wine and then sleep with him and preserve our family line through our father." (33) That night they got their father to drink wine, and the older daughter went in and slept with him. He was not aware of it when she lay down or when she got up. (34) The next day the older daughter said to the younger, "Last night I slept with my father. Let's get him to drink wine again tonight, and you go in and sleep with him so we can preserve our family line through our father." (35) So they got their father to drink wine that night also, and the younger daughter went in and slept with him. Again he was not aware of it when she lay down or when she got up. (36) So both of Lot's daughters became pregnant by their father. (37) The older daughter had a son, and she named him Moab; he is the father of the Moabites of today. (38) The younger daughter also had a son, and she named him Ben-Ammi; he is the father of the

Ammonites of today.

COMMENTARY. GENESIS CHAPTER 19

The two visitors were angels. We must state that artistic licence has over many centuries allowed artists to portray angels as men, women, and children with all sorts of extra features such as wings. The Bible does not tell us what angels look like. Abraham and Sarah would surely have noticed if their visitors had wings or a halo. It seems that angels look like ordinary men when they come to Earth. Lot treated them as ordinary men. He did not know who they were. We shall for the time being refer to them as 'the visitors.'

What do we know about Lot? When he left Abraham, he lived near Sodom. We now read that he had a house in Sodom and sat at its entrance. Historians tell us that the chief men of the city sat at its entrances to monitor visitors. Presumably Lot, with all his wealth, had become a prominent figure in Sodom. We read in Genesis 14 that Lot was captured when Sodom was attacked. When he was freed, he returned to Sodom.

The visitors at first declined Lot's offer of hospitality. Maybe Lot failed to appreciate that however he behaved, choosing to live with the unrighteous meant that he would be regarded as unrighteous. We read there were not even ten righteous people in Sodom and Gomorrah. The Bible does not hide from us the shameful events that occurred that night.

The meal that Lot prepared for the visitors was interrupted by the Sodomites, who wanted to rape the visitors. Read Lot's discussion with these evil men. His moral judgement had sunk to a low level. His daughters were entitled to his protection. They were not goods to be bought, sold or bargained with.

We do not excuse what Lot did, but Abraham had been a bad example to him. We read In Genesis 12 that when Abraham went to Egypt, he feared he would be killed because Sarah was beautiful. He asked her to say that she was his sister. We shall read In Genesis 20 of another occasion when Abraham and Sarah pretended to be brother and sister. Acting innocently, the King of Gerar sent for Sarah. God intervened and Sarah was unharmed.

Genesis confirms that God's view of sin is correct. All sin is evil. God detests it and unforgiven sinners will be punished eternally in The Lake of Fire. Respectability usually hides sin. It must not be confused with righteousness. It seems that Lot was deceived by sin. Naivety is not a virtue. Do not be deceived by sin. John's First Letter will be well worth the time you spend reading it, especially if you are not aware of the cleansing power of the blood shed by Jesus at Calvary.

Lot did not appreciate that the Sodomites thought that those who dwelt in Sodom were unrighteous. They would not be told how to behave by someone who chose to live with them. Believers should know that the difference between believers and unbelievers is not theoretical. God's Salvation has a life changing effect. Believers repent and turn their backs on their former sinful way of life. They stop pleasing themselves and live to please God. Unbelievers neither appreciate nor approve of faithful believers' lifestyles. Hence, The Bible teaches that faithful believers will always be persecuted.

We might not know what angels look like, but we do know from The Bible that angels are God's servants. They are numerous, strong and use divine power. They emphasised to Lot the urgency of their mission. The destruction of Sodom was imminent. Lot wanted more time to save his future sons-in-law but he had lost his credibility. His warnings were ignored. The visitors would not delay. They dragged Lot and his family out of Sodom. We read a wonderful statement that summed up God's involvement in saving Lot and his family:

'the LORD was merciful to them' Genesis 19:16.

We read later of the Sodomites' punishment. Some might question how God could be said to be, 'merciful,' when He punished the Sodomites. It is so important that readers should know three vital truths about God's attitude to sin. God:

1. detests sin.
2. cannot overlook or ignore sin.
3. must judge sin.

Sinners must repent to avoid God's eternal judgment for their sins. Sinners who never repent will never be forgiven. Many years' experience teaches three facts about unbelievers who allege that God is not loving and merciful:

1. Most will not listen to The Gospel.
2. Some do listen to The Gospel, but few are willing to repent.
3. Even when told of God's eternal judgment for sin in The Lake of Fire, most unbelievers do not stop loving their sin.

All could repent and accept Jesus as their Saviour, but only those who do will escape God's eternal judgment. The vast majority choose to ignore The Gospel's warning of judgment. They remain unsaved. Have you realised that The Gospel is like the warning given by the visitors? It was precise, clear and simple. We consider each part:

"FLEE FOR YOUR LIVES"

If Lot and his family ignored this warning, staying near Sodom would have ensured their destruction. Note that the visitors did not drag them to a place of safety. We quote Genesis 19:17:

'As soon as they had brought them out, one of them said, "Flee for your lives! Don't look back, and don't stop anywhere in the plain! Flee to the mountains or you will be swept away!"

God did not force Lot and his family to be saved from His judgment and no one will be forced to accept God's Salvation.

"DO NOT LOOK BACK"

No reason is given for this warning. But we know that when God gave Noah instructions about the ship's windows, they had to be installed at the top of the ark's sides so that Noah and his family could not see God punish those who were not in the ark. Note also that Abraham only saw the result of God's judgment. He did not see God's punish the Sodomites. Maybe God did not want Abraham, Noah and Lot and their families to see Him punish unforgiven sinners.

It is only right that we state that there is little information about Hell and The Lake of Fire in The Bible. However, there are enough warnings about the awful punishment that unforgiven sinners will suffer for eternity.

"ESCAPE TO THE MOUNTAINS"

Lot and his family had been dragged out of Sodom, but they were still not safe. They had to choose whether to escape or stay where they were. "Escape" only has one meaning. It is easily understood. However, experience teaches that many know they need God's Salvation but, they choose God's punishment instead by remaining unforgiven sinners.

"DO NOT STAY HERE"

These simple words stressed the warnings already given. You might think that the words 'flee' and 'escape' were enough, but God is merciful and loving. He repeats His warnings. God does not give sinners only one chance to repent. He wants to forgive them, no matter how evil they have been but He cannot forgive those who will not repent. He must punish them.

There have been other occasions recorded in The Bible when God, or one of His chosen servants, have issued simple warnings with a choice of only one of two alternatives. There is never a third option. God always lets us choose. For example, we read in Deuteronomy 30 that Moses spoke to the Israelites before they crossed the River Jordan to live in the 'promised land of Canaan.' For the sake of space, we have abridged Deuteronomy 30:11-19. ERV.

"'This command that I give you today is not too hard for you

.... So you can obey it .... Today I have given you a choice between life and death .... I command you today to love the LORD your God. I command you to follow him and to obey his commands, laws, and rules. Then you will live, and your nation will grow larger. And the LORD your God will bless you in the land that you are entering to take for your own. But if you turn away from your God and refuse to listen, if you are led away to worship and serve other gods, you will be destroyed. I am warning you today, if you turn away from God, you will not live long in that land across the Jordan River that you are ready to enter and take for your own. Today I am giving you a choice of two ways. And I ask heaven and earth to be witnesses of your choice. You can choose life or death. The first choice will bring a blessing. The other choice will bring a curse. So choose life ...'"

As you read the remainder of Genesis 19, you might conclude that Lot and his family were unworthy recipients of God's love and mercy, but no one has ever merited them.

Lot thanked the visitors for saving his life, but he still wanted to decide his own future. Although the visitors agreed to his request, his decision turned out to be disastrous, both for himself and his family. It seems that Lot never realised that his former decisions had always ended in catastrophes. Believers who make decisions without seeking God's Will take the same risks that Lot took. We ask a general question that we trust will make believers consider how they live.

Question: If believers realised how much God wants to be involved and bless them in their daily lives, would they still insist on being in charge of their own lives?

When Lot and Abraham separated, neither would have envisaged the trouble that befell Lot, but he could only blame himself for His willingness to take risks:

- Lot chose to live with wicked idolaters, rather than his own people who worshipped God. Abraham told Sarah that they lived amongst men who killed husbands so that they could acquire their beautiful wives.

- Lot did not care about his own safety. He knew that living in Sodom was unsafe when he was captured.
- After being saved from Sodom, Lot chose to live in Zoar. It also had evil inhabitants. Lot did not know that God had already decided to destroy Zoar but God spared it when Lot decided to live there.
- Even when Lot was told that God had spared Zoar because he was there, he did not choose another place to live or go back to the safety of Abraham's home.
- When Lot left Zoar because he was afraid, he did not return to the safety of Abraham's home.

Question: Why did Lot choose to live with wicked people rather than those who put their trust in God?

We do not know. But we do know that many make a conscious choice to remain unforgiven sinners, even though they know that their choice will result in God's eternal judgment for their sin. Perhaps what the Prophet Jeremiah preached to the Jews who belonged to The Tribe of Judah, centuries after Abraham and Lot, explains why so many decisions are made that mystify us. In Jeremiah 17:9. NLT we read these solemn words:

"The human heart is the most deceitful of all things, and desperately wicked. Who really knows how bad it is?

As nobody told Lot what to do, or what not to do, we ask two questions. Why did he choose to:

1. be associated with wicked people?

2. live in places where wicked people lived?

Was Lot deceived by his own heart? He was not ignorant of the facts. He knew what he should do. Experience teaches that many are like Lot. The Jews that Jeremiah preached to were. They knew what God required them to do. They chose not to do it.

Genesis records the shameful behaviour of Lot's daughters. Living in Sodom, away from the moral influence of Abraham's home, had repercussions that Lot could never have imagined.

We have considered historical events, but the warnings and the lessons are up to date. The Bible still states the eternal consequences for those who remain unforgiven sinners.

GENESIS CHAPTER 20

Now Abraham moved on from there into the region of the Negev and lived between Kadesh and Shur. For a while he stayed in Gerar, (2) and there Abraham said of his wife Sarah, "She is my sister." Then Abimelek king of Gerar sent for Sarah and took her. (3) But God came to Abimelek in a dream one night and said to him, "You are as good as dead because of the woman you have taken; she is a married woman." (4) Now Abimelek had not gone near her, so he said, "Lord, will you destroy an innocent nation? (5) Did he not say to me, 'She is my sister,' and didn't she also say, 'He is my brother'? I have done this with a clear conscience and clean hands." 6) Then God said to him in the dream, "Yes, I know you did this with a clear conscience, and so I have kept you from sinning against me. That is why I did not let you touch her. (7) Now return the man's wife, for he is a prophet, and he will pray for you and you will live. But if you do not return her, you may be sure that you and all who belong to you will die." (8) Early the next morning Abimelek summoned all his officials, and when he told them all that had happened, they were very much afraid. (9) Then Abimelek called Abraham in and said, "What have you done to us? How have I wronged you that you have brought such great guilt upon me and my kingdom? You have done things to me that should never be done." (10) And Abimelek asked Abraham, "What was your reason for doing this?" (11) Abraham replied, "I said to myself, 'There is surely no fear of God in this place, and they will kill me because of my wife.' (12) Besides, she really is my sister, the daughter of my father though not of my mother; and she became my wife. (13) And when God had me wander from my father's household, I said to her, 'This is how you can show your love to me: Everywhere we go, say of me, "He is my brother."'" (14) Then Abimelek brought sheep and cattle and male and female slaves and gave them to Abraham, and he returned Sarah his wife to him. (15) And Abimelek said, "My land is before you; live wherever you like." (16) To Sarah he said, "I am giving your brother a thousand shekels of silver. This is to cover the offense against you before all who are with you; you are completely vindicated." (17) Then Abraham prayed to God, and God healed Abimelek, his wife and his female slaves so they could have children again, (18) for the LORD had kept all the women in Abimelek's household from conceiving because of Abraham's wife Sarah.

COMMENTARY. GENESIS CHAPTER 20

The events of this chapter are similar to those in Genesis 12 when we read that Abraham and Sarah travelled to Egypt to avoid a severe famine. They knew the dangers of travelling to new areas where the locals murdered husbands to kidnap their wives. Sarah was Abraham's half-sister. They agreed once again to say they were brother and sister. As they were both brother and sister and husband and wife, to pretend to be only brother and sister was not only wrong, it showed their lack of faith in what God had promised them on two matters:

1. Abraham would have a long life.
2. Sarah would have a son within a year.

Hence, it was impossible for Abraham to be killed and Sarah to be kidnapped, but they felt unsafe. They deceived King Abimelek. God had to intervene to save the King and his household from judgment. God told the King that Abraham was a prophet who would pray for him. He did as God said.

As a result of God's intervention Abraham prospered materially by the King's gifts.

Once again, Abraham's faith in God's faltered. He had already been expelled from Egypt for telling the same lie. Had he not learnt that God was in total control? He would have been safe anywhere. We all prefer others to know only our strengths, but The Bible is concerned with truth. We learn from studying Abraham's life that God will provide us with all the resources we need to do what He asks us to do. God wants believers to enjoy His love and fellowship, and to rely on His promise that He will never leave nor forsake those who belong to Him.

GENESIS CHAPTER 21

Now the LORD was gracious to Sarah as he had said, and the LORD did for Sarah what he had promised. (2) Sarah became pregnant and bore a son to Abraham in his old age, at the very time God had promised him. (3) Abraham gave the name Isaac to the son Sarah bore him. (4) When his son Isaac was eight days old, Abraham circumcised him, as God commanded him. (5) Abraham was a hundred years old when his son Isaac was born to him. (6) Sarah said, "God has brought me laughter, and everyone who hears about this will laugh with me."(7) And she added, "Who would have said to Abraham that Sarah would nurse children? Yet I have borne him a son in his old age." (8) The child grew and was weaned, and on the day Isaac was weaned Abraham held a great feast. (9) But Sarah saw that the son whom Hagar the Egyptian had borne to Abraham was mocking, (10) and she said to Abraham, "Get rid of that slave woman and her son, for that woman's son will never share in the inheritance with my son Isaac." (11) The matter distressed Abraham greatly because it concerned his son. (12) But God said to him, "Do not be so distressed about the boy and your slave woman. Listen to whatever Sarah tells you, because it is through Isaac that your offspring will be reckoned.(13) I will make the son of the slave into a nation also, because he is your offspring."(14) Early the next morning Abraham took some food and a skin of water and gave them to Hagar. He set them on her shoulders and then sent her off with the boy. She went on her way and wandered in the Desert of Beersheba. (15) When the water in the skin was gone, she put the boy under one of the bushes. (16) Then she went off and sat down about a bowshot away, for she thought, "I cannot watch the boy die." And as she sat there, she began to sob. (17) God heard the boy crying, and the angel of God called to Hagar from heaven and said to her, "What is the matter, Hagar? Do not be afraid; God has heard the boy crying as he lies there. (18) Lift the boy up and take him by the hand, for I will make him into a great nation." (19) Then God opened her eyes and she saw a well of water. So she went and filled the skin with water and gave the boy a drink. (20) God was with the boy as he grew up. He lived in the desert and became an archer. (21) While he was living in the Desert of Paran, his mother got a wife for him from Egypt. (22) At that time Abimelek and Phicol the commander of his forces said to Abraham, "God is with you in everything you do. (23) Now swear to me here before God that you will not deal falsely with me or my children or my descendants. Show to me and the country where you now reside as a foreigner the same kindness I have shown to you." (24) Abraham said, "I swear it." (25) Then Abraham complained to Abimelek about a well of water that Abimelek's servants had seized. (26) But Abimelek said, "I don't know who has done this. You did not tell me, and I heard about it only today." (27) So Abraham brought sheep and cattle and gave them to Abimelek, and the two men made a treaty. (28) Abraham set apart seven ewe lambs from the flock, (29) and Abimelek asked Abraham, "What is the meaning of these seven ewe lambs you have set apart by themselves?" (30) He replied, "Accept these seven lambs from my hand as a witness that I dug this well." (31) So that place was called Beersheba, because the two men swore an oath there. (32) After the treaty had been made at

Beersheba, Abimelek and Phicol the commander of his forces returned to the land of the Philistines. (33) Abraham planted a tamarisk tree in Beersheba, and there he called on the name of the LORD, the Eternal God. (34) And Abraham stayed in the land of the Philistines for a long time.

COMMENTARY. GENESIS CHAPTER 21

What did Abraham and Sarah learn? God kept His word. If we are unfaithful and God cannot rely on us, we can rely on Him to keep His word:

- God was gracious and merciful. Our disobedience does not cause God's love for us to cease.
- God knows the future. He said the baby boy would be born within a year. God is always right.
- God has the ability to give life. He can bring life out of death.

Isaac's conception and birth were the same as every other baby. The miracle was that Abraham and Sarah were too old to become parents. Their child-producing days had long gone:

- Abraham was almost one hundred years old. He knew His body's reproductive functions were as good as dead. Sarah, his ninety-year-old wife, had that same honest assessment about her own reproductive functions.
- Abraham laughed when he heard from God that Sarah would give birth to a son. She did too. Isaac means 'laughter.' She thought that everyone who heard that she had given birth would laugh as they rejoiced with her.
- Abraham never forgot God's ability to bring life out of death. We shall refer to this again in the next chapter.

In Genesis 17 we read that God made an agreement with Abraham that required him to circumcise all boys when they were eight days old. Isaac was circumcised. He gave much pleasure to Abraham who arranged a party to celebrate the day Isaac was no longer breast fed. But, as we read,

Abraham's joy turned to sadness. What Sarah wanted was harsh, especially as both boys were Abraham's sons, but it was not part of God's plan that Ishmael would share Abraham's inheritance. God repeated what He said after Ishmael's birth. Ishmael would head his own nation. We now know God referred to the Arabs. Isaac headed the Jews. Hagar left Abraham's home on two occasions:

1. We read in Genesis 16 that Hagar ran away when she was pregnant because Sarah had beaten her for being arrogant.
2. We now read that Abraham expelled Hagar.

God knew Hagar's desperate situation on both occasions, and she knew His personal love and care:

- On the first occasion, she spoke to an angel by a stream.
- On the second occasion, an angel spoke to her from Heaven. She heard the good news that she had no reason to be afraid. God had a great future for her son.

Having read twenty-one chapters of Genesis, we know that nothing is too hard for God. So we ask, did the well exist before Hagar sat down, or did God provide it for her? We are not told, and we know little more about Ishmael as Genesis concentrates on 'Salvation History.' Hence, we only read the history of Abraham and Isaac, and their descendants.

We know the name of the place where Ishmael grew up and a few details of his marriage. We read about him in Genesis 25 after Abraham died, and in Genesis 28 when Esau visited him to acquire more wives.

A NEW START WITH GOD

King Abimelek was materialistic. He was complimentary about Abraham's God, but not about Abraham. Nothing suggests that Abimelek wanted to know the true God, or that he was willing to destroy the false gods he worshipped. The king was not unique. Many accept that God exists, but they do not want the personal relationship with Him that He wants with them.

God loves you. He sent Jesus, His only Son, into the world so that He could die on your behalf. God did this so that you could be eternally saved from His eternal punishment for your sin. As you read the words 'shall not perish, in John 3:16, consider if you have taken advantage of what God did for you:

John 3:16: 'For God so loved the world that he gave his one and only Son, that whoever believes in him shall not perish but have eternal life.'

We need to be blunt. The majority do not want 'A New Start with God.' They enjoy their sin and sinning and do not want to repent. If you have chosen to be one of them, and you do not wish to read about The Gospel 'God's Good News for Sinners' you need not read the remaining part of Genesis 21. You can resume reading Genesis from Chapter 22. But if, unlike the majority, you do want 'A New Start with God:'

- you must admit that you are a sinner and tell God that you want to repent of your sins. This means changing the way you live so that, in the future, you live to please God.
- you must believe that Jesus died for your sins and rose from the dead.

Only Jesus' death and resurrection can provide sinners with forgiveness, and make it possible for them to be 'right with God.' God can then regard them as 'if they had never sinned.'

GENESIS CHAPTER 22

Some time later God tested Abraham. He said to him, "Abraham!" "Here I am," he replied. (2) Then God said, "Take your son, your only son, whom you love—Isaac—and go to the region of Moriah. Sacrifice him there as a burnt offering on a mountain I will show you." (3) Early the next morning Abraham got up and loaded his donkey. He took with him two of his servants and his son Isaac. When he had cut enough wood for the burnt offering, he set out for the place God had told him about. (4) On the third day Abraham looked up and saw the place in the distance. (5) He said to his servants, "Stay here with the donkey while I and the boy go over there. We will worship and then we will come back to you." (6) Abraham took the wood for the burnt offering and placed it on his son Isaac, and he himself carried the fire and the knife. As the two of them went on together, (7) Isaac spoke up and said to his father Abraham, "Father?" "Yes, my son?" Abraham replied. "The fire and wood are here," Isaac said, "but where is the lamb for the burnt offering?" (8) Abraham answered, "God himself will provide the lamb for the burnt offering, my son." And the two of them went on together. (9) When they reached the place God had told him about, Abraham built an altar there and arranged the wood on it. He bound his son Isaac and laid him on the altar, on top of the wood. (10) Then he reached out his hand and took the knife to slay his son. (11) But the angel of the LORD called out to him from heaven, "Abraham! Abraham!" "Here I am," he replied. (12) "Do not lay a hand on the boy," he said. "Do not do anything to him. Now I know that you fear God, because you have not withheld from me your son, your only son."(13) Abraham looked up and there in a thicket he saw a ram caught by its horns. He went over and took the ram and sacrificed it as a burnt offering instead of his son. (14) So Abraham called that place The LORD Will Provide. And to this day it is said, "On the mountain of the LORD it will be provided." (15) The angel of the LORD called to Abraham from heaven a second time (16) and said, "I swear by myself, declares the LORD, that because you have done this and have not withheld your son, your only son, (17) I will surely bless you and make your descendants as numerous as the stars in the sky and as the sand on the seashore. Your descendants will take possession of the cities of their enemies, (18) and through your offspring all nations on earth will be blessed, because you have obeyed me." (19) Then Abraham returned to his servants, and they set off together for Beersheba. And Abraham stayed in Beersheba.

(20) Some time later Abraham was told, "Milkah is also a mother; she has borne sons to your brother Nahor: (21) Uz the firstborn, Buz his brother, Kemuel (the father of Aram), (22) Kesed, Hazo, Pildash, Jidlaph and Bethuel." (23) Bethuel became the father of Rebekah. Milkah bore these eight sons to Abraham's brother Nahor. (24) His concubine, whose name was Reumah, also had sons: Tebah, Gaham, Tahash and Maakah.

COMMENTARY. GENESIS CHAPTER 22

We need to read Genesis 22 carefully. Many have been taught notions, rather than what The Bible teaches. The assumption that Isaac was only a child has passed from generation to generation even though, it seems obvious that he was not a child. Many years must have passed since Abraham had been in contact with Ishmael, because when God spoke to Abraham, He referred to Isaac as his “only son.”

We know that Abraham built altars, but Genesis is silent about what the sacrifices consisted of and exactly what he did. We read that sacrificing Isaac was a test of his obedience to God. Some teach that Abraham usually offered a human sacrifice to God, and God used this event to teach him that such sacrifices were wrong. Those who teach this nonsense have obviously never read Genesis. So, we must read what The Bible teaches and reject what others tell it teaches. But, before we consider Genesis 22, we state two facts:

1. Abraham had two sons, Ishmael and Isaac.
2. When Ishmael was seven years old, and Isaac was a baby, Abraham lost the companionship of Ishmael when he and his mother were expelled.

We now consider Genesis 22. We stated above why it must have been many years after the expulsion of Ishmael that God decided to test Abraham. God asked him to sacrifice Isaac. We are not told Abraham’s thoughts but we do know that He wasted no time preparing to obey God's instruction. He started his journey early the next day. Whether Abraham knew that God was testing his faith we do not know, but Abraham knew that God was loving, gracious and merciful and He was not dealing with a God who was capricious.

We have read the incidents that gave Abraham his confidence to trust God. Abraham knew that despite his sins, God had never abandoned him or his family. Abraham had ample proof that God loved him and his family and cared about them. God was totally trustworthy and did what He said He would do.

We are not told what Abraham thought, only what he said, on the long journey. We know that Isaac was unmarried. God had told Abraham He would fulfil all His promises through Isaac. How could God do this if Isaac died?

We read later that Abraham believed that if Isaac died, God would make him live again. Isaac had been born to parents whose reproductive functions were 'as good as dead' so his birth had already proved that God could bring life out of death. Even before Isaac was born, God asked Abraham this wonderful question:

"Is anything too hard for the Lord?"

Abraham knew that God could do anything. Is there evidence that Abraham believed in life after death? Read his words to the servants. Abraham told them that he and Isaac were going to worship and they would return. Abraham had no lamb for the sacrifice but he had every intention of worshipping and returning with Isaac. Note his words in Genesis 22:5. Abraham had many years' experience of God. He knew truths that we would do well to learn:

- He could not sacrifice and worship unless he did exactly what God said because obedience to God was vital.
- Sacrifices had to be properly prepared. Worship required a sacrifice that satisfied God. Without the correct preparation, there could be no acceptable sacrifice or worship. Genesis

22:3 states what Abraham did at home. He did not start his preparation once he arrived at the place of sacrifice.

In Genesis 22:7-8 we read Isaac's query and Abraham's reply:

- Isaac: "Where is the lamb ..."
- Abraham: "God will provide ..."

God had always provided for Abraham and his family. Abraham never once had reason to doubt that God would keep His word. Four times The Bible tells us that 'Abraham believed.' God's faithfulness to Abraham was not dependant on Abraham's faithfulness. God always keeps His promises.

We now consider how old Isaac was at this time, and whether he was a willing sacrifice. The servants are described as young men. The same word, sometimes translated 'lad,' describes Isaac. He was of similar age to the servants and he was old enough to:

- travel on a journey that lasted at least three days.
- realise that they did not have a lamb to sacrifice.
- worship. Abraham told the servants that he and Isaac would worship and return.
- carry enough wood for a sacrifice.

Was Isaac willing to be sacrificed? Only those who assume that Isaac was a child can ignore what Isaac would have done when he realised that he was the sacrifice. But nothing in Genesis 22 suggests there was a struggle. Isaac could easily have overpowered Abraham. Abraham was an old man. He had travelled for three days. Hence we consider that Isaac was willing to be the sacrifice.

God provided a substitute sacrifice. Abraham named the place 'God provides.' An angel repeated God's promise to Abraham. The basis of the promise was obedience. Abraham was not sinless, but he proved that God was pre-eminent in his life whatever the cost.

GENESIS CHAPTER 23

Sarah lived to be a hundred and twenty-seven years old. (2) She died at Kiriath Arba (that is, Hebron) in the land of Canaan, and Abraham went to mourn for Sarah and to weep over her. (3) Then Abraham rose from beside his dead wife and spoke to the Hittites. He said, (4) "I am a foreigner and stranger among you. Sell me some property for a burial site here so I can bury my dead." (5) The Hittites replied to Abraham, (6) "Sir, listen to us. You are a mighty prince among us. Bury your dead in the choicest of our tombs. None of us will refuse you his tomb for burying your dead." (7) Then Abraham rose and bowed down before the people of the land, the Hittites. (8) He said to them, "If you are willing to let me bury my dead, then listen to me and intercede with Ephron son of Zohar on my behalf (9) so he will sell me the cave of Machpelah, which belongs to him and is at the end of his field. Ask him to sell it to me for the full price as a burial site among you." (10) Ephron the Hittite was sitting among his people and he replied to Abraham in the hearing of all the Hittites who had come to the gate of his city. (11) "No, my lord," he said. "Listen to me; I give you the field, and I give you the cave that is in it. I give it to you in the presence of my people. Bury your dead." (12) Again Abraham bowed down before the people of the land (13) and he said to Ephron in their hearing, "Listen to me, if you will. I will pay the price of the field. Accept it from me so I can bury my dead there." (14) Ephron answered Abraham, (15) "Listen to me, my lord; the land is worth four hundred shekels of silver, but what is that between you and me? Bury your dead." (16) Abraham agreed to Ephron's terms and weighed out for him the price he had named in the hearing of the Hittites: four hundred shekels of silver, according to the weight current among the merchants. (17) So Ephron's field in Machpelah near Mamre—both the field and the cave in it, and all the trees within the borders of the field—was deeded (18) to Abraham as his property in the presence of all the Hittites who had come to the gate of the city. (19) Afterward Abraham buried his wife Sarah in the cave in the field of Machpelah near Mamre (which is at Hebron) in the land of Canaan. (20) So the field and the cave in it were deeded to Abraham by the Hittites as a burial site.

COMMENTARY. GENESIS CHAPTER 23

Note the respect that was shown to Abraham. The reference to, 'mighty prince,' implies a relationship to God.

Abraham wanted to buy a burial place for Sarah. We see the respect that he had for the owners of the land. Although Hebron is in Canaan, the land promised by God to Abraham, Abraham knew that for the time being he was only a foreigner.

Abraham did not want anyone to be able to say that they had given him part of the land that God promised to give him and his family. Note also that he both accepted and refused gifts:

- He would not accept gifts from the evil King of Sodom.
- He accepted gifts from Pharaoh and King Abimelek.

GENESIS CHAPTER 24

Abraham was now very old, and the LORD had blessed him in every way. (2) He said to the senior servant in his household, the one in charge of all that he had, "Put your hand under my thigh. (3) I want you to swear by the LORD, the God of heaven and the God of earth, that you will not get a wife for my son from the daughters of the Canaanites, among whom I am living, (4) but will go to my country and my own relatives and get a wife for my son Isaac." (5) The servant asked him, "What if the woman is unwilling to come back with me to this land? Shall I then take your son back to the country you came from?" (6) "Make sure that you do not take my son back there," Abraham said. (7) "The LORD, the God of heaven, who brought me out of my father's household and my native land and who spoke to me and promised me on oath, saying,

'To your offspring I will give this land'—he will send his angel before you so that you can get a wife for my son from there.(8) If the woman is unwilling to come back with you, then you will be released from this oath of mine. Only do not take my son back there." (9) So the servant put his hand under the thigh of his master Abraham and swore an oath to him concerning this matter. (10) Then the servant left, taking with him ten of his master's camels loaded with all kinds of good things from his master. He set out for Aram Naharaim and made his way to the town of Nahor. (11) He had the camels kneel down near the well outside the town; it was toward evening, the time the women go out to draw water. (12) Then he prayed, "LORD, God of my master Abraham, make me successful today, and show kindness to my master Abraham. (13) See, I am standing beside this spring, and the daughters of the townspeople are coming out to draw water. (14) May it be that when I say to a young woman, 'Please let down your jar that I may have a drink,' and she says, 'Drink, and I'll water your camels too'—let her be the one you have chosen for your servant Isaac. By this I will know that you have shown kindness to my master." (15) Before he had finished praying, Rebekah came out with her jar on her shoulder. She was the daughter of Bethuel son of Milkah, who was the wife of Abraham's brother Nahor. (16) The woman was very beautiful, a virgin; no man had ever slept with her. She went down to the spring, filled her jar and came up again. (17) The servant hurried to meet her and said, "Please give me a little water from your jar." (18) "Drink, my lord," she said, and quickly lowered the jar to her hands and gave him a drink. (19) After she had given him a drink, she said, "I'll draw water for your camels too, until they have had enough to drink." (20) So she quickly emptied her jar into the trough, ran back to the well to draw more water, and drew enough for all his camels. (21) Without saying a word, the man watched her closely to learn whether or not the LORD had made his journey successful. (22) When the camels had finished drinking, the man took out a gold nose ring weighing a beka and two gold bracelets weighing ten shekels. (23) Then he asked, "Whose daughter are you? Please tell me, is there room in your father's house for us to spend the night?" (24) She answered him, "I am the daughter of Bethuel, the son that Milkah bore to Nahor." (25) And she added, "We have plenty of straw and fodder, as well as room for you to spend the night." (26) Then the man bowed down and worshiped the LORD, (27) saying, "Praise be to the LORD, the God of my master Abraham, who has not abandoned his kindness and faithfulness to my master. As for me, the LORD has led me on the journey to the house of my master's relatives." (28) The young woman ran and told her mother's household about these things. (29) Now Rebekah had a brother named Laban, and he hurried out to the man at the spring. (30) As soon as he had seen the nose ring, and the bracelets on his sister's arms, and had heard Rebekah tell what the man said to her, he went out to the man and found him standing by the camels near the spring. (31) "Come, you who are blessed by the LORD," he said. "Why are you standing out here? I have prepared the house and a place for the camels." (32) So the man went to the house, and the camels were unloaded. Straw and fodder were brought for the camels, and water for him and his men to wash their feet. (33) Then food was set before him, but he said, "I will not eat until I have told you what I have to say." "Then tell us," Laban said. (34) So he said, "I am Abraham's servant. (35) The LORD has blessed my master abundantly, and he has become wealthy. He has given him sheep and cattle, silver and gold, male and female servants, and camels and donkeys. (36) My master's wife Sarah has borne him a son in her old age, and he has given him everything he owns. (37) And my master made me swear an oath, and said, 'You must not get a wife for my son from the daughters of the Canaanites, in whose land I live, (38) but go to my father's family and to my own clan, and get a wife for my son.' (39) "Then I asked my master, 'What if the woman will not come back with me?' (40) "He replied, 'The LORD, before whom I have walked faithfully, will send his angel with you and make your journey a success, so that you can get a wife for my son from my own clan and from my father's family. (41) You will be released from my oath if, when you go to my clan, they refuse to give her to you—then you will be released from my oath.' (42) "When I came to the spring today, I said, 'LORD, God of my master Abraham, if you will, please grant success to the journey on which I have come. (43) See, I am standing beside this spring. If a young woman comes out to draw water and I say to her, "Please let me drink a little water from your jar," (44) and if she says to me, "Drink, and I'll draw water for your camels too," let her be the one the LORD has chosen for my master's son.' (45) "Before I finished praying in my heart, Rebekah came out, with her jar on her shoulder. She went down to the spring and drew water, and I said to her, 'Please give me a drink.' (46) "She quickly lowered her jar from her shoulder and said, 'Drink, and I'll water your camels too.' So I drank, and she watered the camels also. (47) "I asked her, 'Whose daughter are you?' "She said, 'The daughter of Bethuel son of Nahor, whom Milkah bore to him.' "Then I put the ring in her nose and the bracelets on her arms, (48) and I bowed down and worshiped the LORD. I praised the LORD, the God of my master Abraham, who had led me on the right road to get the granddaughter of my master's brother for his son. (49) Now if you will show kindness and faithfulness to my master, tell me; and if not, tell me, so I may know which way to turn." (50) Laban and Bethuel answered, "This is from the LORD; we can say nothing to you one way or the other. (51) Here is Rebekah; take her and go, and let her become the wife of your master's son, as the LORD has directed." (52) When Abraham's servant heard what they said, he bowed down to the ground before the LORD. (53) Then the servant brought out gold and silver jewelry and articles of clothing and gave them to Rebekah; he also gave costly gifts to her brother and to her mother. (54) Then he and the men who were with him ate and drank and spent the night there. When they got up the next morning, he said, "Send me on my way to my master." (55) But her brother and her mother replied, "Let the young woman remain with us ten days or so; then you may go." (56) But he said to them, "Do not detain me, now that the LORD has granted success to my journey. Send me on my way so I may go to my master." (57) Then they said, "Let's call the young woman and ask her about it." (58) So they called Rebekah and asked her, "Will you go with this man?" "I will go," she said. (59) So they sent their sister Rebekah on her way, along with her nurse and Abraham's servant and his men. (60) And they blessed Rebekah and said to her, "Our sister, may you increase to thousands upon thousands; may your offspring possess the cities of their enemies." (61) Then Rebekah and her attendants got ready and mounted the camels and went back with the man. So the servant took Rebekah and left. (62) Now Isaac had come from Beer Lahai Roi, for he was living in the Negev. (63) He went out to the field one evening to meditate, and as he looked up, he saw camels approaching. (64) Rebekah also looked up and saw Isaac. She got down from her camel (65) and asked the servant, "Who is that man in the field coming to meet us?" "He is my master," the servant answered. So she took her veil and covered herself. (66) Then the servant told Isaac all he had done. (67) Isaac brought her into the tent of his mother Sarah, and he married Rebekah. So she became his wife, and he loved her; and Isaac was comforted after his mother's death.

COMMENTARY. GENESIS CHAPTER 24

Abraham wanted to ensure that Isaac would not have the problems that intermarriage could result in if he married a Canaanite wife. God promised Abraham and his descendants that they would inherit Canaan. Complications would arise if intermarriage brought about changes of ownership of parts of Canaan. Isaac and his descendants only needed to trust God to fulfil His promise and Canaan would be theirs. They did not need to acquire Canaan by any other means.

Eliezer, is referred to in Genesis 15. He would have inherited everything that Abraham possessed if Isaac had not been born. Note the difference in the views of the two men as to God's ability to provide a wife for Isaac from Abraham's homeland. Eliezer must have been aware of God's promises to Abraham regarding Isaac and Canaan. God had a special interest in Abraham's descendants and Canaan.

Eliezer's idea that Isaac should return to his family's homeland was logical, but unnecessary. So, Abraham and Eliezer reached an agreement that enabled Eliezer to swear an oath and travel without Isaac. In view of all the miracles that Eliezer had witnessed as Abraham's servant, what more could God have done to prove that nothing was too hard for God to do.

Logic does not consider God's power. Abraham believed that God could choose a wife for Isaac from his own people and she would be willing to live in Canaan. We have read Eliezer's views. Experience has taught that unbelievers can mock those who know God's power in their lives. Unbelievers never understand the spiritual change that occurs when a sinner accepts God's Salvation. They do not understand why believers obey God when what He asks them to do is illogical.

Believers will miss God's blessings in their lives if they confuse God's Will with their own logical or good ideas. As Eliezer discovered, believers who trust God will not be disappointed as nothing is beyond God's ability.

Eliezer travelled to Haran to contact Abraham's family. Read his prayer to God as he reached the village where Abraham's brother, Nahor, lived. We do not know Eliezer's relationship to God. Maybe, despite all the miraculous things that he saw in the household he served for many years, he never grasped that his master's God also wanted a personal relationship with him. Whether we are masters or servants makes no difference to God. God hears those who humbly seek His Will:

- Eliezer sought God's help and God answered. Because God prepared the way for him to accomplish his mission, Eliezer received more than he expected.
- What Eliezer thought was almost impossible turned out to be a much easier task.

Eliezer responded to God's help. He fell down on his knees and worshipped. He discovered for himself that God knows all about us. God knows our plans and our problems.

Eliezer was a faithful servant:

- His task was to carry out his master's wishes. Note how he stated his instructions whenever he explained his mission.
- He spoke well of Abraham. He stated that God had blessed him and Isaac had a vast inheritance.
- He did not exaggerate. All that he said was true. Those who heard his story believed him and confirmed that in serving Abraham, he also served God.

We can tell from Rebekah's attitude that despite the problems, she had every confidence in Eliezer. She knew that it was a long journey to Canaan, she would be living among strangers, and be a long way from her loving family.

Eliezer did not want to delay carrying out his instructions and his next task was to return with Rebekah to Canaan. Not until then would he have fulfilled his oath. Rebekah's family wanted her to remain with them for a further ten days. The decision was left to Rebekah. Her answer was short and positive. She had heard her father Bethuel and her brother Laban confirming their belief that her marriage to Isaac was God's Will. Her faith and trust were rewarded. The chapter records that she became Isaac's wife and he loved her.

GENESIS CHAPTER 25

Abraham had taken another wife, whose name was Keturah. (2) She bore him Zimran, Jokshan, Medan, Midian, Ishbak and Shuah. (3) Jokshan was the father of Sheba and Dedan; the descendants of Dedan were the Ashurites, the Letushites and the Leummites. (4) The sons of Midian were Ephah, Epher, Hanok, Abida and Eldaah. All these were descendants of Keturah. (5) Abraham left everything he owned to Isaac. (6) But while he was still living, he gave gifts to the sons of his concubines and sent them away from his son Isaac to the land of the east. (7) Abraham lived a hundred and seventy-five years. (8) Then Abraham breathed his last and died at a good old age, an old man and full of years; and he was gathered to his people. (9) His sons Isaac and Ishmael buried him in the cave of Machpelah near Mamre, in the field of Ephron son of Zohar the Hittite, (10) the field Abraham had bought from the Hittites. There Abraham was buried with his wife Sarah. (11) After Abraham's death, God blessed his son Isaac, who then lived near Beer Lahai Roi. (12) This is the account of the family line of Abraham's son Ishmael, whom Sarah's slave, Hagar the Egyptian, bore to Abraham. (13) These are the names of the sons of Ishmael, listed in the order of their birth: Nebaioth the firstborn of Ishmael, Kedar, Adbeel, Mibsam, (14) Mishma, Dumah, Massa, (15) Hadad, Tema, Jetur, Naphish and Kedemah. (16) These were the sons of Ishmael, and these are the names of the twelve tribal rulers according to their settlements and camps. (17) Ishmael lived a hundred and thirty-seven years. He breathed his last and died, and he was gathered to his people. (18) His descendants settled in the area from Havilah to Shur, near the eastern border of Egypt, as you go toward Ashur. And they lived in hostility toward all the tribes related to them. (19) This is the account of the family line of Abraham's son Isaac. Abraham became the father of Isaac, (20) and Isaac was forty years old when he married Rebekah daughter of Bethuel the Aramean from

Paddan Aram and sister of Laban the Aramean. (21) Isaac prayed to the LORD on behalf of his wife, because she was childless. The LORD answered his prayer, and his wife Rebekah became pregnant. (22) The babies jostled each other within her, and she said, "Why is this happening to me?" So she went to inquire of the LORD. (23) The LORD said to her, "Two nations are in your womb, and two peoples from within you will be separated; one people will be stronger than the other, and the older will serve the younger." (24) When the time came for her to give birth, there were twin boys in her womb. (25) The first to come out was red, and his whole body was like a hairy garment; so they named him Esau. (26) After this, his brother came out, with his hand grasping Esau's heel; so he was named Jacob. Isaac was sixty years old when Rebekah gave birth to them. (27) The boys grew up, and Esau became a skillful hunter, a man of the open country, while Jacob was content to stay at home among the tents. (28) Isaac, who had a taste for wild game, loved Esau, but Rebekah loved Jacob. (29) Once when Jacob was cooking some stew, Esau came in from the open country, famished. (30) He said to Jacob, "Quick, let me have some of that red stew! I'm famished!" (That is why he was also called Edom.) (31) Jacob replied, "First sell me your birthright." (32) "Look, I am about to die," Esau said. "What good is the birthright to me?" (33) But Jacob said, "Swear to me first." So he swore an oath to him, selling his birthright to Jacob. (34) Then Jacob gave Esau some bread and some lentil stew. He ate and drank, and then got up and left. So Esau despised his birthright.

COMMENTARY. GENESIS CHAPTER 25

We read about Abraham's marriage to Keturah and their children and grandchildren.

We have no details as to Abraham's age when these events occurred. We are told that he was very old. We do not know the extent of his extended family. We do know that his God given ability to father children remained until he died when he was one hundred and seventy-five years old. Except for Abraham's gifts to his concubines' sons, Isaac inherited everything. Ishmael did not inherit any gift. Isaac and Ishmael buried Abraham in the same place as Sarah.

We read in Genesis 17 that God promised a great inheritance to Ishmael. It was separate from Isaac's inheritance. Abraham had no obligation to give Ishmael anything. Apart from the brief record of Ishmael's descendants in Genesis 25 and the visit Esau made to him to acquire wives recorded in Genesis 28, we do not read of Ishmael again in Genesis. Genesis only records Isaac's history. Isaac and his family were involved in God's Plan of Salvation. Isaac had Abraham's vast wealth and God's blessing upon his life.

Rebekah had difficulty conceiving. Isaac prayed about the problem. After twenty years of marriage, when Isaac was sixty years old, Rebekah became pregnant with twins. Read the problems associated with the twin's birth and Rebekah's prayer. God told her that:

- the twin boys in her womb would head two rival nations.
- one son would be stronger than the other.
- the elder son would be the servant of the younger son.

We read a detailed account of the birth of the twin boys and what their names meant:

- Esau meant, 'hairy.' He was covered with hair.
- Jacob meant, 'greed and deceit.' It matched his lifestyle.

In Genesis 32 we read why, some sixty years later, God changed Jacob's name to Israel. His new name meant, 'One who had power with God.'

We read why both parents chose different favourite sons. We shall read the consequences of these foolish choices.

We read that Jacob acquired the birthright from Esau. Esau was born first and had the legal right to receive the birthright, but, before they were born, God told their mother that Esau would serve Jacob. We learn that one day, Jacob took advantage of Esau's hunger and he bought the birthright.

What Jacob did was wrong. But, why did Esau so cheaply sell his birthright? Did it mean nothing to him? Esau was also called, Edom. Later chapters of Genesis use both his names. Edom means, 'red stuff,' referring to the stew he bought from Jacob when he sold his birthright.

Like Jacob, Esau had to live with a name that must have embarrassed him. The day came when God changed Jacob's name to Israel. God never changed Esau's name.

GENESIS CHAPTER 26

Now there was a famine in the land—besides the previous famine in Abraham's time—and Isaac went to Abimelek king of the Philistines in Gerar. (2) The LORD appeared to Isaac and said, "Do not go down to Egypt; live in the land where I tell you to live. (3) Stay in this land for a while, and I will be with you and will bless you. For to you and your descendants I will give all these lands and will confirm the oath I swore to your father Abraham. (4) I will make your descendants as numerous as the stars in the sky and will give them all these lands, and through your offspring all nations on earth will be blessed, (5) because Abraham obeyed me and did everything I required of him, keeping my commands, my decrees and my instructions." (6) So Isaac stayed in Gerar. (7) When the men of that place asked him about his wife, he said, "She is my sister," because he was afraid to say, "She is my wife." He thought, "The men of this place might kill me on account of Rebekah, because she is beautiful." (8) When Isaac had been there a long time, Abimelek king of the Philistines looked down from a window and saw Isaac caressing his wife Rebekah.

(9) So Abimelek summoned Isaac and said, "She is really your wife! Why did you say, 'She is my sister'?" Isaac answered him, "Because I thought I might lose my life on account of her." (10) Then Abimelek said, "What is this you have done to us? One of the men might well have slept with your wife, and you would have brought guilt upon us." (11) So Abimelek gave orders to all the people: "Anyone who harms this man or his wife shall surely be put to death." (12) Isaac planted crops in that land and the same year reaped a hundredfold, because the LORD blessed him. (13) The man became rich, and his wealth continued to grow until he became very wealthy. (14) He had so many flocks and herds and servants that the Philistines envied him. (15) So all the wells that his father's servants had dug in the time of his father Abraham, the Philistines stopped up, filling them with earth. (16) Then Abimelek said to Isaac, "Move away from us; you have become too powerful for us." (17) So Isaac moved away from there and encamped in the Valley of Gerar, where he settled. (18) Isaac reopened the wells that had been dug in the time of his father Abraham, which the Philistines had stopped up after Abraham died, and he gave them the same names his father had given them. (19) Isaac's servants dug in the valley and discovered a well of fresh water there. (20) But the herders of Gerar quarreled with those of Isaac and said, "The water is ours!" So he named the well Esek, because they disputed with him. (21) Then they dug another well, but they quarreled over that one also; so he named it Sitnah. (22) He moved on from there and dug another well, and no one quarreled over it. He named it Rehoboth, saying, "Now the LORD has given us room and we will flourish in the land." (23) From there he went up to Beersheba. (24) That night the LORD appeared to him and said, "I am the God of your father Abraham. Do not be afraid, for I am with you; I will bless you and will increase the number of your descendants for the sake of my servant Abraham." (25) Isaac built an altar there and called on the name of the LORD. There he pitched his tent,

and there his servants dug a well. (26) Meanwhile, Abimelek had come to him from Gerar, with Ahuzzath his personal adviser and Phicol the commander of his forces. (27) Isaac asked them, "Why have you come to me, since you were hostile to me and sent me away?" (28) They answered, "We saw clearly that the LORD was with you; so we said, 'There ought to be a sworn agreement between us'—between us and you. Let us make a treaty with you (29) that you will do us no harm, just as we did not harm you but always treated you well and sent you away peacefully. And now you are blessed by the LORD." (30) Isaac then made a feast for them, and they ate and drank. (31) Early the next morning the men swore an oath to each other. Then Isaac sent them on their way, and they went away peacefully. (32) That day Isaac's servants came and told him about the well they had dug. They said, "We've found water!" (33) He called it Shibah, and to this day the name of the town has been Beersheba. (34) When Esau was forty years old, he married Judith daughter of Beeri the Hittite, and also Basemath daughter of Elon the Hittite. (35) They were a source of grief to Isaac and Rebekah.

COMMENTARY. GENESIS CHAPTER 26

It was not unusual at a time of famine for those who relied on the land to travel to a place unaffected by the famine. Isaac and his family went south to Gerar where the Philistines lived.

Isaac had God's blessing on his life but this did not exempt him from the problems of life. The Bible teaches that believers will not have problem-free lives, but they have the assurance of God's presence with them whatever happens.

Isaac would probably have travelled further south to Egypt, a country which generally fared better than her neighbours in times of famine, but God warned him not to go to Egypt. God made Isaac the same promise He made many years earlier to his father, Abraham. We consider the promise later.

Abraham twice faced the dilemma of visiting countries where it was not uncommon for husbands to be killed and their wives taken into the harems of the local rulers.

Abraham and Sarah had different mothers but the same father. They agreed on both visits to say they were brother and sister to save Abraham from being killed. We read the serious consequences that resulted from these half-truths. When Isaac considered the problem, surprisingly, he did what his parents had done, although he and Rebekah were never brother and sister.

King Abimelek uncovered Isaac's deceit. As with Abraham, God turned a potential disaster to a blessing. Isaac prospered. He left Gerar to settle in the Gerar Valley and God continued to bless him. He must have been aware that he was the object of God's blessing. Consider how he dealt with the problem of the wells and the names given to them. When Isaac went to Beer-sheba, God spoke to him. For the second time God confirmed the promise to him. Isaac built his first altar at Beer-sheba and worshipped.

Isaac's prosperity was obvious to his Philistine neighbours. We note the terms of the peace treaty. We do not know for how long Isaac and Rebekah enjoyed a peaceful life before Esau decided to marry two women from the Hethite people. Isaac and Rebekah were not pleased. Esau was married when he was forty years old, as was Isaac, but Isaac married a woman from his own people. That was what Abraham required and God showed His approval by directing Abraham's servant to Rebekah. But, Esau had no regard for what God, or his parents wanted. He pleased himself.

GENESIS CHAPTER 27

When Isaac was old and his eyes were so weak that he could no longer see, he called for Esau his older son and said to him, "My son." "Here I am," he answered. (2) Isaac said, "I am now an old man and don't know the day of my death. (3) Now then, get your equipment—your quiver and bow—and go out to the open country to hunt some wild game for me. (4) Prepare me the kind of tasty food I like and bring it to me to eat, so that I may give you my blessing before I die." (5) Now Rebekah was listening as Isaac spoke to his son Esau. When Esau left for the open country to hunt game and bring it back, (6) Rebekah said to her son Jacob, "Look, I overheard your father say to your brother Esau, (7) 'Bring me some game and prepare me some tasty food to eat, so that I may give you my blessing in the presence of the LORD before I die.' (8) Now, my son, listen carefully and do what I tell you: (9) Go out to the flock and bring me two choice young goats, so I can prepare some tasty food for your father, just the way he likes it. (10) Then take it to your father to eat, so that he may give you his blessing before he dies." (11) Jacob said to Rebekah his mother, "But my brother Esau is a hairy man while I have smooth skin. (12) What if my father touches me? I would appear to be tricking him and would bring down a curse on myself rather than a blessing." (13) His mother said to him, "My son, let the curse fall on me. Just do what I say; go and get them for me." (14) So he went and got them and brought them to his mother, and she prepared some tasty food, just the way his father liked it. (15) Then Rebekah took the best clothes of Esau her older son, which she had in the house, and put them on her younger son Jacob. (16) She also covered his hands and the smooth part of his neck with the goatskins. (17) Then she handed to her son Jacob the tasty food and the bread she had made. (18) He went to his father and said, "My father." "Yes, my son," he answered. "Who is it?" (19) Jacob said to his father, "I am Esau your firstborn. I have done as you told me. Please sit up and eat some of my game, so that you may give me your blessing." (20) Isaac asked his son, "How did you find it so quickly, my son?" "The LORD your God gave me success," he replied. (21) Then Isaac said to Jacob, "Come near so I can touch you, my son, to know whether you really are my son Esau or not." (22) Jacob went close to his father Isaac, who touched him and said, "The voice is the voice of Jacob, but the hands are the hands of Esau." (23) He did not recognize him, for his hands were hairy like those of his brother Esau; so he proceeded to bless him. (24) "Are you really my son Esau?" he asked. "I am," he replied. (25) Then he said, "My son, bring me some of your game to eat, so that I may give you my blessing." Jacob brought it to him and he ate; and he brought some wine and he drank. (26) Then his father Isaac said to him, "Come here, my son, and kiss me." (27) So he went to him and kissed him. When Isaac caught the smell of his clothes, he blessed him and said, "Ah, the smell of my son is like the smell of a field that the LORD has blessed. (28) May God give you heaven's dew and earth's richness— an abundance of grain and new wine. (29) May nations serve you and peoples bow down to you. Be lord over your brothers, and may the sons of your mother bow down to you. May those who curse you be cursed and those who bless you be blessed." (30) After Isaac finished blessing him, and Jacob had scarcely left his father's presence, his brother Esau came in from hunting. (31) He too prepared some tasty food and brought it to his father. Then he said to him, "My father, please sit up and eat some of my game, so that you may give me your blessing." (32) His father Isaac asked him, "Who are you?" "I am your son," he answered, "your firstborn, Esau." (33) Isaac trembled violently and said, "Who was it, then, that hunted game and brought it to me? I ate it just before you came and I blessed him—and indeed he will be blessed!" (34) When Esau heard his father's words, he burst out with a loud and bitter cry and said to his father, "Bless me—me too, my father!" (35) But he said, "Your brother came deceitfully and took your blessing." (36) Esau said, "Isn't he rightly named Jacob? This is the second time he has taken advantage of me: He took my birthright, and now he's taken my blessing!" Then he asked, "Haven't you reserved any blessing for me?"

(37) Isaac answered Esau, "I have made him lord over you and have made all his relatives his servants, and I have sustained him with grain and new wine. So what can I possibly do for you, my son?" (38) Esau said to his father, "Do you have only one blessing, my father? Bless me too, my father!" Then Esau wept aloud. (39) His father Isaac answered him, "Your dwelling will be away from the earth's richness, away from the dew of heaven above. (40) You will live by the sword and you will serve your brother. But when you grow restless, you will throw his yoke from off your neck." (41) Esau held a grudge against Jacob because of the blessing his father had given him. He said to himself, "The days of mourning for my father are near; then I will kill my brother Jacob." (42) When Rebekah was told what her older son Esau had said, she sent for her younger son Jacob and said to him, "Your brother Esau is planning to avenge himself by killing you. (43) Now then, my son, do what I say: Flee at once to my brother Laban in Harran. (44) Stay with him for a while until your brother's fury subsides. (45) When your brother is no longer angry with you and forgets what you did to him, I'll send word for you to come back from there. Why should I lose both of you in one day?" (46) Then Rebekah said to Isaac, "I'm disgusted with living because of these Hittite women. If Jacob takes a wife from among the women of this land, from Hittite women like these, my life will not be worth living."

COMMENTARY. GENESIS CHAPTER 27

God made a Covenant with Abraham. God promised to:

- be with him and bless him.
- give the land of Canaan to him and his descendants who would be too numerous to count.
- bless all nations on earth through his descendants.

The Covenant promises were conditional on Abraham and his descendants being obedient and separated to God. God intended to have the Covenant with each generation of Abraham's descendants, hence, the Covenant was made with Abraham's son, Isaac. These men were not sinless. Genesis discloses their sins. Since Adam sinned, sin has contaminated human nature and no one is exempt. But, unlike the majority, Abraham and Isaac were willing to obey God.

Esau was a rebel who disobeyed the Covenant. He demonstrated by his way of life that he had no interest in God. As Isaac's heir, Esau should have received the Covenant. However, he sold his birthright to Jacob and unlike his father, and against his parents' wishes, he married twice outside the family, showing his contempt for the Covenant.

We read why Isaac's firstborn blessing was given to Jacob and not to Esau. You can read the plot that brought this about. It will surprise those not familiar with it.

Esau was aware of the nasty meaning of Jacob's name. It meant, 'cheat,' and Esau was not slow to mention it to Isaac. We consider Jacob's name again in Genesis 32.

You can read the consequences of these remarkable events. Esau made it known that he intended to kill Jacob after Isaac's death. Rebekah heard this and discussed the matter with Jacob suggesting that he flee to her family in Haran. We shall read more of this in later chapters but before leaving this chapter, we must consider why these events took place.

We start with the statement that we emphasised earlier. Before the twins were born, God told Rebekah that Esau would serve Jacob. God knew what Esau would do when he became a man. Esau was a rebel with no regard for God or His Covenant that was based on obedience and separation.

Esau voluntarily sold his birthright to Jacob and married Canaanite wives. He was Isaac's favourite son and yet he ignored Isaac's wishes. Isaac did not want him to marry Canaanite women. We have unanswered questions about

Isaac's behaviour in Genesis 27:

- Why did he want to bless Esau when Esau had proved he was unworthy of the firstborn's blessing?
- Did his love of the food that Esau caught and cooked, so affect his judgement that no matter what God had said or how badly Esau had behaved, he would have blessed him?

When we consider how much scheming Rebekah had to do to deceive Isaac into blessing Jacob, did she think that deceiving a prejudiced and stubborn old man was the only way of ensuring that her favourite son received the Covenant blessing as God had foretold before Jacob's birth?

We consider that Jacob wanted the birthright and Esau showed how little he valued it. It seems that Rebekah thought that Isaac had chosen to ignore a clear indication from God as to which son should inherit. We ask a question:

Did Rebekah think that deceiving Isaac was the only way that Jacob would receive his rightful inheritance and nothing she did would be as bad as seeing Jacob cheated by:

- Isaac who always favoured Esau?
- Esau who had sold his birthright to Jacob?

Genesis does not answer our questions. However, the result of the deception is as surprising as the event:

- Jacob expected his father to be displeased and curse him when he realised that he had been deceived. Isaac willingly accepted the result of the deception.
- Esau wept when Isaac refused to bless him and told him what he did not want to hear.

Only by being deceived did Isaac confirm the prophecy God made to Rebekah during her pregnancy. The Covenant passed to Jacob and he inherited everything that belonged to Isaac. Esau received nothing and he was told to serve Jacob. Apart from the aggression shown by Esau to Jacob, there is no inference of anger between either Isaac and Rebekah, or Isaac and Jacob. It was God's Will that Isaac should bless Jacob. But, God was not responsible for the parent's favouritism that caused the problem, or:

- Isaac's stubbornness and his desire to bless Esau.
- Rebekah's deceitful answer to Isaac's stubbornness.

In Genesis, as elsewhere in The Bible, we discover that what God had already willed should be done, was done by individuals or groups. Believers and unbelievers alike have free wills. They choose what should happen. They are not compelled by God to do anything but God:

- knows in advance what they will do even if it is sinful.
- uses what they choose to do for His own purposes.

God did not approve of the deception because it produced the result He wanted. We shall read later that Rebekah and Jacob were punished. We shall also learn how wise God was in choosing Jacob in preference to Esau before they were born.

We know that God told Esau's mother before he was born that although older than his brother Jacob, he would serve him. Did God force Esau to sell his birthright and be rebellious so that He could bless Jacob? The answer is, "No." Before Esau was born, God knew what he would do. Esau made choices of his own free will.

Before we consider Genesis 28, readers should think about their futures. Those who possess God's Salvation rejoice that God is eternal. Our mental abilities cannot understand the extent of the blessings that God provides for believers, but they know that their blessings in Heaven will last forever.

Human existence is governed by the limitations of time. Eternity is too difficult for us to understand. Hence God only asks us to do what we can do. We can all repent and believe.

If you are not yet a believer, you might not consider yourself as a person who is defiant to God like Esau. He was an out-and-out rebel. But on the Day of Judgment, only believers will escape God's judgment for their sins. Esau and other out-and-out rebels will be with those who were, 'almost believers.'

GENESIS CHAPTER 28

So Isaac called for Jacob and blessed him. Then he commanded him: "Do not marry a Canaanite woman. (2) Go at once to Paddan Aram, to the house of your mother's father Bethuel. Take a wife for yourself there, from among the daughters of Laban, your mother's brother. (3) May God Almighty bless you and make you fruitful and increase your numbers until you become a community of peoples. (4) May he give you and your descendants the blessing given to Abraham, so that you may take possession of the land where you now reside as a foreigner, the land God gave to Abraham." (5) Then Isaac sent Jacob on his way, and he went to Paddan Aram, to Laban son of Bethuel the Aramean, the brother of Rebekah, who was the mother of Jacob and Esau. (6) Now Esau learned that Isaac had blessed Jacob and had sent him to Paddan Aram to take a wife from there, and that when he blessed him he commanded him, "Do not marry a Canaanite woman," (7) and that Jacob had obeyed his father and mother and had gone to Paddan Aram. (8) Esau then realized how displeasing the Canaanite women were to his father Isaac; (9) so he went to Ishmael and married Mahalath, the sister of Nebaioth and daughter of Ishmael son of Abraham, in addition to the wives he already had. (10) Jacob left Beersheba and set out for Harran. (11) When he reached a certain place, he stopped for the night because the sun had set. Taking one of the stones there, he put it under his head and lay down to sleep. (12) He had a dream in which he saw a stairway resting on the earth, with its top reaching to heaven, and the angels of God were ascending and descending on it. (13) There above it stood the LORD, and he said: "I am the

LORD, the God of your father Abraham and the God of Isaac. I will give you and your descendants the land on which you are lying. (14) Your descendants will be like the dust of the earth, and you will spread out to the west and to the east, to the north and to the south. All peoples on earth will be blessed through you and your offspring. (15) I am with you and will watch over you wherever you go, and I will bring you back to this land. I will not leave you until I have done what I have promised you." (16) When Jacob awoke from his sleep, he thought, "Surely the LORD is in this place, and I was not aware of it." (17) He was afraid and said, "How awesome is this place! This is none other than the house of God; this is the gate of heaven." (18) Early the next morning Jacob took the stone he had placed under his head and set it up as a pillar and poured oil on top of it. (19) He called that place Bethel, though the city used to be called Luz. (20) Then Jacob made a vow, saying, "If God will be with me and will watch over me on this journey I am taking and will give me food to eat and clothes to wear (21) so that I return safely to my father's household, then the LORD will be my God (22) and this stone that I have set up as a pillar will be God's house, and of all that you give me I will give you a tenth."

COMMENTARY. GENESIS CHAPTER 28

Isaac’s advice to Jacob about a wife, agreed with Rebekah’s advice to Jacob after she heard that Esau had threatened to kill him. After he received a further blessing in the terms we are now used to reading, he left to seek a wife in Haran.

Rebekah was parted from her favourite son. Was that her punishment for deceiving Isaac? Jacob no longer lived at home. Was that his punishment for his part in the deception? Jacob was a, ‘home-loving,’ son but he had to travel many hundreds of miles through the desert to Haran to meet relatives he did not know hoping to find a women who would return with him to Canaan and be his wife.

Isaac was old, blind and dying. Rebekah was also old and Jacob must have wondered if he would ever see them again. In human terms, escaping from the wrath of Esau was costly for Jacob. Esau's rebellious nature caused problems for his parents. He married Canaanite wives who brought grief to them. Rebekah loathed Esau's wives. Esau knew that Isaac had advised Jacob not to marry Canaanite wives

A wife who was not one of Abraham's descendants had to accept the terms of the Covenant. It was unlikely that a Canaanite woman would have accepted it because it gave her homeland to Abraham's descendants. So, intermarriage with the Canaanites could have resulted in problems about the ownership of Canaan.

Esau knew the terms of the Covenant. It related only to his father and grandfather and their descendants. Ishmael was Abraham's eldest son, but Sarah was not his mother. Hence, the Covenant did not apply to him or his descendants. Esau went to see his Uncle Ishmael who, on God's instructions, had been expelled from Abraham's family. Esau married wives from Ishmael's family. As we would expect, Esau proved that God's view of him was correct. Even though Esau shed tears when he lost his birthright, he continued to be rebellious and he ignored the terms of the Covenant.

Isaac did not marry a Canaanite. His family lived in Haran and Rebekah had travelled from there to marry him. Abraham's and Isaac's descendants were special to God. Unlike all other nations who worshipped false gods, they worshipped only Him. God wanted His people to be separate from everyone who worshipped false gods. Circumcision was a visible sign of the difference between those who accepted the Covenant and those who did not. Those who were:

- not automatically included in the Covenant could be included if they accepted its obligations.
- automatically included in the Covenant who did not accept

its obligations had to live apart from those who did.

We read about Jacob who camped outside Luz. Despite the lack of home comforts, he not only slept, he had a dream. He saw angels silently going up and down a staircase from Earth to Heaven. He specifically saw that:

- The staircase was from Earth to Heaven.
- The angels ascended before they descended.

We might have expected that:

- Heaven would be mentioned before Earth.
- The angels descended before they ascended.

But, Jacob's dream was a picture of God's Salvation. Jacob needed to know that he could have, 'A New Start with God.' He was fully aware of his sinful life. He had lied to and deceived his own father. He was on the run because his brother wanted to kill him.

In his dream he saw that Heaven can be reached from the Earth. Two questions arise for our consideration.

1. Did Jacob's dream mean that only God and the angels live in Heaven?
2. Did the staircase indicate that it was possible for repentant sinners to enter and live in Heaven?

Answers: Jacob learnt three important truths. There is:

1. a Heaven where God and the angels live.
2. an entrance to Heaven.
3. a way of getting to Heaven.

There have been many over the centuries like Jacob. Conscious of their sin, and willing to repent, they have come to appreciate the truth about the Salvation that God offers to repentant sinners. Experience teaches that God deals with each one individually, but the end result is always the same.

When sinners repent and accept Jesus as their Saviour they receive God's eternal Salvation. Often that is shortened and they say, "I am saved." Unbelievers become believers.

We know that, 'the end result is always the same,' but, as Jacob saw in his dream, there is a starting point. It is on Earth. Those who die unsaved can never be saved. Any wishing to climb the staircase had to start at, 'the first step.' It was the only way the staircase could be climbed. The Bible teaches what, 'the first step,' to God's Salvation is. John's Gospel has for 2000 years stated it:

'For God so loved the world that he gave his one and only Son, that whoever believes in him shall not perish but have eternal life.' John 3:16. NIV.

Those words, 'whoever believes in him,' state what sinners must do to obtain eternal life. A song, once sang in Sunday Schools, also made young people aware of God's Salvation:

'There's a way back to God from the dark paths of sin.
There's a door that is open and you may go in.
At Calvary's Cross is where you begin,
When you come as a sinner to Jesus!'
https://hymnary.org/text/theres_a_way_back_to_god

God wants to forgive and give eternal life to those who repent and accept Jesus as their Saviour. Eternal life begins immediately a sinner receives God's Salvation. Eternal life is both for the here and now and for eternity. God wants to welcome those who are saved into His fellowship now and into Heaven when they die. Many do not realise that when The Bible refers to, 'eternal or everlasting life,' this never-ending divine life starts from the moment a sinner is saved.

God spoke to Jacob from the top of the staircase. God has a personal interest in each one of us because He does not want us to perish. He wants to eternally save us.

God, the God of Jacob's grandfather Abraham, and his father Isaac, spoke to him. What did God say to Jacob?

- God repeated the promises made to Abraham and Isaac regarding, 'the promised land.' Jacob was sleeping on a small part of that special land, but he would soon leave it to continue his journey.
- God promised Jacob that he would always be with him and guaranteed to protect him.

What was Jacob's reaction? He made a personal Covenant with God and built an altar so that he could worship God. This was the start of his, 'New Life with God.' Jacob might have been on the run from Esau, but he must have been so thrilled when he discovered that he could never run away from God.

However, whatever their circumstances, there is no reason for anyone to feel envious of Jacob and his, 'New Life with God.' God offers the same eternal Salvation to everyone but God's offer is made to us individually. Jacob heard God's offer. He very wisely accepted it.

GENESIS CHAPTER 29

Then Jacob continued on his journey and came to the land of the eastern peoples. (2) There he saw a well in the open country, with three flocks of sheep lying near it because the flocks were watered from that well. The stone over the mouth of the well was large. (3) When all the flocks were gathered there, the shepherds would roll the stone away from the well's mouth and water the sheep. Then they would return the stone to its place over the mouth of the well. (4) Jacob asked the shepherds, "My brothers, where are you from?" "We're from Harran," they replied. (5) He said to them, "Do you know Laban, Nahor's grandson?" "Yes, we know him," they answered. (6) Then Jacob asked them, "Is he well?" "Yes, he is," they said, "and here comes his daughter Rachel with the sheep." (7) "Look," he said, "the sun is still high; it is not time for the flocks to be gathered. Water the sheep and take them back to pasture." (8) "We can't," they replied, "until all the flocks are gathered and the stone has been rolled away from the mouth of the well. Then we will water the sheep." (9) While he was still talking with them, Rachel came with her father's sheep, for she was a shepherd. (10) When Jacob saw Rachel daughter of his uncle Laban, and Laban's sheep, he went over and rolled the stone away from the mouth of the well and watered his uncle's sheep. (11) Then Jacob kissed Rachel and began to weep aloud. (12) He had told Rachel that he was a relative of her father and a son of Rebekah. So she ran and told her father. (13) As soon as Laban heard the news about Jacob, his sister's son, he hurried to meet him. He embraced him and kissed him and brought him to his home, and there Jacob told him all these things. (14) Then Laban said to him, "You are my own flesh and blood." After Jacob had stayed with him for a whole month, (15) Laban said to him, "Just because you are a relative of mine, should you work for me for nothing? Tell me what your wages should be." (16) Now Laban had two daughters; the name of the older was Leah, and the name of the younger was Rachel. (17) Leah had weak eyes, but Rachel had a lovely figure and was beautiful. (18) Jacob was in love with Rachel and said, "I'll work for you seven years in return for your younger daughter Rachel." (19) Laban said, "It's better that I give her to you than to some other man. Stay here with me." (20) So Jacob served seven years to get Rachel, but they seemed like only a few days to him because of his love for her. (21) Then Jacob said to Laban, "Give me my wife. My time is completed, and I want to make love to her." (22) So Laban brought together all the people of the place and gave a feast. (23) But when evening came, he took his daughter Leah and brought her to Jacob, and Jacob made love to her. (24) And Laban gave his servant Zilpah to his daughter as her attendant. (25) When morning came, there was Leah! So Jacob said to Laban, "What is this you have done to me? I served you for Rachel, didn't I? Why have you deceived me?" (26) Laban replied, "It is not our custom here to give the younger daughter in marriage before the older one. (27) Finish this daughter's bridal week; then we will give you the younger one also, in return for another seven years of work."(28) And Jacob did so. He finished the week with Leah, and then Laban gave him his daughter Rachel to be his wife. (29) Laban gave his servant Bilhah to his daughter Rachel as her attendant. (30) Jacob made love to Rachel also, and his love for Rachel was greater than his love for Leah. And he worked for Laban another seven years. (31) When the LORD saw that Leah was not loved, he enabled her to conceive, but Rachel remained childless. (32) Leah became pregnant and gave birth to a son. She named him Reuben, for she said, "It is because the LORD has seen my misery. Surely my husband will love me now. (33) She conceived again, and when she gave birth to a son she said, "Because the LORD heard that I am not loved, he gave me this one too." So she named him Simeon. (34) Again she conceived, and when she gave birth to a son she said, "Now at last my husband will become attached to me, because I have borne him three sons." So he was named Levi. (35) She conceived again, and when she gave birth to a son she said, "This time I will praise the LORD." So she named him Judah. Then she stopped having children.

COMMENTARY. GENESIS CHAPTER 29

Prior to this chapter, we thought we knew what Jacob was like. He was his mother's favourite son. He preferred to be at home rather than be involved in outdoor activities. We thought he was a soft and gentle man dominated by his mother.

We have now read about a man who made a solo trek through the desert to Haran. He was strong enough to move a heavy stone from a well when the locals said it was a job for more than one man. We shall discover as we read on that he worked without pay for seven years when he wanted to marry the women he fell in love with. He had expertise as a shepherd and a businessman. He worked hard to be successful.

Some might ask if he was the same man who deceived his father and run away from home as he was afraid of his brother.

Question 1: If this was the same man, what brought about the dramatic changes in his life?

Answer: He had an experience of God. He realised that God knew all about his sins and failures but was willing to forgive him and give him a new start.

Question 2: Why did God do this?

Answer: God wanted a personal relationship with him. God promised to bless him and confirmed that the promises made to Abraham and Isaac now applied to him and they would continue for the benefit of his descendants.

Although in the minority, like Jacob, others have experienced a change in their lives. They look back to a time when they realised that God was willing to forgive them and give them His eternal Salvation. They repented and accepted Jesus as their Saviour. It was the beginning of their new divine life. They once lived to please themselves:

- They now live to please God.
- They do not do the things they once did and to put it bluntly, they are ashamed of their past.

We read that Jacob immediately fell in love with Rachel. He wanted to marry her, and He was willing to pay seven years labour to his Uncle Laban, her father, for her. But, Laban deceived him by switching Leah for Rachel on the wedding night. This was the first of Laban's deceitful acts. Jacob did not merit such treatment from Laban, his uncle and father in law. But we must ask the question:

- Were Laban's deceitful acts punishment for the wrong Jacob did when he deceived his father, Isaac?
- Had the former deceiver been deceived?

We consider the answer must be, "Yes." There is a general principle in The Bible that we reap what we sow. Jacob certainly did.

Jacob became the husband of Leah and Rachel. They were sisters. Jacob was the father of thirteen children, twelve boys and one girl. His twelve sons became the leaders of the tribes that subsequently formed the Jewish Nation. Jacob's two wives competed with each other for his affection. They both wanted to be the mother of his children. What a complicated life Jacob lived. For convenience, we summarise it:

- He worked for Laban for seven years so that he could marry Rachel but, by mistake, he married her sister Leah.
- Rachel, who he did love, was more beautiful than her older sister Leah. He did not love Leah.
- He agreed to work another seven years so that he could marry Rachel. A week later, he was married to both sisters.
- He continued to love Rachel more than Leah. Leah felt slighted. God intervened in Leah's difficult circumstances so that she conceived first.
- Leah gave birth to the first four of Jacob's sons. She gave them names that reflected her thoughts.

In the order of their births, Leah's children were:

REUBEN: His name meant, 'God has noticed my trouble.' How good it is when we realise that God knows our individual problems and cares about us. Leah received the answer to her prayers. She became pregnant for the second time.

SIMEON: His name meant, 'God heard.' Why God is willing to hear us and to meet our needs are questions that must have been asked many times. The simple yet profound answer is that God loves us. God's love for us is mentioned many times in The Bible. Leah discovered that those who humbly seek God will not be ignored. God knows our hearts. Because of His love for us, if it accords with His Will, He will answer us.

LEVI: His name meant, 'Attachment.' Leah thought that as she had given Jacob three sons, he would feel affection for her. We can tell by the names of the first three sons how upset Leah was by Jacob's lack of affection for her and his love for Rachel. God knows everything about each one of us. He was aware of Leah's problem with Jacob and of her unhappiness.

JUDAH: God wonderfully intervened. Leah was thankful for God's involvement. We know this as her fourth son's name meant, 'Praise.' She recognised that God had helped her in her time of need. Unlike Leah, some seek by their own efforts to minimise their problems, and by their good deeds to earn God's approval and blessing. They fail to realise that there is nothing that we can do to impress God. God can only save those who admit that because of their sin, they can never merit His favour. That is why repentance always precedes God's forgiveness and Salvation.

GENESIS CHAPTER 30

When Rachel saw that she was not bearing Jacob any children, she became jealous of her sister. So she said to Jacob, "Give me children, or I'll die!" (2) Jacob became angry with her and said, "Am I in the place of God, who has kept you from having children?" (3) Then she said, "Here is Bilhah, my servant. Sleep with her so that she can bear children for me and I too can build a family through her." (4) So she gave him her servant Bilhah as a wife. Jacob slept with her, (5) and she became pregnant and bore him a son. (6) Then Rachel said, "God has vindicated me; he has listened to my plea and given me a son." Because of this she named him Dan. (7) Rachel's servant Bilhah conceived again and bore Jacob a second son. (8) Then Rachel said, "I have had a great struggle with my sister, and I have won." So she named him Naphtali. (9) When Leah saw that she had stopped having children, she took her servant Zilpah and gave her to Jacob as a wife. (10) Leah's servant Zilpah bore Jacob a son. (11) Then Leah said, "What good fortune!" So she named him Gad. (12) Leah's servant Zilpah bore Jacob a second son. (13) Then Leah said, "How happy I am! The women will call me happy." So she named him Asher. (14) During wheat harvest, Reuben went out into the fields and found some mandrake plants, which he brought to his mother Leah. Rachel said to Leah, "Please give me some of your son's mandrakes." (15) But she said to her, "Wasn't it enough that you took away my husband? Will you take my son's mandrakes too?" "Very well," Rachel said, "he can sleep with you tonight in return for your son's mandrakes." (16) So when Jacob came in from the fields that evening, Leah went out to meet him. "You must sleep with me," she said. "I have hired you with my son's mandrakes." So he slept with her that night. (17) God listened to Leah, and she became pregnant and bore Jacob a fifth son. (18) Then Leah said, "God has rewarded me for giving my servant to my husband." So she named him Issachar. (19) Leah conceived again and bore Jacob a sixth son. (20) Then Leah said, "God has presented me with a precious gift. This time my husband will treat me with honor, because I have borne him six sons." So she named him Zebulun. (21) Some time later she gave birth to a daughter and named her Dinah. (22) Then God remembered Rachel; he listened to her and enabled her to conceive. (23) She became pregnant and gave birth to a son and said, "God has taken away my disgrace." (24) She named him Joseph, and said, "May the LORD add to me another son."(25) After Rachel gave birth to Joseph, Jacob said to Laban, "Send me on my way so I can go back to my own homeland. (26) Give me my wives and children, for whom I have served you, and I will be on my way. You know how much work I've done for you." (27) But Laban said to him, "If I have found favor in your eyes, please stay. I have learned by divination that the LORD has blessed me because of you." (28) He added, "Name your wages, and I will pay them." (29) Jacob said to him, "You know how I have worked for you and how your livestock has fared under my care. (30) The little you had before I came has increased greatly, and the LORD has blessed you wherever I have been. But now, when may I do something for my own household?" (31) "What shall I give you?" he asked. "Don't give me anything," Jacob replied. "But if you will do this one thing for me, I will go on tending your flocks and watching over them: (32) Let me go through all your flocks today and remove from them every speckled or spotted sheep, every dark-colored lamb and every spotted or speckled goat. They will be my wages. (33) And my honesty will testify for me in the future, whenever you check on the wages you have paid me. Any goat in my possession that is not speckled or spotted, or any lamb that is not dark-colored, will be considered stolen." (34) "Agreed," said Laban. "Let it be as you have said." (35) That same day he removed all the male goats that were streaked or spotted, and all the speckled or spotted female goats (all that had white on them) and all the dark-colored lambs, and he placed them in the care of his sons. (36) Then he put a three-day journey between himself and Jacob, while Jacob continued to tend the rest of Laban's flocks. (37) Jacob, however, took fresh-cut branches from poplar, almond and plane trees and made white stripes on them by peeling the bark and exposing the white inner wood of the branches. (38) Then he placed the peeled branches in all the watering troughs, so that they would be directly in front of the flocks when they came to drink. When the flocks were in heat and came to drink, (39) they mated in front of the branches. And they bore young that were streaked or speckled or spotted. (40) Jacob set apart the young of the flock by themselves, but made the rest face the streaked and dark-colored animals that belonged to Laban. Thus he made separate flocks for himself and did not put them with Laban's animals. (41) Whenever the stronger females were in heat, Jacob would place the branches in the troughs in front of the animals so they would mate near the branches, (42) but if the animals were weak, he would not place them there. So the weak animals went to Laban and the strong ones to Jacob.

(43) In this way the man grew exceedingly prosperous and came to own large flocks, and female and male servants, and camels and donkeys.

COMMENTARY. GENESIS CHAPTER 30

We read in Genesis 16 that Sarah, Jacob's grandmother's child–bearing years had passed. So she suggested that Abraham, her husband, sleep with Hagar, her maid. Hagar conceived a child for Abraham.

We now ascertain that while Leah asked God to help her conceive, Rachel did not. She was envious of Leah and desperate to conceive. Rachel unreasonably demanded children from Jacob who told her he was not God and had no life-giving ability.

Jacob had learnt the three lessons that God had been teaching Abraham and his descendants.

1. Only God can create life.
2. God did not need human involvement to assist Him.
3. God can create life out of death.

We have considered these lessons previously and the incidents they relate to. For readers who have not studied the previous chapters of Genesis, we refer to five incidents:

1. The promise of a child that God made to Abraham.
2. The conception and birth of Ishmael.
3. The repeated promise of a son to Abraham when Sarah was advanced in years and unable to conceive.
4. The conception and birth of Isaac when Sarah, his mother, was passed her child-bearing years.
5. Abraham's willingness to sacrifice Isaac.

Like Jacob, we must learn what God wants to teach us. Otherwise, like Rachel, we will be ignorant of the spiritual things that really matter. God has disclosed in The Bible all we need to know. The Bible teaches us about sin, life and, more importantly, God's eternal life, and the consequences of not possessing it when we die. Because we have limited space, we abridge these truths:

- God gave us life, but sin brought us eternal death. Because we all sin, we will all die. Death ends our life, but not our existence. Our eternal future will be spent in Heaven or The Lake of Fire. There is no third option. God wants to give us His eternal life so that we can live in Heaven for eternity.
- As we are sinners from birth, our eternal destiny is The Lake of Fire. But God loves us, even though we are sinners, and He sent Jesus into the world to die to save sinners. Those who repent and accept Jesus as their Saviour will be saved from the consequences of their sin and possess God's eternal life. Their eternal destiny is Heaven.
- God will not force us to choose His gift of eternal life and Heaven. We choose our eternal destiny before we die. There is no further opportunity to be saved after death. Judgment follows the death of those who do not possess eternal life. Hence, the time to be saved is now.

Of the many verses from The Bible that we could quote in support of the above statement that, 'the time to be saved is now,' there is one verse written by Paul to the Corinthians that we must bring to your attention. It is a quotation from Psalm 48. It emphasised a truth that it not often preached today:

'I tell you, now is the time of God's favor, now is the day of salvation.' 2Corinthians 6:2.

Note the emphasis on the word, 'now.' Paul wrote it twice. Until Jesus returns from Heaven to take believers to their home in Heaven for eternity, The Gospel is preached, and the unsaved have the opportunity of being saved. But, after Jesus returns, the opportunity to be saved will end. 'The day of salvation,' will have passed. Hence, if you are not saved, now is the time to be saved.

We now revert to Genesis 30. Rachel's plan worked. Her maid gave birth to two sons. Rachel chose their names, Dan and Naphtali. These names indicated Rachel's motives. This was in contrast to her sister, Leah, who chose names in appreciation of what God had done in her life.

DAN: His name meant, 'Justice.' Maybe Rachel thought that God had judged her favourably, hence, 'justice for her.'

NAPHTALI: His name meant, 'Wrestling.' Did Rachel think that she was in a fierce contest with Leah and assumed she was winning the contest? Genesis 29 clearly states that God helped Leah give birth to her four sons. There are two matters we must mention about Rachel's selfish plan:

1. Did Rachel know that she was trying to compete with God? We do not know but we do know that she had no regard for Leah's problems and her unhappiness.
2. Rachel was not to blame that Jacob loved her more than Leah, but she wanted everything to the detriment of Leah.

Genesis discloses to us that Leah sought God's help and guidance, but Rachel did not. Rachel was selfish and self-seeking. She was living as though God did not exist even though she must have been aware that she was a member of the most privileged family on Earth. Jacob, her husband, had the Covenant blessing. We only have limited information about Rachel and Leah, but it seems that Rachel never learnt that her privileges brought her responsibilities.

God's people have the privilege of seeking God's help and His guidance. To avoid misunderstanding, the unsaved are not, 'God's people,' and do not have these privileges.

We noted the similarity of the strategies that Sarah and Rachel adopted when they were unable to have children. Rachel must have been aware of Abraham's and Sarah's mistake, but she intended to rule her own life and never considered God's Will.

It is so easy to judge others. We need to ask if we choose to please ourselves and ignore God's plans for our lives? We can choose to leave God out of our lives but, God's plans will be the best plans. Our plans will never be better than, 'second best.' Because of God's intimate knowledge of us, only He can satisfy us. We can plan for ease, comfort, leisure and pleasure but the items on our, 'I want them, and I want them now,' list relate to things that will only temporally satisfy us.

What does The Bible tell us about our search for the things we hope will satisfy us? People have been doing it for many centuries. Hence, when God spoke to the Jews through Isaiah, He challenged them to explain why they were spending money on things that did not satisfy them when He was providing, free of charge, things that would. We quote from Isaiah 55:1-7. Note that God will only satisfy those who forsake their evil ways and seek Him.

Isaiah 55:1. "Is anyone thirsty? Come and drink—even if you have no money! Come, take your choice of wine or milk—it's all free! 2. Why spend your money on food that does not give you strength? Why pay for food that does you no good? Listen to me, and you will eat what is good. You will enjoy the finest food. 3. "Come to me with your ears wide open. Listen, and you will find life. I will make an everlasting covenant with you. I will give you all the unfailing love I promised to David. 4. See how I used him to display my power among the peoples. I made him a leader among the nations. 5. You also will command nations you do not know, and peoples unknown to you will come running to obey, because I, the LORD your God, the Holy One of Israel, have made you glorious." 6. Seek the LORD while you can find him. Call on him now while he is near. 7. Let the wicked change their ways and banish the very thought of doing wrong. Let them turn to the LORD that he may have mercy on them. Yes, turn to our God, for he will forgive generously. Isaiah 55:1-7. NLT.

It could be that for years you have been seeking something

that will satisfy you. Maybe you have concluded that nothing ever will. Parts of The Old Testament have been written in, 'picture language,' and the message in Isaiah 55 was written for the Jews in Isaiah's day. But, the satisfaction that God promised then applies today. Consider God's message for us today. We quote the truths that have never changed:

- Come ... — even if you have no money!
- Listen, and you will find life.
- I will give you .... unfailing love.
- Seek the LORD while you can find him. Call on him now while he is near.
- Let the wicked change their ways and banish the very thought of doing wrong. Let them turn to the LORD that he may have mercy on them.
- Yes, turn to our God, for he will forgive generously.

Note that God warned the Jews that there was a, 'time limit,' on His offer. God was then, 'near,' to them, but He did not say for how long it would last. The Good News is that God's offer is still available. But there will come a time when it is not. If you are not saved, the time to repent and accept Jesus as your Saviour is now. There is no guarantee that Salvation will be available to us later today or tomorrow.

We have read about two sisters who married the same man. Both wanted his affection. Leah, the older sister, wanted him to love her as much as he loved Rachel, her younger sister. Leah had given birth to four sons for him, Rachel's maid only two. Rachel considered providing sons for him was a contest between the sisters, and she thought she was winning it.

Before any children were born, Leah had been upset and God had come to her aid. However, Leah decided to disregard what God had done for her and adopted the same tactics as Rachel. Jacob became the father of two more sons through Leah's maid. Leah's names for them reflected her attitude.

GAD: His name meant, 'My fortune has turned.

ASHER: His name meant, 'Happy.' Leah ignore God when she planned to provide more boys for Jacob. After the births of Gad and Asher she did not mention God as she had done after giving birth to her own four sons. Leah exchanged mandrakes with Rachel in exchange for the opportunity of sleeping with Jacob. Read the allegations that passed between the sisters. Their hostility to each other at this time is not hidden from us. Note that when Leah prayed again, God answered. God is not revengeful. We do not deserve His love when we forsake Him, but He does not forsake us or, 'write us off.' So, in answer to Leah's prayers, she became pregnant for the fifth time.

ISSACHAR: His name meant, 'Wages.' Leah considered she had been repaid for letting her maid sleep with Jacob. Leah did not refer to God although she had prayed for a child and God had answered her prayer.

ZEBULUN: Leah then gave birth to Zebulun. His name meant, 'Gifts.' Surprisingly, she did not ask God to assist her to conceive. Her acknowledgement of God was only after the birth. As Leah had done on the first four occasions when she had given birth to sons, she acknowledged God as the giver of the good gifts she had received for Jacob.

DINAH: a girl, born to Leah, was Jacob's only daughter. We shall read about Dinah again in Genesis 34. Leah gave birth to six sons and a daughter, her maid gave birth to two sons.

JOSEPH: We read that God answered Rachel's prayers and gave her a son. Her maid had borne two sons for Jacob, but this was Rachel's first pregnancy. She called her son Joseph. His name meant, 'May I have another.' Rachel asked God for help to become pregnant again. We have read of her desire to bear sons for Jacob. We have noted her competitive nature and her tactics to achieve what she wanted. But now, she again sought God's help. We must consider her prayers. You will recall the first time that Rachel prayed. She wanted God's help to conceive. We ask and answer three questions:

1. Did God reject her prayers because she had previously ignored Him?
2. Did God remind her of the times she had boasted that she was going to give birth to more sons than Leah?
3. Did God mention that Leah had conceived because she had asked for His help?

The Answer to all three questions is the same. "No."

Before we read on, we need to grasp the truth that God does not behave like us. God is holy. He will always act righteously. The good news is that God loves sinners. God loved Rachel. He wanted to be involved in her life, but she had a free will. God waits for us to invite Him into our hearts and lives. You would not expect God to go where He was not wanted. God wanted to bless Rachel. He was gracious and merciful to her. Once again, we state that you would not expect less of the God that believers know to be all that He has promised to be. God loves us, even though no one has ever deserved anything except His eternal punishment for their sins.

It is important to realise that God would not have forced Rachel to seek His help. God did not create robots. God has given all of us a free will. Rachel had the option of seeking God's help or organising her own life and pleasing herself what she did. God has not changed. If we have neglected God, we can do what Rachel did. We can do it in the knowledge that God loves us and will forgive us. He desires fellowship with us:

- God's grace, mercy and love will never cease.
- God wants to be involved in believers' lives because, without His power working in them, they really are, 'going it alone.' They can do nothing of spiritual or eternal value.
- Seeking God's help is an acknowledgement that believers

do not want to organise their own lives. They do not want to please themselves what they do. They belong to God and they want to do His Will.

- trust Him, not only for their eternal blessings, but for His blessings in this life.

Sadly, as has been illustrated in this chapter, it is often only when human efforts have failed that God's help is sought.

Jacob was still working for Laban when Joseph was born:

- Jacob decided to return to Canaan.
- Laban had prospered by Jacob's efforts. He was reluctant to lose Jacob. Read the details of their discussion.
- Jacob would not go without being compensated for his expertise and hard work.

Jacob had no intention of being outwitted by Laban who he knew would do his utmost to defraud him. Jacob set out the terms of a deal that Laban accepted. As Jacob anticipated, Laban tried to defraud him, but Jacob successfully achieved his objective. Genesis 30 ends with details of his vast wealth.

GENESIS CHAPTER 31

Jacob heard that Laban's sons were saying, "Jacob has taken everything our father owned and has gained all this wealth from what belonged to our father." (2) And Jacob noticed that Laban's attitude toward him was not what it had been. (3) Then the LORD said to Jacob, "Go back to the land of your fathers and to your relatives, and I will be with you." (4) So Jacob sent word to Rachel and Leah to come out to the fields where his flocks were. (5) He said to them, "I see that your father's attitude toward me is not what it was before, but the God of my father has been with me. (6) You know that I've worked for your father with all my strength, yet your father has cheated me by changing my wages ten times. However, God has not allowed him to harm me. (8) If he said, 'The speckled ones will be your wages,' then all the flocks gave birth to speckled young; and if he said, 'The streaked ones will be your wages,' then all the flocks bore streaked young. (9) So God has taken away your father's livestock and has given them to me. (10) "In breeding season I once had a dream in which I looked up and saw that the male goats mating with the flock were streaked, speckled or spotted. (11) The angel of God said to me in the dream, 'Jacob.' I answered, 'Here I am.' (12) And he said, 'Look up and see that all the male goats mating with the flock are streaked, speckled or spotted, for I have seen all that Laban has been doing to you. (13) I am the God of Bethel, where you anointed a pillar and where you made a vow to me. Now leave this land at once and go back to your native land.'" (14) Then Rachel and Leah replied, "Do we still have any share in the inheritance of our father's estate? (15) Does he not regard us as foreigners? Not only has he sold us, but he has used up what was paid for us. (16) Surely all the wealth that God took away from our father belongs to us and our children. So do whatever God has told you." (17) Then Jacob put his children and his wives on camels, (18) and he drove all his livestock ahead of him, along with all the goods he had accumulated in Paddan Aram, to go to his father Isaac in the land of Canaan. (19) When Laban had gone to shear his sheep, Rachel stole her father's household gods. (20) Moreover, Jacob deceived Laban the Aramean by not telling him he was running away. (21) So he fled with all he had, crossed the Euphrates River, and headed for the hill country of Gilead. (22) On the third day Laban was told that Jacob had fled. (23) Taking his relatives with him, he pursued Jacob for seven days and caught up with him in the hill country of Gilead. (24) Then God came to Laban the Aramean in a dream at night and said to him, "Be careful not to say anything to Jacob, either good or bad." (25) Jacob had pitched his tent in the hill country of Gilead when Laban overtook him, and Laban and his relatives camped there too. (26) Then Laban said to Jacob, "What have you done? You've deceived me, and you've carried off my daughters like captives in war. (27) Why did you run off secretly and deceive me? Why didn't you tell me, so I could send you away with joy and singing to the music of timbrels and harps? (28) You didn't even let me kiss my grandchildren and my daughters goodbye. You have done a foolish thing. (29) I have the power to harm you; but last night the God of your father said to me, 'Be careful not to say anything to Jacob, either good or bad.'(30) Now you have gone off because you longed to return to your father's household. But why did you steal my gods?" (31) Jacob answered Laban, "I was afraid, because I thought you would take your daughters away from me by force. (32) But if you find anyone who has your gods, that person shall not live. In the presence of our relatives, see for yourself whether there is anything of yours here with me; and if so, take it." Now Jacob did not know that Rachel had stolen the gods. (33) So Laban went into Jacob's tent and into Leah's tent and into the tent of the two female servants, but he found nothing. After he came out of Leah's tent, he entered Rachel's tent. (34) Now Rachel had taken the household gods and put them inside her camel's saddle and was sitting on them. Laban searched through everything in the tent but found nothing. (35) Rachel said to her father, "Don't be angry, my lord, that I cannot stand up in your presence; I'm having my period." So he searched but could not find the household gods. (36) Jacob was angry and took Laban to task. "What is my crime?" he asked Laban. "How have I wronged you that you hunt me down? (37) Now that you have searched through all my goods, what have you found that belongs to your household? Put it here in front of your relatives and mine, and let them judge between the two of us. (38) "I have been with you for twenty years now. Your sheep and goats have not miscarried, nor have I eaten rams from your flocks. (39) I did not bring you animals torn by wild beasts; I bore the loss myself. And you demanded payment from me for whatever was stolen by day or night. (40) This was my situation: The heat consumed me in the daytime and the cold at night, and sleep fled from my eyes. (41) It was like this for the twenty years I was in your household. I worked for you fourteen years for your two daughters and six years for your flocks, and you changed my wages ten times. (42) If the God of my father, the God of Abraham and the Fear of Isaac, had not been with me, you would surely have sent me away empty-handed. But God has seen my hardship and the toil of my hands, and last night he rebuked you." (43) Laban answered Jacob, "The women are my daughters, the children are my children, and the flocks are my flocks. All you see is mine. Yet what can I do today about these daughters of mine, or about the children they have borne? (44) Come now, let's make a covenant, you and I, and let it serve as a witness between us." (45) So Jacob took a stone and set it up as a pillar. (46) He said to his relatives, "Gather some stones." So they took stones and piled them in a heap, and they ate there by the heap. (47) Laban called it Jegar Sahadutha, and Jacob called it Galeed. (48) Laban said, "This heap is a witness between you and me today." That is why it was called Galeed. (49) It was also called Mizpah, because he said, "May the LORD keep watch between you and me when we are away from each other. (50) If you mistreat my daughters or if you take any wives besides my daughters, even though no one is with us, remember that God is a witness between you and me." (51) Laban also said to Jacob, "Here is this heap, and here is this pillar I have set up between you and me. (52) This heap is a witness, and this pillar is a witness, that I will not go past this heap to your side to harm you and that you will not go past this heap and pillar to my side to harm me. (53) May the God of Abraham and the God of Nahor, the God of their father, judge between us." So Jacob took an oath in the name of the Fear of his father Isaac. (54) He offered a sacrifice there in the hill country and invited his relatives to a meal. After they had eaten, they spent the night there. (55) Early the next morning Laban kissed his grandchildren and his daughters and blessed them. Then he left and returned home.

COMMENTARY. GENESIS CHAPTER 31

Jacob had previously been the victim of Laban's cruel and deceitful ways and this deceit had made Laban a wealthy man. That was now to cease. Laban's sons were not pleased. Jacob heard them make false allegations about him.

Jacob told his two wives that he intended to return to Canaan, and disclosed their father's deceit. He stated that God had looked after him and guided him and he had successfully obtained what was due to him. He disclosed his dream and the words spoken by God's angel. Because the angel said to him, "I am the God you met at Bethel," all three believed that God Himself had instructed them to travel to Canaan.

We know that some twenty years separated Jacob's two dreams and proof that God's timing is always right can be seen in the attitude of Leah and Rachel. Laban, their father, had unfairly treated them too. So, without hesitation they agreed to go and live in Canaan. God was aware of what Jacob and his wives had suffered.

Jacob told Laban the many wrongs he had endured.

Question: Why did Jacob accept ill-treatment for so long?

Answer: Jacob knew from his dream at Bethel that:

- God had a plan for his life.
- God would decide when he must return to Canaan.

We have noted elsewhere in Genesis that:

- God's people are not exempt from hardship and suffering.
- God's plans can often be long term.

Hence, over thirty verses in The New Testament require God's people to learn patience and perseverance. Even a cursory reading of them will teach believers to be patient until it is

God's time for action. In the meantime, God promises His continuous presence and blessings to those who trust Him.

It must be wrong to presume that God will respond quickly to prayer. Wrong and false assumptions often lead believers to be disappointed. God has never promised that the, 'Christian Life,' will be, 'a bed of roses.' Some preach this spurious teaching. God has a Will, and a timetable. Hence, those who teach that believers can pray and tell God what they want, and when they want it, not only teach error about God, they do spiritual harm to those they mislead.

It was not only Laban's sons who would be less prosperous when Jacob departed, so would Laban. When Laban left home for a few days, Jacob and his family secretly departed. Laban returned and discovered that Jacob had left three days earlier. Laban decided to give chase. Rachel, unknown to Jacob, had taken some idols so, in addition to losing Jacob's services and his large family, Laban had also lost his household idols. We shall consider these idols again.

Since Jacob had so cheaply bought the birthright from Esau, and then deceived his own father, he had been careful not to take or remove anything that belonged to another. We had an example of this when Jacob negotiated with Laban over the ownership of the flocks.

After seven days, Laban caught up with Jacob and his family at Mount Gilead. Laban was warned in a dream not to harm, bless, or curse Jacob. Read what happened when Laban and Jacob met and what they said. Note that:

- Jacob emphasised that God had been good to him.
- Rachel appeared determined that Laban, her father, would never again have the household idols.
- Laban returned home after kissing and blessing his family. Because of the warning he received, he did not harm, bless or curse Jacob.

We need to consider Laban as both a man and a worshipper. Genesis discloses to us that Laban was a liar and a cheat. We first read of him in Genesis 24. He was Rebekah's brother. He was very impressed with the jewellery that she received, and his materialism is emphasised in Genesis. From time to time he gave the impression that he was a spiritual man who worshipped God. However, there are a number of erroneous statements in what he said. In reality, Laban was an idolatrous, selfish, cheat and liar.

Perhaps Laban thought that by constantly referring to God, he could fool people into thinking that he worshipped God. But there is a contrast in what Laban and Jacob said about God:

- Jacob correctly said, "The God of my grandfather Abraham" and "The God of my father Isaac." He swore an oath to, "The God of Isaac."
- Laban erroneously said, "The God of Abraham, The God of Nahor and The God of their fathers." Nahor was Abraham's brother and Laban's father. God was not Nahor's God, nor their fathers' God.

Laban had seen Jacob's God bestow blessings on Jacob despite the cruelty and the deceptions inflicted on him for some twenty years. Was Laban hoping that because he was related to, 'God's special family,' the family that we know were part of God's Salvation History, he would receive some divine blessings? We do not know Laban's motives, but we do know that while he was going through the motions of acknowledging God, he was also very concerned about his stolen idols:

- He obviously thought that worshipping these idols brought good fortune and the loss of them would be to his detriment.
- If he wanted to be blessed like Jacob, who admitted that God had blessed him, why did he not repent of his idolatrous past and sin and put his trust in Jacob's God?

Did Laban think that he could continue to sin and have God's blessings on his life? If he did, experience teaches that he would be like the many today who have his wrong opinions of God's holiness and the fact that He detests sin. So many:

- want to sin and please themselves how they live, but at the same time, they want God's blessings.
- live unconcerned that God demands they repent, and Jesus died to save sinners from God's Judgment.
- hope that if there is life after death, Hell does not exist, or if it does, that as in their own opinion they have done more good things than bad things, God will be loving enough to overlook their sin and welcome them into Heaven.

Note that only Jacob presented a sacrifice to God. Laban did not take part.

GENESIS CHAPTER 32

Jacob also went on his way, and the angels of God met him.
(2) When Jacob saw them, he said, "This is the camp of God!"
So he named that place Mahanaim. (3) Jacob sent
messengers ahead of him to his brother Esau in the land of
Seir, the country of Edom. (4) He instructed them: "This is
what you are to say to my lord Esau: 'Your servant Jacob says,
I have been staying with Laban and have remained there till
now. (5) I have cattle and donkeys, sheep and goats, male
and female servants. Now I am sending this message to my
lord, that I may find favor in your eyes.'" (6) When the
messengers returned to Jacob, they said, "We went to your
brother Esau, and now he is coming to meet you, and four
hundred men are with him." (7) In great fear and distress
Jacob divided the people who were with him into two groups,
and the flocks and herds and camels as well. (8) He thought,
"If Esau comes and attacks one group, the group that is left
may escape." (9) Then Jacob prayed, "O God of my father
Abraham, God of my father Isaac, LORD, you who said to me,
'Go back to your country and your relatives, and I will make
you prosper,' (10) I am unworthy of all the kindness and

faithfulness you have shown your servant. I had only my staff when I crossed this Jordan, but now I have become two camps. (11) Save me, I pray, from the hand of my brother Esau, for I am afraid he will come and attack me, and also the mothers with their children. (12) But you have said, 'I will surely make you prosper and will make your descendants like the sand of the sea, which cannot be counted.'" (13) He spent the night there, and from what he had with him he selected a gift for his brother Esau: (14) two hundred female goats and twenty male goats, two hundred ewes and twenty rams, (15) thirty female camels with their young, forty cows and ten bulls, and twenty female donkeys and ten male donkeys. (16) He put them in the care of his servants, each herd by itself, and said to his servants, "Go ahead of me, and keep some space between the herds." (17) He instructed the one in the lead: "When my brother Esau meets you and asks, 'Who do you belong to, and where are you going, and who owns all these animals in front of you?' (18) then you are to say, 'They belong to your servant Jacob. They are a gift sent to my lord Esau, and he is coming behind us.'" (19) He also instructed the second, the third and all the others who followed the herds: "You are to say the same thing to Esau when you meet him. (20) And be sure to say, 'Your servant Jacob is coming behind us.'" For he thought, "I will pacify him with these gifts I am sending on ahead; later, when I see him, perhaps he will receive me." (21) So Jacob's gifts went on ahead of him, but he himself spent the night in the camp. (22) That night Jacob got up and took his two wives, his two female servants and his eleven sons and crossed the ford of the Jabbok. (23) After he had sent them across the stream, he sent over all his possessions. (24) So Jacob was left alone, and a man wrestled with him till daybreak. (25) When the man saw that he could not overpower him, he touched the socket of Jacob's hip so that his hip was wrenched as he wrestled with the man. (26) Then the man said, "Let me go, for it is daybreak." But Jacob replied, "I will not let you go unless you bless me."

(27) The man asked him, "What is your name?" "Jacob," he answered. (28) Then the man said, "Your name will no longer be Jacob, but Israel, because you have struggled with God and with humans and have overcome." (29) Jacob said, "Please tell me your name." But he replied, "Why do you ask my name?" Then he blessed him there. (30) So Jacob called the place Peniel, saying, "It is because I saw God face to face, and yet my life was spared." (31) The sun rose above him as he passed Peniel, and he was limping because of his hip. (32) Therefore to this day the Israelites do not eat the tendon attached to the socket of the hip, because the socket of Jacob's hip was touched near the tendon.

COMMENTARY. GENESIS CHAPTER 32

Once Laban departed Jacob continued his journey:

- Jacob knew that God wanted him to return to Canaan, his homeland, and with God's intervention he had survived the wrath of Laban.
- God ensured that Jacob was aware of the angels who were with him. Jacob acknowledged God's presence with him by calling the place where he became aware of the angels, Mahanaim. It means, 'God's camp.' This name suggests that God's army was present.

The Bible mentions very little about angels. In Matthew 26:53 we read that Jesus said:

"Do you think I cannot call on my Father, and he will at once put at my disposal more than twelve legions of angels?"

Historians tell us that there were some 5000 soldiers in a Roman Legion.

God knew that Jacob would have to meet Esau and He knew that Jacob would be concerned when told that Esau and four hundred men were coming to meet him. More than twenty years had passed since Jacob fled from Esau and Jacob did not know if he still wanted to kill him. We read about the preparations that Jacob made for the meeting with Esau, the messages that he sent on ahead and the tactics he used to improve his chances of survival.

Jacob's prayer gives us a wonderful insight into the character of the man we have read about in the last six chapters. To consider his prayer in its context, we must realise that God made exactly the same Covenant with Abraham, Isaac, and Jacob. God wanted each of them to know that He was their personal God. He was not blessing Isaac and Jacob because He had blessed their fathers. Abraham was not more important to God than Isaac or Jacob as he received the Covenant first. There was no hierarchy. Each of them were part of God's Plan of Salvation. This is not a Bible name, but it helps us to understand that Genesis and The Old Testament disclose a period in God's Eternal Plan of Salvation.

Note that when God referred to Abraham, Isaac, and Jacob hundreds of years after they died, God used the present tense. So we read in The Bible that God said, "I am the God of Abraham ..." not, "I was the God of Abraham ..." Because God used the present tense, it proves that the three men existed, even though dead for centuries. This also proves that we too will always exist. We are considering three men, but you would be well advised to consider this vital question:

Question: Will you spend eternity in Heaven with Abraham, Isaac, and Jacob, or in The Lake of Fire with others who never wanted or possessed God's Salvation?

Jacob began his prayer by stating his belief that he addressed the God of his father and grandfather. Jacob was aware of the wonderful things that God had done for them. These two ordinary men experienced extraordinary events in their lives.

When others, even their own families worshipped idols, they honoured God by worshipping and obeying Him. God wanted a special people who were separate from the rest of mankind because they only worshipped Him. God's purpose was that this special people would evangelise the rest of mankind so that through them the whole world would be blessed. This purpose was part of the Covenant that God made with His people through Abraham, Isaac and Jacob.

God's Covenant people were promised wonderful blessings for the present and the future, but only if they continued to obey God. They were and remained ordinary people. They were just the same as us. They were not given any divine or special resource that enabled them to believe in God, be obedient to God and stop sinning. We read about their sins in The Bible. Nothing has been hidden.

God is loving and merciful. Believers belong to God. He does not disown them when they sin. Jacob knew this important truth. After he addressed God, he acknowledged his own unworthiness and God's mercy to him. Jacob was some sixty years old. His knowledge of God came from his personal experience over many years. He never needed to be reminded of his sin. He knew that, although he did not deserve it, God had been merciful to him.

What Esau might do to get his revenge worried Jacob. Jacob had sinned against Esau and others, but he had learnt that all sin is first and foremost against God. Sin offends a holy God who detests it. Because God loves us, His forgiveness is freely available to those who confess their sin and repent. Jacob did this. We can do the same. Then, like Jacob, we can mention the past, the present and the future to God:

- The Past: Jacob acknowledged God's goodness to him. Jacob fled from Esau and Canaan with only his staff. He was returning a wealthy family man.
- The Present: There were serious problems for Jacob to deal with and he mentioned them to God.
- The Future: Jacob referred to God's promise that He would

maintain His goodness to him, and his descendants would be so many in number, they would be uncountable.

Because Jacob's prayer contains teaching and guidance that is relevant to believers' prayers today, we précis it. Jacob:

- spoke to God on a personal basis because he belonged to God. Do not misunderstand this. He was not over familiar with God. Hence, Jacob:
  - admitted his unworthiness.
  - acknowledged God's mercy and past blessings.
- he told God his problems and acknowledged that his future was in God's hands.

After Jacob prayed, he prepared gifts for Esau and a plan of action. He instructed his servants to move his family across the River Jordan and during the night, Jacob wrestled with a Man who Jacob did not know.

At dawn, the Man realised that Jacob had not been defeated. So, the Man struck Jacob's hip knocking it out of joint. But, Jacob held on to Him and the Man asked Jacob his name. Even though it implied awful things about him, he replied, "Jacob." Readers who have not read recent chapters of Genesis will question why Jacob's name was so awful.

In Genesis 25 we read that he was the last of twin boys to be born. During his brother's birth, he held one of his heels. His mother, Rebekah, named him, 'Jacob.' It meant a, 'heel, cheat, deceiver or grabber.' In Genesis 27, we read that after Jacob deceived his father, Isaac, Esau said that Jacob had been correctly named.

How wonderful it must have been for Jacob to be told that he was now to be called, 'Israel,' a name meaning, 'One who has power with God.' To save any confusion in this book, we, like Genesis, continue to use the name, 'Jacob.'

The chapter concludes by informing us that Jacob knew he

had wrestled with God. He had received the blessing he both prayed and wrestled for. He named the place, 'Peniel,' It meant, 'The Face of God.'

GENESIS CHAPTER 33

Jacob looked up and there was Esau, coming with his four hundred men; so he divided the children among Leah, Rachel and the two female servants. (2) He put the female servants and their children in front, Leah and her children next, and Rachel and Joseph in the rear. (3) He himself went on ahead and bowed down to the ground seven times as he approached his brother. (4) But Esau ran to meet Jacob and embraced him; he threw his arms around his neck and kissed him. And they wept. (5) Then Esau looked up and saw the women and children. "Who are these with you?" he asked. Jacob answered, "They are the children God has graciously given your servant." (6) Then the female servants and their children approached and bowed down. (7) Next, Leah and her children came and bowed down. Last of all came Joseph and Rachel, and they too bowed down. (8) Esau asked, "What's the meaning of all these flocks and herds I met?" "To find favor in your eyes, my lord," he said. (9) But Esau said, "I already have plenty, my brother. Keep what you have for yourself." (10) "No, please!" said Jacob. "If I have found favor in your eyes, accept this gift from me. For to see your face is like seeing the face of God, now that you have received me favorably. (11) Please accept the present that was brought to you, for God has been gracious to me and I have all I need." And because Jacob insisted, Esau accepted it. (12) Then Esau said, "Let us be on our way; I'll accompany you." (13) But Jacob said to him, "My lord knows that the children are tender and that I must care for the ewes and cows that are nursing their young. If they are driven hard just one day, all the animals will die. (14) So let my lord go on ahead of his servant, while I move along slowly at the pace of the flocks and herds before me and the pace of the children, until I come to my lord in Seir." (15) Esau said, "Then let me leave some of my men with you." "But why do that?" Jacob asked. "Just let me find favor in the eyes of my lord." (16) So that day Esau started on his way back to Seir. (17) Jacob, however, went to Sukkoth, where he built a place for himself and made shelters for his livestock. That is why the place is called Sukkoth. (18) After Jacob came from Paddan Aram, he arrived safely at the city of Shechem in Canaan and camped within sight of the city. (19) For a hundred pieces of silver, he bought from the sons of Hamor, the father of Shechem, the plot of ground where he pitched his tent. (20) There he set up an altar and called it El Elohe Israel.

COMMENTARY. GENESIS CHAPTER 33

Jacob met Esau after a separation of over twenty years. We are not told why Esau considered it necessary to have four hundred men with him. Genesis 32 gives us the impression that these were fighting men, Esau's private army:

- Maybe Esau thought that as Jacob had the Covenant blessing, Jacob would take Canaan by force and make servants of him, his family and other inhabitants.
- Isaac had told Esau that he would serve Jacob for a time and then be free. Maybe Esau decided that this was an opportunity to ensure he never served Jacob.

You will recall that Jacob was terrified when told that four hundred men were approaching, and he mentioned his fears to God in his prayer. Contrary to Jacob's fears, Esau ran to him, welcomed and embraced him. What brought about such a change in Esau? Why did a man who thought it prudent to have a private army with him embrace a man he thought was his enemy? The Answers are in the verses we read:

- Jacob mentioned the problem to God.
- God changed Esau's plans.

Prior to Esau embracing Jacob, Jacob bowed low to Esau seven times. Esau did not bow to Jacob:

- Was Esau too proud to bow to Jacob?
- Did Esau think that if he bowed to Jacob, it might give the men with him the impression that he was acknowledging that Jacob was their new leader?

Esau's men must have been puzzled. They must have been anticipating a fight and would not expect to see their leader embrace his enemy and weep.

It would have been appropriate for Esau to bow to Jacob. Esau knew that under the terms of the blessing Jacob received from Isaac, he was to be Jacob's servant as contrary to custom, God had indicated that in Isaac's family, the eldest son would serve the youngest son. Genesis has already disclosed Esau's sinful and rebellious attitude and lifestyle. We assume that Esau had not told his family, friends and neighbours that when Jacob came home, Jacob would be the head of his family.

We do not know why Jacob bowed to Esau, but we do know what Jacob said, and his words disclose his attitude. He knew that God had given Canaan to him and his descendants. He had returned to Canaan because God required it and made it possible. He owed everything to God. Without God's help, he would have returned with nothing.

Jacob admitted his dependence upon God to Esau and those who were present. Jacob was a humble and obedient servant of God. Unlike his proud brother Esau, Jacob had no desire to impress people with his wealth and accomplishments.

Jacob had tactically arranged for his family to walk in order in a line that would best suit his purposes should things go wrong. This line of four women and twelve children must have puzzled Esau. He had been brought up in a household of only four people. Isaac, their father, only had one wife, their mother, Rebecca. So, Jacob introduced his family. Jacob had sent his servants in advance with many animals as a gift for Esau. When Esau asked about the animals, Jacob admitted that his gift was intended to find favour. From their conversation, it seems that both men had prospered during their separation, but only Jacob admitted that his prosperity came from God's goodness to him.

Jacob wanted to remain in control of his own family and people and to decide where they camped and settled. He was reluctant to go with Esau to his home in Seir, or to accept assistance from Esau's men. After a temporary stay in Succoth, Jacob finally settled at Shechem in Canaan.

Even though God had given him all the land, Jacob bought the land he needed, as did Abraham when he wanted a burial place for Sarah. Some might wonder why Jacob bought what God had given him but, we read in Genesis 34 that it was important to Jacob that he had a good name with the existing inhabitants of Canaan. He had no instructions from God to take Canaan by force. As Jacob now lived in Canaan, he built an altar naming it, 'The altar to the God of Israel.' We mentioned above that Israel was Jacob's new name.

GENESIS CHAPTER 34

Now Dinah, the daughter Leah had borne to Jacob, went out to visit the women of the land. (2) When Shechem son of Hamor the Hivite, the ruler of that area, saw her, he took her and raped her. (3) His heart was drawn to Dinah daughter of Jacob; he loved the young woman and spoke tenderly to her. (4) And Shechem said to his father Hamor, "Get me this girl as my wife." (5) When Jacob heard that his daughter Dinah had been defiled, his sons were in the fields with his livestock; so he did nothing about it until they came home. (6) Then Shechem's father Hamor went out to talk with Jacob. (7) Meanwhile, Jacob's sons had come in from the fields as soon as they heard what had happened. They were shocked and furious, because Shechem had done an outrageous thing in Israel by sleeping with Jacob's daughter—a thing that should not be done. (8) But Hamor said to them, "My son Shechem has his heart set on your daughter. Please give her to him as his wife. (9) Intermarry with us; give us your daughters and take our daughters for yourselves. (10) You can settle among us; the land is open to you. Live in it, trade in it, and acquire property in it."(11) Then Shechem said to Dinah's father and brothers, "Let me find favor in your eyes, and I will give you whatever you ask. (12) Make the price for the bride and the gift I am to bring as great as you like, and I'll pay whatever you ask me. Only give me the young woman as my wife." (13) Because their sister Dinah had been defiled, Jacob's sons replied deceitfully as they spoke to Shechem and his father Hamor. (14) They said to them, "We can't do such a thing; we can't give our sister to a man who is not circumcised. That would be a disgrace to us. (15) We will enter into an agreement with you on one condition only: that you become like us by circumcising all your males. (16) Then we will give you our daughters and take your daughters for ourselves. We'll settle among you and become one people with you. (17) But if you will not agree to be circumcised, we'll take our sister and go." (18) Their proposal seemed good to Hamor and his son Shechem. (19) The young man, who was the most honored of all his father's family, lost no time in doing what they said, because he was delighted with Jacob's daughter. (20) So Hamor and his son Shechem went to the gate of their city to speak to the men of their city. (21) "These men are friendly toward us," they said. "Let them live in our land and trade in it; the land has plenty of room for them. We can marry their daughters and they can marry ours. (22) But the men will agree to live with us as one people only on the condition that our males be circumcised, as they themselves are. (23) Won't their livestock, their property and all their other animals become ours? So let us agree to their terms, and they will settle among us." (24) All the men who went out of the city gate agreed with Hamor and his son Shechem, and every male in the city was circumcised. (25) Three days later, while all of them were still in pain, two of Jacob's sons, Simeon and Levi, Dinah's brothers, took their swords and attacked the unsuspecting city, killing every male. (26) They put Hamor and his son Shechem to the sword and took Dinah from Shechem's house and left. (27) The sons of Jacob came upon the dead bodies and looted the city where their sister had been defiled. (28) They seized their flocks and herds and donkeys and everything else of theirs in the city and out in the fields. (29) They carried off all their wealth and all their women and children, taking as plunder everything in the houses. (30) Then Jacob said to Simeon and Levi, "You have brought trouble on me by making me obnoxious to the Canaanites and Perizzites, the people living in this land. We are few in number, and if they join forces against me and attack me, I and my household will be destroyed." (31) But they replied, "Should he have treated our sister like a prostitute?"

COMMENTARY. GENESIS CHAPTER 34

When we read Genesis, we often do not know:

- When some of the recorded events occurred.
- Why, when we are considering a person's life, many years pass about which we know nothing.
- Why we read about events that at first seem to contain little guidance for us today.

Jacob and his family camped outside Shechem. We last read of Dinah in Genesis 30 when she was born. She was Jacob's eleventh child and his only daughter. Jacob may have lived in Canaan for some years, when Shechem, the son of King Hamor, raped Dinah and then fell in love with her.

King Hamor and Shechem expressed no regret for Dinah's

rape when they met Jacob and his sons to suggest marriage. King Hamor wanted to be wealthier. Shechem wanted to marry Dinah. King Hamor was a liar. Compare what he said to Jacob and his sons with what he said to the rulers of Shechem. King Hamor needed the rulers to agree to an alliance with Jacob's family. An alliance required that every male in Shechem be circumcised. King Hamor told Jacob and his sons that an alliance would benefit them and make them richer. However, King Hamor thought that as the people of Shechem would acquire Jacob's possessions they, and not Jacob and his sons, would be richer.

We are not told what Jacob thought when he heard that Dinah had been raped. We know that he waited for his sons to return. How old were they at this time? When Dinah was raped, she was of marriageable age. Ten of her brothers were older than her. We can therefore assume that the majority of Jacob's sons, if not all of them, were men or young men. They were old enough to be outraged when their sister was raped.

Despite the incident being very serious, Jacob's sons received no guidance from him, and he did not seek God's guidance. His sons conducted the meeting with Shechem and Hamor. Jacob remained silent. Jacob let Dinah return to Shechem's home. Her brothers subsequently rescued her.

We might also wonder why Jacob said nothing when his sons behaved deceitfully to fool Shechem and King Hamor. Jacob must have known that the suggested solution would never solve the problem or have God's approval. Circumcision was evidence of the Covenant between God and Abraham's descendants. It signified that they were God's people. It could never be a prerequisite to intermarriage with non-Covenant peoples who did not accept all the Covenant's obligations.

Jacob's sons knew God's law regarding the Covenant's obligations. Their motive in suggesting circumcision must have been obvious to him. They wanted the men of Shechem to be unable to defend themselves after each male had undergone painful circumcision. Their plan required Dinah to return to Shechem's home. Her safety was secondary to their murderous intentions. In the absence of guidance from Jacob, his sons decided what the appropriate retribution should be.

Only Simeon and Levi are mentioned as killing King Hamor, Shechem, and the men in Shechem. Jacob's other sons plundered the city and the surrounding area. Jacob only blamed Simeon and Levi. Although Jacob rather belatedly disapproved of his son's actions, telling them of his desire to maintain a good name and to avoid conflict, we do not know what action, if any, he would have taken.

We have read how God's people dealt with serious problems in the past, but on this occasion no one sought God's guidance about the rape of Dinah. There were times when we would have expected Jacob to take control and speak but he did neither. Jacob and his sons had different views. This does not surprise us. Jacob had many years' experience of handling problems. His sons had none. Despite the novel situation, and the potentially disastrous outcome, no one suggested seeking God's guidance. We read the consequences of God's peoples' human judgement.

What happened to Dinah was disgraceful and her brothers cannot be criticised for feeling outraged. It was right that Shechem should be punished. Jacob's only concern was his family's wellbeing. Not only were they foreigners, they were outnumbered by the Canaanites. This was a legitimate serious consideration in times of conflict. Shechem was the King's son. The killings and the thefts could have resulted in serious repercussions. Jacob and his family were camped outside Shechem. They had no city wall to protect them.

Consider the question recorded in the last verse of the chapter. Jacob's sons were clearly not pleased with Jacob's lack of action, and his criticism of their actions. Readers might think it unjust that the only time Jacob spoke about the matter, he chose to condemn his sons even though he said nothing to Shechem and his father about the rape. As the head of the family, Jacob should have dealt with the problem and given guidance to his sons. Jacob failed them. His lack of guidance, and non-intervention enabled his sons to deceive the Hivites into being circumcised so that they would be defenceless.

We are sure that each reader will wonder how the problem might have been resolved. But there is surely one matter on which we will all agree. Jacob should have sought God's guidance as he had done previously. We are not told why he did not. Surely he could not have forgotten the times that he faced difficulties and prayed, and God intervened. God had protected him, his ancestors, and his family over many years and dealt with those who could so easily have destroyed God's people. We have more questions about Jacob:

- Why was he so afraid of the Canaanites when God promised him that Canaan belonged to him and to his descendants?
- Why did he say that the family were few and could be wiped out when God had said that his descendants would be so numerous, they could not be counted?

Until this problem occurred, Genesis is silent as to what happened to Jacob after he and Esau were reunited. Had Jacob's reliance on God lessened when times were good? We do not know but there is a vital lessons that all believers need to learn. Like Jacob, they need God's continual guidance.

What happens when believers do not seek God's guidance? They either rely on their own planning and ingenuity or do nothing and wait for events to unfold. So, they should not be surprised when overwhelming problems arise. They should never forget that God wants fellowship with them in the good times, as well as the times when life is difficult, and problems seem insurmountable.

GENESIS CHAPTER 35

Then God said to Jacob, "Go up to Bethel and settle there, and build an altar there to God, who appeared to you when you were fleeing from your brother Esau." (2) So Jacob said to his household and to all who were with him, "Get rid of the foreign gods you have with you, and purify yourselves and change your clothes. (3) Then come, let us go up to Bethel, where I will build an altar to God, who answered me in the day of my distress and who has been with me wherever I have gone." (4) So they gave Jacob all the foreign gods they had and the rings in their ears, and Jacob buried them under the oak at Shechem. (5) Then they set out, and the terror of God fell on the towns all around them so that no one pursued them.(6) Jacob and all the people with him came to Luz (that is, Bethel) in the land of Canaan. (7) There he built an altar, and he called the place El Bethel, because it was there that God revealed himself to him when he was fleeing from his brother. (8) Now Deborah, Rebekah's nurse, died and was buried under the oak outside Bethel. So it was named Allon Bakuth. (9) After Jacob returned from Paddan Aram, God appeared to him again and blessed him. (10) God said to him, "Your name is Jacob, but you will no longer be called Jacob; your name will be Israel." So he named him Israel. (11) And God said to him, "I am God Almighty; be fruitful and increase in number. A nation and a community of nations will come from you, and kings will be among your descendants. (12) The land I gave to Abraham and Isaac I also give to you, and I will give this land to your descendants after you." (13) Then God went up from him at the place where he had talked with him. (14) Jacob set up a stone pillar at the place where God had talked with him, and he poured out a drink offering on it; he also poured oil on it. (15) Jacob called the place where God had talked with him Bethel. (16) Then they moved on from Bethel. While they were still some distance from Ephrath, Rachel began to give birth and had great difficulty. (17) And as she was having great difficulty in childbirth, the midwife said to her, "Don't despair, for you have another son." (18) As she breathed her last—for she was dying—she named her son Ben-Oni. But his father named him Benjamin. (19) So Rachel died and was buried on the way to Ephrath (that is, Bethlehem). (20) Over her tomb Jacob set up a pillar, and to this day that pillar marks Rachel's tomb. (21) Israel moved on again and pitched his tent beyond Migdal Eder. (22) While Israel was living in that region, Reuben went in and slept with his father's concubine Bilhah, and Israel heard of it. Jacob had twelve sons: (23) The sons of Leah: Reuben the firstborn of Jacob, Simeon, Levi, Judah, Issachar and Zebulun. (24) The sons of Rachel: Joseph and Benjamin. (25) The sons of Rachel's servant Bilhah: Dan and Naphtali. (26) The sons of Leah's servant Zilpah: Gad and Asher. These were the sons of Jacob, who were born to him in Paddan Aram. (27) Jacob came home to his father Isaac in Mamre, near Kiriath Arba (that is, Hebron), where Abraham and Isaac had stayed. (28) Isaac lived a hundred and eighty years. (29) Then he breathed his last and died and was gathered to his people, old and full of years. And his sons Esau and Jacob buried him.

COMMENTARY. GENESIS CHAPTER 35

The story so far:

- Jacob settled at Shechem. He was reconciled to Esau his brother. We are not told why he did not return to his parents who lived in the Gerar Valley.
- When Jacob left home, he thought his father, Isaac, was dying but he was still alive. However, we do not know if Rebekah, his mother, had died.
- It appears from Genesis that Jacob and his family were wealthy, self-sufficient and independent. There was no reference to God or their relatives in the last chapter.

We now read that God spoke to Jacob. God wanted to remind

him of former times. God asked him to return to Bethel for a third time. What happened on the previous occasions?

- First Occasion: He dreamt about a staircase from Earth to Heaven. God spoke to him and confirmed he possessed the Covenant blessing. He set up a stone as a memorial.
- Second Occasion: A Man fought with him and God changed his name to Israel.

Jacob wanted his third visit to Bethel to be a new beginning and he immediately prepared for the journey. His response reminds us of what happens when unbelievers repent and receive God's Salvation. They are born again, receive God's eternal life and begin living to please God and not themselves.

Jacob intended to return to Bethel, build another altar and worship. We can feel his excitement as we read. Note that his new beginning involved so much more than just an outward show of cleanliness. Why he previously permitted household members to have idols we are not told. Worshipping idols has always been offensive to God. Jacob made sure that the idols were buried before the journey to Bethel began.

When Jacob's daughter Dinah had been raped, his sons took revenge on the Hivites. Jacob expected the Canaanites to retaliate but God made them afraid of doing so and Jacob need not have worried about this problem. God protected His people and they arrived at Bethel where Jacob built another altar and named it, 'To the God who met me here at Bethel.'

As we have studied Genesis, believers should have learnt that God does not fail us when we fail Him. Even if they fail to stay in touch with God and seek to live without His involvement in their lives, He does not stop wanting them to return to Him. Maybe you once prayed regularly, read your Bible, and knew God's presence with you. Now, because your life is relatively problem free, is it only when you feel vulnerable and unable to handle problems that you pray? Experience teaches that even unbelievers pray when facing danger and death.

God wants to be involved in believers' lives.

We read about Deborah's death. We read In Genesis 24 that when Rebekah travelled to Canaan, her servants went with her. One unnamed servant is referred to as, 'Rebekah's childhood nurse.' She might have been Deborah.

This was Jacob's third visit to Bethel. He needed to return there to be reminded that it was there that:

- God gave him the same Covenant blessing He had given to Abraham and Isaac.
- God changed his name from Jacob, with all its degrading implications, to Israel. It clearly meant that whatever he had done that was wrong, he now had, 'A New Start with God.'

Jacob's story is but one of many that prove everyone can have, 'A New Start with God.' God wants to forgive those who repent, and accept Jesus as their Saviour. God can then give them His Salvation. God can forgive because Jesus was punished for our sins on the Cross. He died, was buried, but rose again. Jesus is now in Heaven. He can save anyone, and everyone, anywhere who accept Him as their Saviour. Consider these vital words from Hebrews 7:24-25. GW:

'... Jesus lives forever .... That is why he is always able to save those who come to God through him.'

The above vital words from Hebrews 7:24-25 necessitate that we ask each Reader two vital question. We want to ensure that every reader is saved and on their way to Heaven.

1. Have you ever come to God through Jesus for God's eternal Salvation?
2. Is your eternal destiny The Lake of Fire because you have chosen not come to God through Jesus for God's eternal Salvation?

The choice is simple. It is either God's Eternal Salvation or God's Eternal Judgment for sin. The eternal consequences of choosing wisely or unwisely, although also uncomplicated, should not be ignored or considered and dismissed. This is because every Reader will either spend eternity in the bliss of Heaven or the horrendous agony of The Lake of Fire.

The last event in the chapter is the difficult birth of Rachel's second baby. Leah and Rachel, Jacob's wives, had named all of his previous children, and Rachel wanted the baby called Ben-oni, meaning, 'Son of my sorrow.' But, Jacob chose the name, 'Benjamin,' meaning, 'Son of my right hand.'

Rachel died near Ephrath. She was buried at an unnamed place. Jacob set up a pillar of stone to mark her tomb.

After Rachel died, Genesis uses either the name, 'Israel,' or Jacob.' We shall still refer to him as Jacob to avoid confusion, but note when Genesis uses the name, 'Israel.'

We have considered elsewhere in Genesis that although God wants to bless us and be with us constantly, we will not be exempt from the problems of life. God will comfort and sustain those who belong to Him in difficult times but the blessings that God bestowed on Jacob at Bethel did not stop his beloved Rachel from dying, or Reuben committing adultery with Bilhah, Jacob's concubine, who was the mother of his sons Dan and Naphtali, Reuben's brothers.

It seems that Jacob did nothing when he was told what Reuben had done, just as he did nothing when Shechem the Hivite raped his daughter, Dinah. We considered that incident in Genesis 34. Remember that at this time, there was no written law. The only mandatory punishment was death and it only applied to murderers. We considered this in Genesis 9.

As all sin is against God, Jacob might have taken the view that as God will judge wrongdoers, he could leave the matter to God. We will read later that Jacob disinherited Reuben. He should have received the firstborn's inheritance.

Benjamin was the last of Jacob's thirteen children and as the chapter concludes, we have a complete list of Jacob's children and their respective mothers.

Genesis states that all Jacob's children were born in Paddan-aram, where Jacob's Uncle Laban lived. At first reading, this appears inaccurate. Benjamin was born many years after Jacob left Paddan-aram to live in Canaan. As we consider in Genesis 48, Jacob seemed to have regarded the journey from Paddan-aram to Ephrath as one continuous journey. He ignored the places where he camped in-between Paddan-aram and Ephrath, however long he spent there. Reaching Ephrath meant arriving at his real earthly home. So, anything that happened pre-Ephrath happened in Paddan-aram.

We have details of what happened when Jacob arrived at Mamre, later called Hebron, where Isaac lived. Genesis states that Abraham had also lived there. Isaac died there when he was one hundred and eighty years old and Esau and Jacob buried him.

GENESIS. CHAPTER 36

This is the account of the family line of Esau (that is, Edom). (2) Esau took his wives from the women of Canaan: Adah daughter of Elon the Hittite, and Oholibamah daughter of Anah and granddaughter of Zibeon the Hivite— (3) also Basemath daughter of Ishmael and sister of Nebaioth. (4) Adah bore Eliphaz to Esau, Basemath bore Reuel, (5) and Oholibamah bore Jeush, Jalam and Korah. These were the sons of Esau, who were born to him in Canaan. (6) Esau took his wives and sons and daughters and all the members of his household, as well as his livestock and all his other animals and all the goods he had acquired in Canaan, and moved to a land some distance from his brother Jacob.(7) Their possessions were too great for them to remain together; the land where they were staying could not support them both because of their livestock. (8) So Esau (that is, Edom) settled in the hill country of Seir. (9) This is the account of the family line of Esau the father of the Edomites in the hill country of Seir. (10) These are the names of Esau's sons: Eliphaz, the son of Esau's wife Adah, and Reuel, the son of Esau's wife Basemath. (11) The sons of Eliphaz: Teman, Omar, Zepho, Gatam and Kenaz. (12) Esau's son Eliphaz also had a concubine named Timna, who bore him Amalek. These were grandsons of Esau's wife Adah. (13) The sons of Reuel: Nahath, Zerah, Shammah and Mizzah. These were grandsons of Esau's wife Basemath. (14) The sons of Esau's wife Oholibamah daughter of Anah and granddaughter of Zibeon, whom she bore to Esau: Jeush, Jalam and Korah. (15) These were the chiefs among Esau's descendants: The sons of Eliphaz the firstborn of Esau: Chiefs Teman, Omar, Zepho, Kenaz, (16) Korah, Gatam and Amalek. These were the chiefs descended from Eliphaz in Edom; they were grandsons of Adah. (17) The sons of Esau's son Reuel: Chiefs Nahath, Zerah, Shammah and Mizzah. These were the chiefs descended from Reuel in Edom; they were grandsons of Esau's wife Basemath. (18) The sons of Esau's wife Oholibamah: Chiefs Jeush, Jalam and Korah. These were the chiefs descended from Esau's wife Oholibamah daughter of Anah. (19) These were the sons of Esau (that is, Edom), and these were their chiefs. (20) These were the sons of Seir the Horite, who were living in the region: Lotan, Shobal, Zibeon, Anah, (21) Dishon, Ezer and Dishan. These sons of Seir in Edom were Horite chiefs. (22) The sons of Lotan: Hori and Homam. Timna was Lotan's sister. (23) The sons of Shobal: Alvan, Manahath, Ebal, Shepho and Onam. (24) The sons of Zibeon: Aiah and Anah. This is the Anah who discovered the hot springs in the desert while he was grazing the donkeys of his father Zibeon. (25) The children of Anah: Dishon and Oholibamah daughter of Anah. (26) The sons of Dishon: Hemdan, Eshban, Ithran and Keran. (27) The sons of Ezer: Bilhan, Zaavan and Akan. (28) The sons of Dishan: Uz and

Aran. (29) These were the Horite chiefs: Lotan, Shobal, Zibeon, Anah, (30) Dishon, Ezer and Dishan. These were the Horite chiefs, according to their divisions, in the land of Seir. (31) These were the kings who reigned in Edom before any Israelite king reigned: (32) Bela son of Beor became king of Edom. His city was named Dinhabah. (33) When Bela died, Jobab son of Zerah from Bozrah succeeded him as king. (34) When Jobab died, Husham from the land of the Temanites succeeded him as king. (35) When Husham died, Hadad son of Bedad, who defeated Midian in the country of Moab, succeeded him as king. His city was named Avith. (36) When Hadad died, Samlah from Masrekah succeeded him as king. (37) When Samlah died, Shaul from Rehoboth on the river succeeded him as king. (38) When Shaul died, Baal-Hanan son of Akbor succeeded him as king. (39) When Baal-Hanan son of Akbor died, Hadad succeeded him as king. His city was named Pau, and his wife's name was Mehetabel daughter of Matred, the daughter of Me-Zahab. (40) These were the chiefs descended from Esau, by name, according to their clans and regions: Timna, Alvah, Jetheth, (41) Oholibamah, Elah, Pinon, (42) Kenaz, Teman, Mibzar, (43) Magdiel and Iram. These were the chiefs of Edom, according to their settlements in the land they occupied. This is the family line of Esau, the father of the Edomites.

COMMENTARY. GENESIS CHAPTER 36

We read in Genesis 25 that Esau sold his birthright for Jacob's stew. So, he was also called, 'Edom.' It means, 'red stuff.' Genesis focusses on Jacob's life. Esau is only mentioned when events involved them both. Why then is there a list of Esau's descendants? Maybe the answer is that without it we would not have known that Esau's family were so numerous.

We do not read about Esau or his family again in Genesis, although they are referred to elsewhere in The Bible. Genesis concentrates on Jacob's family history as Jacob's family had a Covenant relationship with God.

We know from Genesis that Esau considered the things that mattered to God of little value:

- Esau knew what God wanted, but chose to please himself.
- There is no evidence in The Bible to indicate that Esau was ever obedient to God, repented or sought forgiveness.
- God knew before Esau was born that although he would be the firstborn, he would be rebellious. So God chose Jacob to receive His Covenant blessings.

Genesis 36 refers to Esau's wives being from the locality. Isaac and Jacob married wives from their homeland in Haran. Esau, unlike Isaac and Jacob, showed a complete disregard for God's Covenant. Esau's descendants became known as the Edomites. Genesis 25 states that Edom means, 'red stuff.' It refers to the stew for which Esau sold his birthright to Jacob.

Genesis 36 ends the story of Esau by telling us that a whole nation was named after a man who regarded God's Covenant of little value.

GENESIS. CHAPTER 37

Jacob lived in the land where his father had stayed, the land of Canaan. (2) This is the account of Jacob's family line. Joseph, a young man of seventeen, was tending the flocks with his brothers, the sons of Bilhah and the sons of Zilpah, his father's wives, and he brought their father a bad report about them. (3) Now Israel loved Joseph more than any of his other sons, because he had been born to him in his old age; and he made an ornate robe for him. (4) When his brothers saw that their father loved him more than any of them, they hated him and could not speak a kind word to him. (5) Joseph had a dream, and when he told it to his brothers, they hated him all the more. (6) He said to them, "Listen to this dream I had: (7) We were binding sheaves of grain out in the field when suddenly my sheaf rose and stood upright, while your sheaves gathered around mine and bowed down to it." (8) His brothers said to him, "Do you intend to reign over us? Will you actually rule us?" And they hated him all the more because of his dream and what he had said. (9) Then he had another dream, and he told it to his brothers. "Listen," he said, "I had another dream, and this time the sun and moon and eleven stars were bowing down to me." (10) When he told his father as well as his brothers, his father rebuked him and said, "What is this dream you had? Will your mother and I and your brothers actually come and bow down to the ground before you?" (11) His brothers were jealous of him, but his father kept the matter in mind. (12) Now his brothers had gone to graze their father's flocks near Shechem, (13) and Israel said to Joseph, "As you know, your brothers are grazing the flocks near Shechem. Come, I am going to send you to them." "Very well," he replied. (14) So he said to him, "Go and see if all is well with your brothers and with the flocks, and bring word back to me." Then he sent him off from the Valley of Hebron. When Joseph arrived at Shechem, (15) a man found him wandering around in the fields and asked him, "What are you looking for?" (16) He replied, "I'm looking for my brothers. Can you tell me where they are grazing their flocks?" (17) "They have moved on from here," the man answered. "I heard them say, 'Let's go to Dothan.'" So Joseph went after his brothers and found them near Dothan. (18) But they saw him in the distance, and before he reached them, they plotted to kill him. (19) "Here comes that dreamer!" they said to each other. (20) "Come now, let's kill him and throw him into one of these cisterns and say that a ferocious animal devoured him. Then we'll see what comes of his dreams." (21) When Reuben heard this, he tried to rescue him from their hands. "Let's not take his life," he said. (22) "Don't shed any blood. Throw him into this cistern here in the wilderness, but don't lay a hand on him." Reuben said this to rescue him from them and take him back to his father. (23) So when Joseph came to his brothers, they stripped him of his robe—the ornate robe he was wearing— (24) and they took him and threw him into the cistern. The cistern was empty; there was no water in it. (25) As they sat down to eat their meal, they looked up and saw a caravan of Ishmaelites coming from Gilead. Their camels were loaded with spices, balm and myrrh, and they were on their way to take them down to Egypt. (26) Judah said to his brothers, "What will we gain if we kill our brother and cover up his blood? (27) Come, let's sell him to the Ishmaelites and not lay our hands on him; after all, he is our brother, our own flesh and blood." His brothers agreed. (28) So when the Midianite merchants came by, his brothers pulled Joseph up out of the cistern and sold him for twenty shekels of silver to the Ishmaelites, who took him to Egypt. (29) When Reuben returned to the cistern and saw that Joseph was not there, he tore his clothes. (30) He went back to his brothers and said, "The boy isn't there! Where can I turn now?" (31) Then they got Joseph's robe, slaughtered a goat and dipped the robe in the blood. (32) They took the ornate robe back to their father and said, "We found this. Examine it to see whether it is your son's robe." (33) He recognized it and said, "It is my son's robe! Some ferocious animal has devoured him. Joseph has surely been torn to pieces." (34) Then Jacob tore his clothes, put on sackcloth and mourned for his son many days. (35) All his sons and daughters came to comfort him, but he refused to be comforted. "No," he said, "I will continue to mourn until I join my son in the grave." So his father wept for him. (36) Meanwhile, the Midianites sold Joseph in Egypt to Potiphar, one of Pharaoh's officials, the captain of the guard.

COMMENTARY. GENESIS CHAPTER 37

Jacob had thirteen children. Genesis now tells us in some detail about Joseph, Jacob's twelfth and Rachel's first child. He was Jacob’s second youngest child.

Benjamin was the youngest child. His difficult birth resulted in his mother Rachel's death. We recall that Esau was the favourite son of Isaac, and Jacob was the favourite son of Rebekah. We have considered the problems that this favouritism caused. Jacob must have been aware of these problems but, surprisingly, he favoured Joseph more than his other children as Joseph was born when Jacob was old. Jacob unwisely made his affection for Joseph known. He gave Joseph a brightly coloured coat when he was seventeen. This favouritism made Joseph unpopular with his brothers. Joseph's morality, honesty and trustworthiness also distinguished him from his older brothers and made him even more unpopular with them.

Joseph lived to please God. He did not ignore his older brothers' sins. They were shepherds, often living away from home. Joseph told Jacob of their immorality. We know about Jacob's general lack of discipline as well as some specific incidents where he should have acted but he did nothing:

- His daughter, Dinah, was raped by Shechem.
- His son, Reuben, committed adultery with Jacob's concubine.
- Some members of his household worshipped idols.

Maybe Jacob's general lack of discipline led his sons to think that they could sin without fearing punishment. There is nothing to indicate that Jacob took any action when he knew about their immorality. We read in Genesis 28:14 God's promise to Jacob:

'All peoples on earth will be blessed through you and your offspring.'

But the sinful behaviour of Jacob's family did not appear to have been a matter of concern to him.

Joseph had the ability to dream about the future and to interpret the dreams of other people. Divine dreams were not new. God told Abraham and Jacob about His plans in their dreams. In his own dreams, and those he interpreted, no one spoke. Only Joseph could interpret, 'silent dreams.'

We discover that similar dreams could have either different or identical interpretations. Jacob and Joseph's brothers thought that Joseph's two dreams had the same meaning, but they were wrong. His brothers would bow to him, but not his father and mother. Years later, Joseph was in charge of Egypt. Joseph's brothers bowed to him, but he bowed to Jacob. Joseph's mother, Rachel, was dead when Joseph had his dreams. So why did Jacob refer to her? Jacob believed in resurrection. He knew that Rachel would live again.

We cannot leave this part of Genesis without noting that Jacob rebuked Joseph for mentioning the second dream to him. Jacob condemned Joseph before thinking about what he said. Jacob's actions will surprise you when you recall that Joseph was his favourite son and Jacob had said nothing to Shechem, Reuben, and Joseph's older brothers about their sexual sins. Was Jacob more concerned with his pride than with the meaning of the dream? We know that Jacob was no stranger to God disclosing the future in dreams. We are not surprised that later, Jacob thought about what Joseph said and what it could mean. But that appears to be all the did.

Thinking, but doing nothing, changes nothing. When we are dealing with the mundane, this complacently might not have serious consequences for us but if we do the same with spiritual matters, like Jacob and his family, we might one day regret that we chose to be so unwise. Experience teaches that the majority have no interest in and do nothing about spiritual matters. Paul told us why:

'Satan, who is the god of this world, has blinded the minds of those who don't believe.' 2Corinthians 4:4. NLT.

We next read of the plot to kill Joseph. We read how wicked human nature is. Unbelievers do not accept God's opinion that sin is evil, and sin and sinners are under the control of Satan. Many blame society, bad housing and the like. But few would disagree that because they hated Joseph, his older brothers intended to commit a cruel, 'cold-blooded murder,' and then deceive their father about Joseph's death.

Our curiosity would have compelled us to find out the background to this crime. We would want to know what heinous act warranted such callousness and be surprised to learn that the victim was an honest young man who exposed the murderers' sins to their father. He was to be murdered by his brothers to ensure that his dream, which indicated he was going to their ruler, could not happen.

We know about the brothers' immorality. They had every reason to expect that their father would not take any action, but this would change if their righteous younger brother was in charge of the family. So they had to get rid of him.

Reuben, Jacob's eldest son and heir, changed his mind about killing Joseph but he had no control over his brothers. If he had, he would have stopped them planning to kill Joseph. Reuben deceived his younger brothers into thinking that he wanted to murder Joseph in a way that would save them from having to kill him with their own hands. We ask two questions:

1. What difference did it make to their guilt whether they murdered Joseph with their own hands or put him in a pit and left him to die?

   Answer: None.

2. Why was what the brothers thought so wrong?

Answer: Satan and sin control and darken the mind. We repeat what Paul wrote:

'Satan, who is the god of this world, has blinded the minds of those who don't believe.' 2Corinthians 4:4. NLT.

Only The Gospel shines light into our hearts. It enables us

to grasp that sin is evil and God detests it. In The Bible, God is always linked with light and sin with darkness. God is light, there is no darkness in God. God wants us to live in the light. When we receive His light, our darkness departs because light and darkness do not mix. The Bible teaches that:

- we either live in the light or in the darkness.
- truth is associated with light and untruth with darkness.
- the light exposes things that are done in the dark.

Judah foolishly told his brothers that they would only have guilty consciences if they killed Joseph. As we shall read in Genesis 45, it was only many years later that Jacob discovered Joseph was alive.

None of Joseph's older brothers confessed their involvement in the deceit that fooled Jacob, even though he grieved for Joseph for many weeks. Even when the brothers' sin was exposed, neither Jacob nor Joseph received an apology.

Genesis 37 ends with Joseph being sold in Egypt to Potiphar.

GENESIS CHAPTER 38

At that time, Judah left his brothers and went down to stay with a man of Adullam named Hirah. (2) There Judah met the daughter of a Canaanite man named Shua. He married her and made love to her; (3) she became pregnant and gave birth to a son, who was named Er. (4) She conceived again and gave birth to a son and named him Onan. (5) She gave birth to still another son and named him Shelah. It was at Kezib that she gave birth to him. (6) Judah got a wife for Er, his firstborn, and her name was Tamar. (7) But Er, Judah's firstborn, was wicked in the LORD's sight; so the LORD put him to death. (8) Then Judah said to Onan, "Sleep with your brother's wife and fulfill your duty to her as a brother-in-law to raise up offspring for your brother." (9) But Onan knew that the child would not be his; so whenever he slept with his brother's wife, he spilled his semen on the ground to keep from providing offspring for his brother. (10) What he did was wicked in the LORD's sight; so the LORD put him to death also. (11) Judah then said to his daughter-in-law Tamar, "Live as a widow in your father's household until my son Shelah grows up." For he thought, "He may die too, just like his brothers." So Tamar went to live in her father's household. (12) After a long time Judah's wife, the daughter of Shua, died. When Judah had recovered from his grief, he went up to Timnah, to the men who were shearing his sheep, and his friend Hirah the Adullamite went with him. (13) When Tamar was told, "Your father-in-law is on his way to Timnah to shear his sheep," (14) she took off her widow's clothes, covered herself with a veil to disguise herself, and then sat down at the entrance to Enaim, which is on the road to Timnah. For she saw that, though Shelah had now grown up, she had not been given to him as his wife. (15) When Judah saw her, he thought she was a prostitute, for she had covered her face. (16) Not realizing that she was his daughter-in-law, he went over to her by the roadside and said, "Come now, let me sleep with you." "And what will you give me to sleep with you?" she asked. (17) "I'll send you a young goat from my flock," he said. "Will you give me something as a pledge until you send it?" she asked. (18) He said, "What pledge should I give you?" "Your seal and its cord, and the staff in your hand," she answered. So he gave them to her and slept with her, and she became pregnant by him. (19) After she left, she took off her veil and put on her widow's clothes again. (20) Meanwhile Judah sent the young goat by his friend the Adullamite in order to get his pledge back from the woman, but he did not find her. (21) He asked the men who lived there, "Where is the shrine prostitute who was beside the road at Enaim?" "There hasn't been any shrine prostitute here," they said. (22) So he went back to Judah and said, "I didn't find her. Besides, the men who lived there said, 'There hasn't been any shrine prostitute here.'" (23) Then

Judah said, "Let her keep what she has, or we will become a laughingstock. After all, I did send her this young goat, but you didn't find her." (24) About three months later Judah was told, "Your daughter-in-law Tamar is guilty of prostitution, and as a result she is now pregnant." Judah said, "Bring her out and have her burned to death!" (25) As she was being brought out, she sent a message to her father-in-law. "I am pregnant by the man who owns these," she said. And she added, "See if you recognize whose seal and cord and staff these are." (26) Judah recognized them and said, "She is more righteous than I, since I wouldn't give her to my son Shelah." And he did not sleep with her again. (27) When the time came for her to give birth, there were twin boys in her womb. (28) As she was giving birth, one of them put out his hand; so the midwife took a scarlet thread and tied it on his wrist and said, "This one came out first." (29) But when he drew back his hand, his brother came out, and she said, "So this is how you have broken out!" And he was named Perez. (30) Then his brother, who had the scarlet thread on his wrist, came out. And he was named Zerah.

COMMENTARY. GENESIS CHAPTER 38

Genesis temporarily leaves Joseph's story. We now read about Jacob's fourth son, Judah. He suggested to his brothers that Joseph be sold into slavery. Genesis discloses the history of this callous man. A word of caution. Do not consider that Judah was more responsible than his brothers for what happened to Joseph as Genesis only reviews his life and family history. Genesis teaches us that all the brothers agreed to kill Joseph. Only Reuben changed his mind, but he was absent when Joseph was sold into slavery.

Prior to this selling Joseph, the brothers discussed various ways of killing him. Genesis does not tell us which brother made which suggestion, but it does name Judah as the one who suggested that Joseph be sold rather than killed. He said that selling Joseph would save the brothers from having guilty consciences. Did Judah live with a guilt-free conscience? The answer might be in this chapter that discloses his life and sins, his son's lives and their sins and the consequences.

What do we know about Judah? We know he left home, but not why. He married a Canaanite wife. We studied the problems of such marriages when we read about his rebellious Uncle Esau who did the same. God's Covenant with Jacob descendants required that they would always be a non-idolatrous people. Marriage to the idolatrous breached the Covenant. Judah had little regard for God's Covenant even though, like Esau, his family had ample evidence that obedience to God resulted in God's blessings.

Nothing we read suggests that Judah showed any interest in those matters that God regards as imperative. We read about the eldest two of his three sons. They had Judah's rebellious attitude. His eldest son, Er, was so wicked that God killed him.

Judah must have been aware of his family's history and that he belonged to God's special people whose blessings were based on their obedience to God. We ask questions:

1. Did his eldest son's unusual death cause Judah to think about God's judgment on those who sin?
2. Did Judah not realise that because of his disobedience:
    1) he was living without God's help and would continue to face life's problems alone?
    2) he needed to repent to receive God's blessings?

The Answer to each question appears to be, "No."

Judah's second eldest son was Onan. We read about the problem that arose on the death of Er. Judah spoke to Onan about his legal duty. He told him what the law required.

You might find it strange that a man who conspired to kill his brother and instead sold him as a slave insisted on his son doing his duty and obeying the law. Hypocrisy is but one of many common sins. How many bring up their children with a, 'Do as I say' and not, 'do as I do,' code of moral instruction? Unsurprisingly, Onan refused to obey Judah and we read he:

- ignored his legal obligations.
- deceived his recently widowed sister-in-law, Tamar, into a sexual relationship.

God took Onan's life as He had taken the life of Er, his brother. Although Judah did not want a guilty conscience regarding his evil treatment of Joseph, he must have been concerned when God killed his eldest and second eldest evil sons:

- Question: Did Judah seek God after the death of Onan?
- Answer: "No."

Judah deceived Tamar regarding marriage to his third son, Shelah. So, not only did Onan deceive Tamar, a young childless widow, so did his father, Judah. Let us consider the background to these shameful deceits on Tamar.

Judah told Onan that because his sister-in-law, Tamar, was a childless widow, he was required to marry her and to produce sons that would inherit from his deceased brother Er. God was displeased with what Onan actually did. Onan had no intention of producing sons that would not be counted as his own sons. He had sexual intercourse with Tamar but ensured she remained childless. Tamar was deceived into believing that Onan was fulfilling his legal and moral obligations to her.

The remainder of Genesis 38 does nothing to improve Judah's image. It does not hide his immorality, arrogance and hypocrisy. Twice, he made others fulfil their legal obligations but disobeyed the law himself:

- First Occasion: When God killed Er, Judah told Onan that he must marry Tamar, as it was both his duty and his legal obligation. But, when Onan died, he had no intention of letting Shelah marry Tamar. He thought that Shelah would also die. Judah was unconcerned that Shelah was in breach of both his duty and his legal obligation.

It seems that Judah thought his sons died because they married Tamar. We know they were so wicked that God killed them. We ask three questions that have the same answer to emphasise sins ability to deceive:

1) Why was Judah's belief so wrong?

2) Did Judah not know how evil his sons were?

3) Was Judah so evil he could not recognise sin?

The Answers: Although Judah knew what his sons had done, his conscience was so polluted with sin, he did not realise that God killed them because they were so evil.

Judah had told his brothers that if they sold Joseph instead of killing him, they could all have clear consciences. Judah made a number of statements. He thought they were right, but they were wrong. He never realised that:

- he was constantly being deceived by his own sin.
- sin is real and active. It grows in our lives. Only the foolish would trifle with it.
- he could never have a clear conscience because he never repented of his sin.

Without God's Salvation, sin cannot be mastered.

Judah could not rely on his conscience to distinguish, 'right and wrong.' He was like the people Paul mentioned when he wrote to Timothy. These four words described them:

'… their consciences are dead.' 1Timothy 4:2.

Before we look at the second occasion when Judah was hypocritical about the law, experience teaches there is a widely held but that we can control sin. So this incorrect belief considers that we can resolve to stop sinning when we choose to. But, 'sin continually grows,' within us. It is like a malignant cancer tumour that spreads within our bodies. To prove that this is true, we consider children and criminals and crime.

- As children grow, so does the gravity of their sins and yet no one teaches them how to sin. They need to be taught many things, but sin is in their nature. It is as natural for a child to sin as it is for them to cry or smile.
- Criminals and crimes are categorised as petty criminals and hardened criminals, petty crime and serious crime. But who would deny the progression from petty criminals to hardened criminals, petty crime to serious crime?

Sin deceives many about God's judgment. Experience teaches that unbelievers usually have one of two beliefs:

1. God's judgment for sin and Hell do not exist.
2. God will only judge us after we die and take our, 'good deeds,' into account.

We cannot in this book deal with what The Bible teaches about God's judgment, but both of the above beliefs are wrong.

We revert to Judah's hypocrisy.

- Second Occasion: Judah was hypocritical when Tamar became pregnant. Judah declared that she was a prostitute and should be executed.

  She knew that Judah used the services of prostitutes, so she pretended to be one. She entrapped him when he was away from home. He paid for her sexual services. She kept proof that he was the father of her twins.

Genesis records Judah's words when he was publicly disgraced. Judah also admitted that years earlier he had deceived Tamar into believing that Shelah would marry her so that she could have sons. How many other sins had Judah committed that would in due time be made known? We consider this again but in concluding this chapter, we note that

Judah deceived Tamar and she deceived him.

We have the second example in Genesis of a deceiver being deceived. The first was Jacob. In The Bible, there is a principle that, ‘we reap what we sow.’

GENESIS CHAPTER 39

Now Joseph had been taken down to Egypt. Potiphar, an Egyptian who was one of Pharaoh's officials, the captain of the guard, bought him from the Ishmaelites who had taken him there. (2) The LORD was with Joseph so that he prospered, and he lived in the house of his Egyptian master. (3) When his master saw that the LORD was with him and that the LORD gave him success in everything he did, (4) Joseph found favor in his eyes and became his attendant. Potiphar put him in charge of his household, and he entrusted to his care everything he owned. (5) From the time he put him in charge of his household and of all that he owned, the LORD blessed the household of the Egyptian because of Joseph. The blessing of the LORD was on everything Potiphar had, both in the house and in the field. (6) So Potiphar left everything he had in Joseph's care; with Joseph in charge, he did not concern himself with anything except the food he ate. Now Joseph was well-built and handsome, (7) and after a while his master's wife took notice of Joseph and said, "Come to bed with me!" (8) But he refused. "With me in charge," he told her, "my master does not concern himself with anything in the house; everything he owns he has entrusted to my care. (9) No one is greater in this house than I am. My master has withheld nothing from me except you, because you are his wife. How then could I do such a wicked thing and sin against God?" (10) And though she spoke to Joseph day after day, he refused to go to bed with her or even be with her. (11) One day he went into the house to attend to his duties, and none of the household servants was inside. (12) She caught him by his cloak and said, "Come to bed with me!" But he left his cloak in her hand and ran out of the house. (13) When she saw that he had left his cloak in her hand and had run out of the house, (14) she called her household servants. "Look," she said to them, "this Hebrew has been brought to us to make sport of us! He came in here to sleep with me, but I screamed. (15) When he heard me scream for help, he left his cloak beside me and ran out of the house." (16) She kept his cloak beside her until his master came home. (17) Then she told him this story: "That Hebrew slave you brought us came to me to make sport of me. (18) But as soon as I screamed for help, he left his cloak beside me and ran out of the house." (19) When his master heard the story his wife told him, saying, "This is how your slave treated me," he burned with anger. (20) Joseph's master took him and put him in prison, the place where the king's prisoners were confined. But while Joseph was there in the prison, (21) the LORD was with him; he showed him kindness and granted him favor in the eyes of the prison warden. (22) So the warden put Joseph in charge of all those held in the prison, and he was made responsible for all that was done there. (23) The warden paid no attention to anything under Joseph's care, because the LORD was with Joseph and gave him success in whatever he did.

COMMENTARY. GENESIS CHAPTER 39

In this and the remaining chapters of Genesis we read about Joseph's many years in Egypt. He arrived there as a slave and was sold to Potiphar, a senior army officer on Pharaoh's personal staff. What do we know about Joseph?

- He was the second youngest member of a large family. When he was seventeen, his dreams upset his father and brothers. They thought his dreams indicated that one day all members of the family would bow down to him.
- When he was in Egypt, an idolatrous country, he maintained his desire to please God. He had integrity. God blessed him in everything he did.

- He was only a young slave, but those he worked for realised that his God was blessing him. Hence, he was promoted by Potiphar. He was in charge of all Potiphar's personal and business affairs. For his sake, God blessed the whole household. He was a handsome young man, competent at his job and faithful to his master.

The Bible does not hide the sins of those we read about but there is no reference to wrongdoing in the story of Joseph.

Even Potiphar's wife could not seduce him, despite her best daily efforts. Joseph's replies to her immoral suggestions represented his righteous view of the way he should live. He mentioned two matters. With regard to:

1. God, he would not commit sin.
2. Potiphar, his earthly master, he would not abuse his position of trust.

He wanted to live to please and honour God, and that included being totally trustworthy in his daily work. He worked for Potiphar for some ten years. We mentioned in Genesis 37 that those who live to please God incur the wrath and hatred of those who do not. We read how Joseph, though he was innocent, was imprisoned in Pharaoh's prison.

This was the second time Joseph suffered for being righteous. The first time was when he was sold into slavery. But Joseph's objective was not to have a comfortable life. He chose to please God and he accepted the consequences.

Experience teaches that believers can be discouraged when things go wrong. Some teach that believers should be exempt from hardship. Joseph had no such false belief. His godly life brought him much suffering. There are other examples in The Bible of those who suffered because of their faithfulness to God. Many centuries after Joseph, Paul wrote to Timothy:

'... everyone who wants to live a godly life in Christ Jesus will be persecuted ...' 2Timothy 3:12.

Joseph was falsely accused of rape. It appears that he was detained in a part of the prison for common criminals that was reserved for Pharaoh's own prisoners. As expected of a man who lived to please God, Joseph was, 'a perfect prisoner.' He was so trusted that he was promoted by the chief jailor to the Prison Administrator. Even in times of adversity, good things happened to him. We know why. God was with Joseph and blessed him. So, the prison was properly administered.

We have considered thirty-nine chapters of Genesis in some detail. Genesis has disclosed the sins and weaknesses of those we have read about. There are details of sins in Genesis that, for the benefit of younger readers, we have mentioned but not detailed. We state this to emphasise that we have not censored Joseph's story. He lived to please God.

There is a reason why God wants believers to know about the sins and weaknesses of the people we read about in The Bible. God wants believers to learn two truths:

1. How they can avoid the situations and relationships that caused the downfall of others.
2. How that keeping in a close relationship with God will enable them to live godly lives and resist sin.

GENESIS CHAPTER 40

Some time later, the cupbearer and the baker of the king of Egypt offended their master, the king of Egypt. (2) Pharaoh was angry with his two officials, the chief cupbearer and the chief baker, (3) and put them in custody in the house of the captain of the guard, in the same prison where Joseph was confined. (4) The captain of the guard assigned them to Joseph, and he attended them. After they had been in custody for some time, (5) each of the two men—the cupbearer and the baker of the king of Egypt, who were being held in prison—had a dream the same night, and each dream had a meaning of its own. (6) When Joseph came to them the next morning, he saw that they were dejected. (7) So he asked Pharaoh's officials who were in custody with him in his master's house, "Why do you look so sad today?" (8) "We both had dreams," they answered, "but there is no one to interpret them." Then Joseph said to them, "Do not interpretations belong to God? Tell me your dreams." (9) So the chief cupbearer told Joseph his dream. He said to him10) and on the vine were three branches. As soon as it budded, it blossomed, and its clusters ripened into grapes. (11) Pharaoh's cup was in my hand, and I took the grapes, squeezed them into Pharaoh's cup and put the cup in his hand." (12) "This is what it means," Joseph said to him. "The three branches are three days. (13) Within three days Pharaoh will lift up your head and restore you to your position, and you will put Pharaoh's cup in his hand, just as you used to do when you were his cupbearer. (14) But when all goes well with you, remember me and show me kindness; mention me to Pharaoh and get me out of this prison. (15) I was forcibly carried off from the land of the Hebrews, and even here I have done nothing to deserve being put in a dungeon." (16) When the chief baker saw that Joseph had given a favorable interpretation, he said to Joseph, "I too had a dream: On my head were three baskets of bread. (17) In the top basket were all kinds of baked goods for Pharaoh, but the birds were eating them out of the basket on my head." (18) "This is what it means," Joseph said. "The three baskets are three days. (19) Within three days Pharaoh will lift off your head and impale your body on a pole. And the birds will eat away your flesh." (20) Now the third day was Pharaoh's birthday, and he gave a feast for all his officials. He lifted up the heads of the chief cupbearer and the chief baker in the presence of his officials: (21) He restored the chief cupbearer to his position, so that he once again put the cup into Pharaoh's hand— (22) but he impaled the chief baker, just as Joseph had said to them in his interpretation. (23) The chief cupbearer, however, did not remember Joseph; he forgot him.

COMMENTARY. GENESIS CHAPTER 40

Joseph was in prison. Pharaoh's chief baker and his wine taster, who had both offended Pharaoh, joined him. Joseph was put in charge of them. We read about their dreams.

Because some teach false and weird doctrines about dreams, note the words we read about the dreams that Joseph interpreted. He told the two men that the interpretation of dreams belonged to God. We recall that when Joseph told his dreams to his father and brothers, although they had no ability to, they sought to interpret Joseph's dreams. They thought they meant that one day they would all bow down to him. Joseph was the only one present with the God given ability to interpret dreams. He was not asked what his dreams meant.

Joseph interpreted the men's dreams. and what he predicted occurred. Joseph asked the wine taster to remember him but, he forgot Joseph for two years. God did not forget him. God was always with Joseph in the awful situations he endured.

We have mentioned before that God's Salvation does not guarantee that believers will have a life of ease exempt from hardship. God offers His Salvation to all. Those who accept it will receive spiritual, not material, blessings. Believers will one day be in God's presence in Heaven for eternity. But, until then, believers will live in a world that:

- loves sin and unrighteousness.
- hates God and righteousness.
- hates and persecutes believers.
- offers believers numerous temptations to sin.

Paul wrote to the believers in Rome. They were suffering because they had accepted God's Salvation. They remained faithful to God in an idolatrous city. We read in Romans 8:18.

'Yet what we suffer now is nothing compared to the glory he

will reveal to us later.' Romans 8:18.

Reader, reject the foolish teaching that believers should have an easy life and not suffer. Do not be misled. God's Salvation gives believers God's continuous presence in both good and bad times. Unbelievers do not have this amazing blessing.

How does what we have written about God's continuous presence apply to Joseph?

- He never blamed God for his problems and sufferings.
- His suffering resulted from living righteously to please God

If Joseph had chosen to live like others, he could have committed the sins his older brothers committed or lived in Potiphar's comfortable home committing adultery with his wife. But he would not have known God's presence with him, and the blessings that God gives to those who honour Him.

GENESIS CHAPTER 41

When two full years had passed, Pharaoh had a dream: He was standing by the Nile, (2) when out of the river there came up seven cows, sleek and fat, and they grazed among the reeds. (3) After them, seven other cows, ugly and gaunt, came up out of the Nile and stood beside those on the riverbank. (4) And the cows that were ugly and gaunt ate up the seven sleek, fat cows. Then Pharaoh woke up. (5) He fell asleep again and had a second dream: Seven heads of grain, healthy and good, were growing on a single stalk. (6) After them, seven other heads of grain sprouted—thin and scorched by the east wind. (7) The thin heads of grain swallowed up the seven healthy, full heads. Then Pharaoh woke up; it had been a dream. (8) In the morning his mind was troubled, so he sent for all the magicians and wise men of Egypt. Pharaoh told them his dreams, but no one could interpret them for him. (9) Then the chief cupbearer said to Pharaoh, "Today I am reminded of my shortcomings. (10) Pharaoh was once angry with his servants, and he imprisoned me and the chief baker in the house of the captain of the guard. (11) Each of us had a dream the same night, and each dream had a meaning of its own. (12) Now a young Hebrew was there with us, a servant of the captain of the guard. We told him our dreams, and he interpreted them for us, giving each man the interpretation of his dream. (13) And things turned out exactly as he interpreted them to us: I was restored to my position, and the other man was impaled." (14) So Pharaoh sent for Joseph, and he was quickly brought from the dungeon. When he had shaved and changed his clothes, he came before Pharaoh. (15) Pharaoh said to Joseph, "I had a dream, and no one can interpret it. But I have heard it said of you that when you hear a dream you can interpret it." (16) "I cannot do it," Joseph replied to Pharaoh, "but God will give Pharaoh the answer he desires." (17) Then Pharaoh said to Joseph, "In my dream I was standing on the bank of the Nile, (18) when out of the river there came up seven cows, fat and sleek, and they grazed among the reeds. (19) After them, seven other cows came up—scrawny and very ugly and lean. I had never seen such ugly cows in all the land of Egypt. (20) The lean, ugly cows ate up the seven fat cows that came up first. (21) But even after they ate them, no one could tell that they had done so; they looked just as ugly as before. Then I woke up. (22) "In my dream I saw seven heads of grain, full and good, growing on a single stalk. (23) After them, seven other heads sprouted—withered and thin and scorched by the east wind. (24) The thin heads of grain swallowed up the seven good heads. I told this to the magicians, but none of them could explain it to me." (25) Then Joseph said to Pharaoh, "The dreams of Pharaoh are one and the same. God has revealed to Pharaoh what he is about to do. (26) The seven good cows are seven years, and the seven good heads of grain are seven years; it is one and the same dream. (27) The seven lean, ugly cows that came up afterward are seven years, and so are the seven worthless heads of grain scorched by the east wind: They are seven years of famine. (28) "It is just as I said to Pharaoh: God has shown Pharaoh what he is about to do. (29) Seven years of great abundance are coming throughout the land of Egypt, (30) but seven years of famine will follow them. Then all the abundance in Egypt will be forgotten, and the famine will ravage the land. (31) The abundance in the land will not be remembered, because the famine that follows it will be so severe. (32) The reason the dream was given to Pharaoh in two forms is that the matter has been firmly decided by God, and God will do it soon. (33) "And now let Pharaoh look for a discerning and wise man and put him in charge of the land of Egypt. (34) Let Pharaoh appoint commissioners over the land to take a fifth of the harvest of Egypt during the seven years of abundance. (35) They should collect all the food of these good years that are coming and store up the grain under the authority of Pharaoh, to be kept in the cities for food. (36) This food should be held in reserve for the country, to be used during the seven years of famine that will come upon Egypt, so that the country may not be ruined by the famine." (37) The plan seemed good to Pharaoh and to all his officials. (38) So Pharaoh asked them, "Can we find anyone like this man, one in whom is the spirit of God?" (39) Then Pharaoh said to Joseph, "Since God has made all this known to you, there is no one so discerning and wise as you. (40) You shall be in charge of my palace, and all my people are to submit to your orders. Only with respect to the throne will I be greater than you." (41) So Pharaoh said to Joseph, "I hereby put you in charge of the whole land of Egypt." (42) Then Pharaoh took his signet ring from his finger and put it on Joseph's finger. He dressed him in robes of fine linen and put a gold chain around his neck. (43) He had him ride in a chariot as his second-in-command, and people shouted before him, "Make way!" Thus he put him in charge of the whole land of Egypt. (44) Then Pharaoh said to Joseph, "I am Pharaoh, but without your word no one will lift hand or foot in all Egypt." (45) Pharaoh gave Joseph the name Zaphenath-Paneah and gave him Asenath daughter of Potiphera, priest of On, to be his wife. And Joseph went throughout the land of Egypt. (46) Joseph was thirty years old when he entered the service of Pharaoh king of Egypt. And Joseph went out from Pharaoh's presence and traveled throughout Egypt. (47) During the seven years of abundance the land produced plentifully. (48) Joseph collected all the food produced in those seven years of abundance in Egypt and stored it in the cities. In each city he put the food grown in the fields surrounding it. (49) Joseph stored up huge quantities of grain, like the sand of the sea; it was so much that he stopped keeping records because it was beyond measure. (50) Before the years of famine came, two sons were born to Joseph by Asenath daughter of Potiphera, priest of On. (51) Joseph named his firstborn Manasseh and said, "It is because God has made me forget all my trouble and all my father's household." (52) The second son he named Ephraim and said, "It is because God has made me fruitful in the land of my suffering." (53) The seven years of abundance in Egypt came to an end, (54) and the seven years of famine began, just as Joseph had said. There was famine in all the other lands, but in the whole land of Egypt there was food. (55) When all Egypt began to feel the famine, the people cried to Pharaoh for food. Then Pharaoh told all the Egyptians, "Go to Joseph and do what he tells you." (56) When the famine had spread over the whole country, Joseph opened all the storehouses and sold grain to the Egyptians, for the famine was severe throughout Egypt. (57) And all the world came to Egypt to buy grain from Joseph, because the famine was severe everywhere.

COMMENTARY. GENESIS CHAPTER 41

Although he awakened between them, Pharaoh had two similar dreams. He had to know their meaning. All Egypt's wise men were summoned to the palace to interpret the dreams, but no one could.

After forgetting Joseph for two years, the wine taster

remembered him. Joseph was thirty when he was summoned to appear before one of the most powerful rulers on Earth.

There was no pretence with Joseph. He told Pharaoh that he had no ability to interpret dreams, but that his God would interpret Pharaoh's dreams. As Joseph did not then know what Pharaoh had dreamt, this was a brave statement to make to a man who was regarded as a god by the Egyptians. But, wherever Joseph was, or whoever he spoke to, he was never afraid to tell the truth and speak about his God.

When Joseph heard the two dreams, he immediately confirmed that they had the same interpretation. God was warning Pharaoh about a severe famine that would begin in seven years, last for seven years, and be preceded by seven years of surplus food.

Without being asked to, Joseph said what Pharaoh should do. His kingdom should be divided into five areas. During the next seven years, surplus food should be stored. Joseph added that a wise man should implement his seven year plan.

Pharaoh must have been impressed by Joseph's confidence in his God. Joseph was a self-educated Hebrew. Genesis 43:32 tells us that the Egyptians despised Hebrews. Joseph had never pretended to be an Egyptian. In Potiphar's household he was called, 'the Hebrew slave.'

Pharaoh knew Joseph was not relying on any Egyptian god for his ability to interpret dreams. Pharaoh's wise men had not interpreted his dreams. So with the approval of all his royal assistants, Pharaoh appointed Joseph to administer his plan.

Pharaoh stated to those present that Joseph had received his wisdom from God. Whether he realised that Joseph's God was the God of Creation, the only true God, we do not know but Pharaoh's actions support the view that he recognised that Joseph's God's ability was unique. The Egyptian wise men who could not assist Pharaoh, so he knew that Joseph's God's ability was not available in Egypt. The words, 'all the wise men,' included those, so-called, 'wise men,' who were familiar with the supernatural and the paranormal.

We cannot consider these, 'wise men,' in detail now. We have not read about Satan since Genesis 3, but do not assume that he had been inactive since the days of Adam and Eve. The opposite is true. Satan had continued his evil activities. For millennia some have practiced divination. The Bible does not hide from us the evil powers that Satan and his angels possess, and humans seek and receive from Satan.

Joseph married into one of the high-ranking families of the day, a family chosen for him by Pharaoh but despite his fame and the good things that happened to him, he was humble and acknowledged that God was working through him. He was not an Egyptian but he was the second most important person in Egypt. Only Pharaoh outranked him. Pharaoh was content to leave every aspect of his kingdom's administration to Joseph.

Since the age of seventeen, Joseph had faithfully managed the affairs of those he was subservient to:

- Potiphar's household and business affairs.
- The administration of the jail for the chief jailer.

At home he was a shepherd. His progress in the thirteen years he lived in Egypt is amazing. He proved that he could:

- run an army officer's household and his business affairs.
- organise a prison that contained Pharaoh's prisoners.
- be entrusted with the task of administering Egypt.

God had prepared Joseph for the enormous task of saving Egypt and her neighbours from the devastating consequences of a seven year famine. Predicting it was just the beginning.

God wanted Joseph to be in a position where he could avert a disaster. Because Joseph was faithful and gained practical experience in smaller undertakings, he was able to take on the huge and difficult task required by Pharaoh. We know that some reading Joseph's story would:

- Regard him as fortunate and use a word like, 'lucky,' to describe his meteoric rise to fame and fortune.
- Consider that he was, 'in the right place at the right time,' indicating their view that it was providence or something similar that gave him a, 'once-in-a-lifetime,' opportunity.

These are the views of those who do not know God and they are wrong because they ignore God's plan for Joseph. We need to be blunt about this. Joseph did not live to please God so that he would become important or obtain earthly benefits.

Genesis makes it clear that God was always with Joseph, blessing him and making a success of whatever he did. There is no suggestion in Genesis that an illiterate young Hebrew shepherd miraculously received the ability to speak the Egyptian language or received accountancy, management and administrative abilities superior to those possessed by the Egyptians, who were, 'world leaders,' in administration.

Question: Do many believers have Joseph's abilities?

Answer: The Bible and experience teach that the answer is, "No." It is not, "Maybe," or "Possibly." It is definitely, "No."

When Paul, who was a highly respected scholar and lawyer, wrote to the Corinthians 2000 years ago, he was under no illusion about the social standing, academic abilities, and the ability of the vast majority of believers.

Paul travelled and preached The Gospel in many countries and he knew that well-bred, well-educated, and influential believers were in the minority.

Read his candid words in 1Corinthians 1:26:

'Brothers and sisters, think of what you were when you were called. Not many of you were wise by human standards; not many were influential; not many were of noble birth.'

Paul wrote that the majority of believers were, 'nobodies.' For his actual comments read 1Corinthians 1:26-28.

Question: Did Joseph's success enable him to make a lot of money, retire early and have a very pleasant and easy life sunbathing and swimming in the River Nile?

Answer: "No." From the age of seventeen, until he was thirty, Joseph was either a slave or a prisoner. He worked for a:

- Master: He should not have been a slave.
- Jailor: He should not have been a prisoner.

Would we have been as diligent and as faithful as Joseph was if we had suffered not one serious injustice, but two?

Some might have been faithful if they had served in an influential household and received respect. But, would they have been as faithful a second time when they were wrongly imprisoned, even if respected by those in charge?

Previously, when we mentioned Joseph's progress, we only considered the scope and extent of his administrative duties. Although no one would consider that being removed from an influential household and imprisoned was progress, God wanted Joseph to be in that particular prison when the chief baker and the wine taster were also imprisoned and Pharaoh had his two dreams.

Joseph did not know that during the previous thirteen years, whether as slave or prisoner, God had been preparing him to be in charge of Egypt at a time when his administrative abilities would prove to be vital to the survival of his own family, God's earthly people.

Pharaoh gave Joseph a new name, Zaphenath-Paneah. It means, 'He has the god-like power of life and death.' To save confusion, we will continue to call him Joseph. In due course his brothers appeared before him although they were unaware of who he was. We read Reuben's view.

Pharaoh also gave Joseph clothes and jewellery, a wife, Asenath, from an influential family and a chariot that indicated that he was Pharaoh's second-in-command.

Joseph's father-in-law was Potiphera, the priest of the sun god Ra. Nothing more is written about him, but we discuss the Egyptian priests when we study Genesis 47.

Joseph began his work with his usual diligence and he had the success we have come to associate with him. He had two sons. He named them Manasseh: meaning, 'Made to forget,' and Ephraim: meaning, 'Fruitful.' Joseph acknowledged that God had compensated him for the loss of his home life in Canaan and had made him fruitful in a land where he had been a slave.

Joseph's interpretation of Pharaoh's dreams was accurate. The seven years of surplus came to an end and a universal famine followed. Only in Egypt was there plenty of grain. Though we are pleased that Joseph's story had, 'a happy ending,' readers must not miss the spiritual lesson that the story teaches us. It can be simply stated:

- God warned Pharaoh of an impending disaster.
- Pharaoh wisely heeded God's warning and let Joseph save the Egyptians from starvation.

Think of the human consequences if Pharaoh had:

- ignored God's warning.
- not let Joseph save the Egyptians.

Think of the awful consequences that will result to unbelievers who fail to heed God's warning of eternal judgment.

GENESIS CHAPTER 42

When Jacob learned that there was grain in Egypt, he said to his sons, "Why do you just keep looking at each other?" (2) He continued, "I have heard that there is grain in Egypt. Go down there and buy some for us, so that we may live and not die." (3) Then ten of Joseph's brothers went down to buy grain from Egypt. (4) But Jacob did not send Benjamin, Joseph's brother, with the others, because he was afraid that harm might come to him. (5) So Israel's sons were among those who went to buy grain, for there was famine in the land of Canaan also. (6) Now Joseph was the governor of the land, the person who sold grain to all its people. So when Joseph's brothers arrived, they bowed down to him with their faces to the ground. (7) As soon as Joseph saw his brothers, he recognized them, but he pretended to be a stranger and spoke harshly to them. "Where do you come from?" he asked. "From the land of Canaan," they replied, "to buy food." (8) Although Joseph recognized his brothers, they did not recognize him. (9) Then he remembered his dreams about them and said to them, "You are spies! You have come to see where our land is unprotected." (10) "No, my lord," they answered. "Your servants have come to buy food. (11) We are all the sons of one man. Your servants are honest men, not spies." (12) "No!" he said to them. "You have come to see where our land is unprotected." (13) But they replied, "Your servants were twelve brothers, the sons of one man, who lives in the land of Canaan. The youngest is now with our father, and one is no more." (14) Joseph said to them, "It is just as I told you: You are spies! (15) And this is how you will be tested: As surely as Pharaoh lives, you will not leave this place unless your youngest brother comes here. (16) Send one of your number to get your brother; the rest of you will be kept in prison, so that your words may be tested to see if you are telling the truth. If you are not, then as surely as Pharaoh lives, you are spies!" (17) And he put them all in custody for three days. (18) On the third day, Joseph said to them, "Do this and you will live, for I fear God: (19) If you are honest men, let one of your brothers stay here in prison, while the rest of you go and take grain back for your starving households. (20) But you must bring your youngest brother to me, so that your words may be verified and that you may not die." This they proceeded to do. (21) They said to one another, "Surely we are being punished because of our brother. We saw how distressed he was when he pleaded with us for his life, but we would not listen; that's why this distress has come on us." (22) Reuben replied, "Didn't I tell you not to sin against the boy? But you wouldn't listen! Now we must give an accounting for his blood." (23) They did not realize that Joseph could understand them, since he was using an interpreter. (24) He turned away from them and began to weep, but then came back and spoke to them again. He had Simeon taken from them and bound before their eyes. (25) Joseph gave orders to fill their bags with grain, to put each man's silver back in his sack, and to give them provisions for their journey. After this was done for them, (26) they loaded their grain on their donkeys and left. (27) At the place where they stopped for the night one of them opened his sack to get feed for his donkey, and he saw his silver in the mouth of his sack. (28) "My silver has been returned," he said to his brothers. "Here it is in my sack." Their hearts sank and they turned to each other trembling and said, "What is this that God has done to us?" (29) When they came to their father Jacob in the land of Canaan, they told him all that had happened to them. They said, (30) "The man who is lord over the land spoke harshly to us and treated us as though we were spying on the land. (31) But we said to him, 'We are honest men; we are not spies. (32) We were twelve brothers, sons of one father. One is no more, and the youngest is now with our father in Canaan.' (33) "Then the man who is lord over the land said to us, 'This is how I will know whether you are honest men: Leave one of your brothers here with me, and take food for your starving households and go. (34) But bring your youngest brother to me so I will know that you are not spies but honest men. Then I will give your brother back to you, and you can trade in the land.'" (35) As they were emptying their sacks, there in each man's sack was his pouch of silver! When they and their father saw the money pouches, they were frightened. (36) Their father Jacob said to them, "You have deprived me of my children. Joseph is no more and Simeon is no more, and now you want to take Benjamin. Everything is against me!" (37) Then Reuben said to his father, "You may put both of my sons to death if I do not bring him back to you. Entrust him to my care, and I will bring him back." (38) But Jacob said, "My son will not go down there with you; his brother is dead and he is the only one left. If harm comes to him on the journey you are taking, you will bring my gray head down to the grave in sorrow."

COMMENTARY. GENESIS CHAPTER 42

While the events predicted in the dreams of the chief baker, the wine taster and Pharaoh occurred shortly after their dreams, Joseph had to wait over twenty years for the events predicted in his own dreams to occur.

The famine resulted in problems for Jacob and his family in Canaan, but he would not let Benjamin travel with his brothers to Egypt. It seems that Jacob's family had no grain in the first year of the famine as when the brothers visited Egypt, one year after their previous visit, Joseph told them that the famine would last for another five years.

Joseph was at least twenty years older than when his brothers last saw him. They did not recognise him, but he knew them instantly. Their dialogue was translated so they would not recognise him. He said that they were spies and pretended not to accept their story. He wanted them to bring his younger brother Benjamin to Egypt:

- Benjamin and Joseph were Rachel's sons.
- Jacob loved Rachel, and her sons were born much later than his other children.
- Benjamin was not involved in the plan to kill Joseph.

Joseph's plan was simple. He would make his brothers

believe that only one of them could return to Canaan to bring Benjamin to Egypt. He would put them in prison. After they had spent three days in prison, he would change his demand so that all but one of them could return home to bring Benjamin to him.

In Genesis 38 we discussed the brothers' consciences. Even after twenty years, they recalled exactly what they had done and every word they had said. Joseph understood what they said to each other as they admitted their treatment of him. As second only to Pharaoh, he could have punished them without having to answer to anyone. We only have to consider the meaning of his new name to realise the retribution he could have inflicted on his wicked brothers.

Joseph had no intention of seeking revenge. He left the room and wept. We are not told what caused his sorrow, but he was a righteous man and he heard his unrighteous brothers talk about their wickedness. Not one of them was repentant. They were only concerned about retribution. Joseph's sorrow, and an absence of retribution, suggests to us that although he now possessed fame, fortune and power, Joseph:

'loved righteousness and hated wickedness.' Hebrews 1:9.

Those who live to please God do not change their spiritual values when their earthly circumstances change.

After three days in prison, as Joseph anticipated, his brothers agreed to his demand that Simeon stay. Simeon was the second eldest brother. Reuben, the eldest brother, had attempted to save Joseph from being killed. He was not chosen to stay. Maybe Joseph thought that his brothers would need him to organise the return journey home.

We note the brothers' surprise as they travelled home. They discovered the additional free grain and the money they paid for the grain. Once again they thought that God was punishing them for selling Joseph. When they arrived home, they told Jacob that Benjamin must travel to Egypt but did not confess to Jacob their fears that God was punishing them for selling Joseph. Jacob's concern was that of any father. He had lost Joseph, and Simeon was in prison in Egypt. To additionally lose Benjamin was unthinkable.

GENESIS CHAPTER 43

Now the famine was still severe in the land. (2) So when they had eaten all the grain they had brought from Egypt, their father said to them, "Go back and buy us a little more food." (3) But Judah said to him, "The man warned us solemnly, 'You will not see my face again unless your brother is with you.' (4) If you will send our brother along with us, we will go down and buy food for you. (5) But if you will not send him, we will not go down, because the man said to us, 'You will not see my face again unless your brother is with you.'" (6) Israel asked, "Why did you bring this trouble on me by telling the man you had another brother?" (7) They replied, "The man questioned us closely about ourselves and our family. 'Is your father still living?' he asked us. 'Do you have another brother?' We simply answered his questions. How were we to know he would say, 'Bring your brother down here'?" (8) Then Judah said to Israel his father, "Send the boy along with me and we will go at once, so that we and you and our children may live and not die. (9) I myself will guarantee his safety; you can hold me personally responsible for him. If I do not bring him back to you and set him here before you, I will bear the blame before you all my life. (10) As it is, if we had not delayed, we could have gone and returned twice." (11) Then their father Israel said to them, "If it must be, then do this: Put some of the best products of the land in your bags and take them down to the man as a gift—a little balm and a little honey, some spices and myrrh, some pistachio nuts and almonds. (12) Take double the amount of silver with you, for you must return the silver that was put back into the mouths of your sacks. Perhaps it was a mistake. (13) Take your brother also and go back to the man at once. (14) And may God Almighty grant you mercy before the man so that he will let your other brother and Benjamin come back with you. As for me, if I am bereaved, I am bereaved." (15) So the men took the gifts and double the amount of silver, and Benjamin also. They hurried down to Egypt and presented themselves to Joseph. (16) When Joseph saw Benjamin with them, he said to the steward of his house, "Take these men to my house, slaughter an animal and prepare a meal; they are to eat with me at noon." The man did as Joseph told him and took the men to Joseph's house. (18) Now the men were frightened when they were taken to his house. They thought, "We were brought here because of the silver that was put back into our sacks the first time. He wants to attack us and overpower us and seize us as slaves and take our donkeys." (19) So they went up to Joseph's steward and spoke to him at the entrance to the house. (20) "We beg your pardon, our lord," they said, "we came down here the first time to buy food. (21) But at the place where we stopped for the night we opened our sacks and each of us found his silver—the exact weight—in the mouth of his sack. So we have brought it back with us. (22) We have also brought additional silver with us to buy food. We don't know who put our silver in our sacks."(23) "It's all right," he said. "Don't be afraid. Your God, the God of your father, has given you treasure in your sacks; I received your silver." Then he brought Simeon out to them. (24) The steward took the men into Joseph's house, gave them water to wash their feet and provided fodder for their donkeys. (25) They prepared their gifts for Joseph's arrival at noon, because they had heard that they were to eat there. (26) When Joseph came home, they presented to him the gifts they had brought into the house, and they bowed down before him to the ground. (27) He asked them how they were, and then he said, "How is your aged father you told me about? Is he still living?" (28) They replied, "Your servant our father is still alive and well." And they bowed down, prostrating themselves before him. (29) As he looked about and saw his brother Benjamin, his own mother's son, he asked, "Is this your youngest brother, the one you told me about?" And he said, "God be gracious to you, my son."(30) Deeply moved at the sight of his brother, Joseph hurried out and looked for a place to weep. He went into his private room and wept there. (31) After he had washed his face, he came out and, controlling himself, said, "Serve the food." (32) They served him by himself, the brothers by themselves, and the Egyptians who ate with him by themselves, because Egyptians could not eat with Hebrews, for that is detestable to Egyptians. (33) The men had been seated before him in the order of their ages, from the firstborn to the youngest; and they looked at each other in astonishment. (34) When portions were served to them from Joseph's table, Benjamin's portion was five times as much as anyone else's. So they feasted and drank freely with him.

COMMENTARY. GENESIS CHAPTER 43

When they had no grain, Jacob had to change his mind about Benjamin going to Egypt. As they had not paid for the previous grain, Jacob sent Joseph the previous payment and a gift of the produce still available in Canaan.

We do not know how long elapsed between the two journeys to Egypt. Judah told Jacob they could have been there and back twice. We do not know if this was true or derisive, but both journeys were within two years of the famine.

The brothers were troubled when they had to visit Joseph's Palace. He intended to give them a free meal, but they thought he intended to make them slaves. They told the house manager of their surprise at finding their money when they were returning home from their last visit. The house manager said that Joseph had remained true to God. He had not worshipped the local gods or the sun god Re. This was the god worshipped by his Egyptian family. Simeon was reunited with his brothers. They were given water to wash their feet and their donkeys were fed. When Joseph arrived the brothers gave him the gifts. They all bowed to him. Joseph's first dream had come true.

Joseph immediately questioned them about their own health and that of their father and again they bowed to him. He spoke to Benjamin and then overcome with love and emotion he left them and wept in private. He regained his composure, returned, and ate with them. Read about the food, the wine, the table arrangements and the good-natured conversation.

GENESIS CHAPTER 44

Now Joseph gave these instructions to the steward of his house: "Fill the men's sacks with as much food as they can carry, and put each man's silver in the mouth of his sack. (2) Then put my cup, the silver one, in the mouth of the youngest one's sack, along with the silver for his grain." And he did as Joseph said. (3) As morning dawned, the men were sent on their way with their donkeys. (4) They had not gone far from the city when Joseph said to his steward, "Go after those men at once, and when you catch up with them, say to them, 'Why have you repaid good with evil? (5) Isn't this the cup my master drinks from and also uses for divination? This is a wicked thing you have done.'" (6) When he caught up with them, he repeated these words to them. (7) But they said to him, "Why does my lord say such things? Far be it from your servants to do anything like that! (8) We even brought back to you from the land of Canaan the silver we found inside the mouths of our sacks. So why would we steal silver or gold from your master's house? (9) If any of your servants is found to have it, he will die; and the rest of us will become my lord's slaves." (10) "Very well, then," he said, "let it be as you say. Whoever is found to have it will become my slave; the rest of you will be free from blame." (11) Each of them quickly lowered his sack to the ground and opened it. (12) Then the steward proceeded to search, beginning with the oldest and ending with the youngest. And the cup was found in Benjamin's sack. (13) At this, they tore their clothes. Then they all loaded their donkeys and returned to the city. (14) Joseph was still in the house when Judah and his brothers came in, and they threw themselves to the ground before him. (15) Joseph said to them, "What is this you have done? Don't you know that a man like me can find things out by divination?" (16) "What can we say to my lord?" Judah replied. "What can we say? How can we prove our innocence? God has uncovered your servants' guilt. We are now my lord's slaves—we ourselves and the one who was found to have the cup." (17) But Joseph said, "Far be it from me to do such a thing! Only the man who was found to have the cup will become my slave. The rest of you, go back to your father in peace." (18) Then Judah went up to him and said: "Pardon your servant, my lord, let me speak a word to my lord. Do not be angry with your servant, though you are equal to Pharaoh himself. (19) My lord asked his servants, 'Do you have a father or a brother?' (20) And we answered, 'We have an aged father, and there is a young son born to him in his old age. His brother is dead, and he is the only one of his mother's sons left, and his father loves him.' (21) "Then you said to your servants, 'Bring him down to me so I can see him for myself.' (22) And we said to my lord, 'The boy cannot leave his father; if he leaves him, his father will die.' (23) But you told your servants, 'Unless your youngest brother comes down with you, you will not see my face again.' (24) When we went back to your servant my father, we told him what my lord had said. (25) "Then our father said, 'Go back and buy a little more food.' (26) But we said, 'We cannot go down. Only if our youngest brother is with us will we go. We cannot see the man's face unless our youngest brother is with us.' (27) "Your servant my father said to us, 'You know that my wife bore me two sons. (28) One of them went away from me, and I said, "He has surely been torn to pieces." And I have not seen him since. (29) If you take this one from me too and harm comes to him, you will bring my gray head down to the grave in misery.' (30) "So now, if the boy is not with us when I go back to your servant my father, and if my father, whose life is closely bound up with the boy's life, (31) sees that the boy isn't there, he will die. Your servants will bring the gray head of our father down to the grave in sorrow. (32) Your servant guaranteed the boy's safety to my father. I said, 'If I do not bring him back to you, I will bear the blame before you, my father, all my life!' (33) "Now then, please let your servant remain here as my lord's slave in place of the boy, and let the boy return with his brothers. (34) How can I go back to my father if the boy is not with me? No! Do not let me see the misery that would come on my father."

COMMENTARY. GENESIS CHAPTER 44

Joseph gave orders that would cause problems for his brothers as they returned home. He had to ensure that they returned and so the cup was discovered in Benjamin's sack. Judah spoke to Joseph on behalf of the brothers. Judah had guaranteed the safety of Benjamin to Jacob, so he nominated himself as a slave in Benjamin's place. Read the discourse between Judah and Joseph.

Judah eloquently explained why the brothers could not return to their father without Benjamin. For a second time, Joseph was told the family's history. We do not know which brother spoke to Joseph previously. Maybe more than one did but Joseph knew that he was listening to lies when he was told by Judah that one of their brothers had died and he inferred that a wild animal killed him.

Maybe Judah was confusing the lie told to Joseph on their first visit with the lie told to Jacob some twenty years earlier. Experience teaches that liars have problems remembering exactly what they previously said.

We read in Genesis 42 that on their first visit, Joseph heard his brothers talking. They did not know that he understood every word. They admitted their wrongdoing and discussed why disposing of him had brought them problems.

Joseph had twice caused them problems. Was he waiting for them to stop telling lies, and confess their wrongdoing? Did he expect that Judah would be honest and state that their problems had arisen because of their mistreatment of their father's favourite son? We do not know. However, we do know that in all the years Jacob had suffered the loss of Joseph, not one of his brothers had confessed what they had done.

We shall consider what effect this had on Joseph in our next chapter. Fortunately for his brothers, Joseph loved them despite their callous and despicable sin:

- Joseph's love for his evil brothers is a wonderful picture of God's love for us.
- God loves us and wants to save us from His eternal judgment despite our sin that He detests.

God's Salvation is offered to all sinners, notwithstanding the degree of their sin. It is in language we can all understand. God does not require us to understand His thoughts, actions and reasons. We would never be able to. But we are all capable of understanding that we are sinners and obeying God's demands. We are all capable of:

- repenting of our sin and changing how we live so that we live to please God and not ourselves.
- accepting Jesus as our Saviour.

God does not distinguish between us. His eternal Salvation is available to all who repent and accept Jesus as their Saviour.

None are too bad that they cannot be saved and none are too good that they do not need to be saved. We ask questions:

- Has the truth of God's love for you ever thrilled you?
- Does reflecting on God's love for you bring you joy?

- Do you recall a time when you were filled with joy as you realised that:
  - Jesus was your Saviour and God had forgiven your sins?
  - You possessed God's eternal Salvation and Heaven was your eternal home?
- Did God's Salvation result in a lasting change in your attitude to sin and your lifestyle?

Only you know the answers to these soul-searching questions. Regrettably, experience teaches that so many unbelievers have been misled, or have misled themselves, into thinking that they are right with God and going to Heaven because they were baptised as infants, or are churchgoers, or do their best to keep The Ten Commandments.

The above three examples are just some of the reasons that fool unbelievers into thinking that they do not need to repent and accept Jesus as their Saviour because they are going to Heaven. Experience teaches that even Sunday School teachers have been surprised when they heard The Gospel for the first time and realised they were sinners who needed Jesus to save them from God's judgment for their sins.

Believer love each other because they belong to God's family. Joseph loved his family. Do you love God's family?

GENESIS CHAPTER 45

Then Joseph could no longer control himself before all his attendants, and he cried out, "Have everyone leave my presence!" So there was no one with Joseph when he made himself known to his brothers. (2) And he wept so loudly that the Egyptians heard him, and Pharaoh's household heard about it. (3) Joseph said to his brothers, "I am Joseph! Is my father still living?" But his brothers were not able to answer him, because they were terrified at his presence. (4) Then Joseph said to his brothers, "Come close to me." When they had done so, he said, "I am your brother Joseph, the one you sold into Egypt! (5) And now, do not be distressed and do not be angry with yourselves for selling me here, because it was to save lives that God sent me ahead of you. (6) For two years now there has been famine in the land, and for the next five years there will be no plowing and reaping. (7) But God sent me ahead of you to preserve for you a remnant on earth and to save your lives by a great deliverance. (8) "So then, it was not you who sent me here, but God. He made me father to Pharaoh, lord of his entire household and ruler of all Egypt. (9) Now hurry back to my father and say to him, 'This is what your son Joseph says: God has made me lord of all Egypt. Come down to me; don't delay. (10) You shall live in the region of Goshen and be near me—you, your children and grandchildren, your flocks and herds, and all you have. (11) I will provide for you there, because five years of famine are still to come. Otherwise you and your household and all who belong to you will become destitute.' (12) "You can see for yourselves, and so can my brother Benjamin, that it is really I who am speaking to you. (13) Tell my father about all the honor accorded me in Egypt and about everything you have seen. And bring my father down here quickly." (14) Then he threw his arms around his brother Benjamin and wept, and Benjamin embraced him, weeping. (15) And he kissed all his brothers and wept over them. Afterward his brothers talked with him. (16) When the news reached Pharaoh's palace that Joseph's brothers had come, Pharaoh and all his officials were pleased. (17) Pharaoh said to Joseph, "Tell your brothers, 'Do this: Load your animals and return to the land of Canaan, (18) and bring your father and your families back to me. I will give you the best of the land of Egypt and you can enjoy the fat of the land.' (19) "You are also directed to tell them, 'Do this: Take some carts from Egypt for your children and your wives, and get your father and come. (20) Never mind about your belongings, because the best of all Egypt will be yours.'" (21) So the sons of Israel did this. Joseph gave them carts, as Pharaoh had commanded, and he also gave them provisions for their journey. (22) To each of them he gave new clothing, but to Benjamin he gave three hundred shekels of silver and five sets of clothes. (23) And this is what he sent to his father: ten donkeys loaded with the best things of Egypt, and ten female donkeys loaded with grain and bread and other provisions for his journey. (24) Then he sent his brothers away, and as they were leaving he said to them, "Don't quarrel on the way!" (25) So they went up out of Egypt and came to their father Jacob in the land of Canaan. (26) They told him, "Joseph is still alive! In fact, he is ruler of all Egypt." Jacob was stunned; he did not believe them. (27) But when they told him everything Joseph had said to them, and when he saw the carts Joseph had sent to carry him back, the spirit of their father Jacob revived. (28) And Israel said, "I'm convinced! My son Joseph is still alive. I will go and see him before I die."

COMMENTARY. GENESIS CHAPTER 45

We will never know what Joseph had planned to do because he found it impossible to continue to pretend that he was aggrieved with his brothers. He disclosed to them who he was. You can read their reaction.

As we read the story of how Joseph and his family were reunited and reconciled, and why the Hebrews left Canaan to live in Egypt, we could so easily miss the important spiritual lessons that this chapter contains for us today. We mention these important matters later.

Those reading this chapter will be pleased that after over twenty years, Joseph was reunited with Benjamin and he would soon be reunited with his father, Jacob. If we had spoken to those involved, each would have had their own story to tell. Jacob and Benjamin did not know what Joseph's older brothers had done to him, whereas each one of them knew every detail of their wickedness. For the sake of space, we only consider the lessons that apply to Joseph's older brothers as Joseph's love for them is obvious throughout this chapter and it reminds us of God's love for sinners. We write this because Joseph's love was:

1. unconditional.

2. bestowed without limit.

3. totally undeserved.

Ponder on these three statements a moment. They describe God's love for us.

Whenever we have heard or read a story, there has been something within us that hopes there will be a happy ending. It pleases us that the hero triumphs over the villain and the villain is punished, or has an unpleasant end.

But, in the story of Joseph and his older brothers, the villains are forgiven, treated as though they had never sinned, and become richer than they ever imagined was possible.

This story of Joseph and his older brothers reminds us of:

- God's love for sinners.
- God's forgiveness for sinners who repent and accept Jesus as their Saviour.

The wonderful truth is that not one sinner ever deserved either God's love or His forgiveness. We both ask and answer three questions to make the story of Joseph and his older brothers pertinent to two matters that every reader should think about:

1. Jesus' death for our sins.

2. God's offer of Salvation.

Question 1. Did Joseph's brothers expect to be punished?

Answer: "Yes."

Question 2. Did Joseph's brothers deserve to be punished?

Answer: "Yes."

Question 3. What did Joseph's brothers receive from him?

Answer: Joseph's undeserved love and his total forgiveness.

Joseph could have ordered the execution of his older brothers. They deserved nothing less. But, he:

- dealt with them as if they had never sinned against him.
- gave them gifts.
- promised them a home where they would always have abundant supplies of everything they needed.

We have more questions for you to consider:

Questions: What must Joseph's evil brothers have thought when they knew that:

1) they had been forgiven?

2) their futures could not be better?

Consider your answers to these questions. It will prepare you to think about your answer to our next question:

Question: If you had been one of Joseph's evil brothers, what would you have said to Joseph for his love and forgiveness?

We have asked these questions to prepare you to carefully consider God's love, and the forgiveness He offers to those who repent and accept Jesus as their Saviour.

Joseph's forgiveness was amazing but, it was only human forgiveness. It ensured that his older brothers were not punished during his lifetime. But, if they were not also forgiven by God, they will forever suffer God's punishment for their sin.

God loves all His creatures, but their sin is first and foremost against Him and He detests it. The brothers sinned against God as well as Joseph and Jacob.

But there is Good News for every sinner. It is called, "The Gospel." It states that Jesus died for our sins. He was buried and resurrected. He finished the work that God had sent Him into the world to accomplish. He returned to Heaven and He now occupies God's Throne.

Genesis 45 has given us the opportunity of mentioning God's love and forgiveness by stating that the forgiveness of sins that God offers those who repent and receive Jesus as their Saviour enables God to regard them as never having sinned. God can regard them as righteous, 'right with Him.'

Paul wrote: 'Christ had no sin, but God made him become sin so that in Christ we could be right with God.'

2Corinthians 5:21.ERV.

We ask you a soul-searching question:

Question: Does God regard you as, 'right with Him?'

GENESIS CHAPTER 46

So Israel set out with all that was his, and when he reached Beersheba, he offered sacrifices to the God of his father Isaac. (2) And God spoke to Israel in a vision at night and said, "Jacob! Jacob!" "Here I am," he replied. (3) "I am God, the God of your father," he said. "Do not be afraid to go down to Egypt, for I will make you into a great nation there. (4) I will go down to Egypt with you, and I will surely bring you back again. And Joseph's own hand will close your eyes." (5) Then Jacob left Beersheba, and Israel's sons took their father Jacob and their children and their wives in the carts that Pharaoh had sent to transport him. (6) So Jacob and all his offspring went to Egypt, taking with them their livestock and the possessions they had acquired in Canaan. (7) Jacob brought with him to Egypt his sons and grandsons and his daughters and granddaughters—all his offspring. (8) These are the names of the sons of Israel (Jacob and his descendants) who went to Egypt: Reuben the firstborn of Jacob. (9) The sons of Reuben: Hanok, Pallu, Hezron and Karmi. (10) The sons of Simeon: Jemuel, Jamin, Ohad, Jakin, Zohar and Shaul the son of a Canaanite woman. (11) The sons of Levi: Gershon, Kohath and Merari. (12) The sons of Judah: Er, Onan, Shelah, Perez and Zerah (but Er and Onan had died in the land of Canaan). The sons of Perez: Hezron and Hamul. (Genesis 46:13) The sons of Issachar: Tola, Puah, Jashub and Shimron. (14) The sons of Zebulun: Sered, Elon and Jahleel. (15) These were the sons Leah bore to Jacob in Paddan Aram, besides his daughter Dinah. These sons and daughters of his were thirty-three in all. (16) The sons of Gad: Zephon, Haggi, Shuni, Ezbon, Eri, Arodi and Areli. (17) The sons of Asher: Imnah, Ishvah, Ishvi and Beriah. Their sister was Serah. The sons of Beriah: Heber and Malkiel. (18) These were the children born to Jacob by Zilpah, whom Laban had given to his daughter Leah—sixteen in all. (19) The sons of Jacob's wife Rachel: Joseph and Benjamin. (20) In Egypt, Manasseh and Ephraim were born to Joseph by Asenath daughter of Potiphera, priest of On. (21) The sons of Benjamin: Bela, Beker, Ashbel, Gera, Naaman, Ehi, Rosh, Muppim, Huppim and Ard. (22) These were the sons of Rachel who were born to Jacob—fourteen in all. (23) The son of Dan: Hushim. (24) The sons of Naphtali: Jahziel, Guni, Jezer and Shillem. (25) These were the sons born to Jacob by Bilhah, whom Laban had given to his daughter Rachel—seven in all. (26) All those who went to Egypt with Jacob—those who were his direct descendants, not counting his sons' wives—numbered sixty-six persons. (27) With the two sons who had been born to Joseph in Egypt, the members of Jacob's family, which went to Egypt, were seventy in all. (28) Now Jacob sent Judah ahead of him to Joseph to get directions to Goshen. When they arrived in the region of Goshen, (29) Joseph had his chariot made ready and went to Goshen to meet his father Israel. As soon as Joseph appeared before him, he threw his arms around his father and wept for a long time. (30) Israel said to Joseph, "Now I am ready to die, since I have seen for myself that you are still alive." (31) Then Joseph said to his brothers and to his father's household, "I will go up and speak to Pharaoh and will say to him, 'My brothers and my father's household, who were living in the land of Canaan, have come to me. (32) The men are shepherds; they tend livestock, and they have brought along their flocks and herds and everything they own.' (33) When Pharaoh calls you in and asks, 'What is your occupation?' (34) you should answer, 'Your servants have tended livestock from our boyhood on, just as our fathers did.' Then you will be allowed to settle in the region of Goshen, for all shepherds are detestable to the Egyptians."

COMMENTARY. GENESIS CHAPTER 46

We read in Genesis 35 that God changed Jacob's name to Israel and we read God's reasons for doing this. Genesis 46 uses both his names. He travelled to Egypt to be with Joseph and when he reached Beersheba, God spoke to him in a vision. God referred to him by his former name, Jacob. He made sacrifices to God. Since we learnt of the Covenant that God originally made with Abraham and then Isaac, Genesis has concentrated our thoughts on the lives of Isaac and Jacob. God dealt in a special way with all three. They each agreed the terms of God's Covenant. To inherit the land God promised them, their descendants had to abide by the terms of the Covenant, We considered this in detail in Genesis

It is so important that we realise that everyone must have their own experience of God. God dealt with Abraham, Isaac and Jacob. Although related, they each knew God individually.

God still forgives and saves us individually. God's Salvation is not inherited. Family connections will not save us. Jacob and Esau were Isaac's sons. We have read what happened to Esau. In Exodus, the next book of The Bible, we read that Esau's family were the enemies of God's peoples.

When we considered Abraham's life, we read about:

- the five altars he built in various places, the sacrifices he made to worship God, and the times he revisited those altars and worshipped again.

- God having to reassure him that He would fulfil His promises to him.
- the different ways that God spoke to him:
    - he had dreams.
    - God and two angels visited him.

If we compare Abraham with Isaac, we are told that Isaac only built two altars and sacrificed twice. God spoke to him twice, but we are not told how.

If we then compare Isaac with Jacob, Jacob only built one altar. It consisted of stone and later, a column of stones. Instead of sacrificing an animal, he poured oil over the stones. We read that God spoke to Jacob in his dreams.

These three men were grandfather, father and son but God dealt with them in different ways. What do we conclude from these differences? They illustrate a wonderful truth about a wonderful God. Put simply it is this:

- We are all different, even if closely related by birth, so God deals with each one of us as individuals.
- God cares about each one of us and He wants to be our personal God.

God promised to give His people Canaan. During famines, both Abraham and Isaac left Canaan to travel south for food.

- Abraham travelled to Egypt. We read about the problems he encountered in Genesis 12 and the following chapters that mention Lot.
- When Isaac planned to go as far south as Egypt, God warned him not to do so. Isaac obeyed and in Genesis 26 we noted that God confirmed the Covenant blessing to him.

Jacob must have known of these incidents as they involved his grandfather and father when they faced famines in Canaan and there was food in Egypt. To eliminate any doubts that

Jacob might have about going to Egypt, God told him that he should go there with his family. God also promised Him that:

- his family would become a great nation in Egypt.
- he would die in Egypt with Joseph at his side.
- He would be with him.
- his descendants would return to Canaan.

Jacob obeyed God and he and all his family took everything and went to live in Egypt. You can read the names of Jacob's descendants in the chapter. Jacob retained control. As they were on their way, Jacob told Judah to travel ahead to tell Joseph that they would soon arrive in Goshen. Pharaoh wanted to give Jacob's family the best land in Egypt. Joseph knew that unless they resided in Goshen, the Egyptians would hate them as they were shepherds. Only in Goshen were shepherds welcome. We will consider this subject again.

Joseph's wisdom regarding relationships and favouritism, and the consequences that ensue if we get these two matters wrong, is vital to our relationships and friendships today.

GENESIS CHAPTER 47

Joseph went and told Pharaoh, "My father and brothers, with their flocks and herds and everything they own, have come from the land of Canaan and are now in Goshen." (2) He chose five of his brothers and presented them before Pharaoh. (3) Pharaoh asked the brothers, "What is your occupation?" "Your servants are shepherds," they replied to Pharaoh, "just as our fathers were." (4) They also said to him, "We have come to live here for a while, because the famine is severe in Canaan and your servants' flocks have no pasture. So now, please let your servants settle in Goshen." (5) Pharaoh said to Joseph, "Your father and your brothers have come to you, (6) and the land of Egypt is before you; settle your father and your brothers in the best part of the land.

Let them live in Goshen. And if you know of any among them with special ability, put them in charge of my own livestock." (7) Then Joseph brought his father Jacob in and presented him before Pharaoh. After Jacob blessed Pharaoh, (8) Pharaoh asked him, "How old are you?" (9) And Jacob said to Pharaoh, "The years of my pilgrimage are a hundred and thirty. My years have been few and difficult, and they do not equal the years of the pilgrimage of my fathers." (10) Then Jacob blessed Pharaoh and went out from his presence. (11) So Joseph settled his father and his brothers in Egypt and gave them property in the best part of the land, the district of Rameses, as Pharaoh directed. (12) Joseph also provided his father and his brothers and all his father's household with food, according to the number of their children. (13) There was no food, however, in the whole region because the famine was severe; both Egypt and Canaan wasted away because of the famine. (14) Joseph collected all the money that was to be found in Egypt and Canaan in payment for the grain they were buying, and he brought it to Pharaoh's palace. (15) When the money of the people of Egypt and Canaan was gone, all Egypt came to Joseph and said, "Give us food. Why should we die before your eyes? Our money is all gone." (16) "Then bring your livestock," said Joseph. "I will sell you food in exchange for your livestock, since your money is gone."(17) So they brought their livestock to Joseph, and he gave them food in exchange for their horses, their sheep and goats, their cattle and donkeys. And he brought them through that year with food in exchange for all their livestock. (18) When that year was over, they came to him the following year and said, "We cannot hide from our lord the fact that since our money is gone and our livestock belongs to you, there is nothing left for our lord except our bodies and our land. (19) Why should we perish before your eyes—we and our land as well? Buy us and our land in exchange for food, and we with our land will be in bondage to Pharaoh. Give us seed so that we may live and not die, and that the land may not become desolate." (20)

So Joseph bought all the land in Egypt for Pharaoh. The Egyptians, one and all, sold their fields, because the famine was too severe for them. The land became Pharaoh's, (21) and Joseph reduced the people to servitude, from one end of Egypt to the other. (22) However, he did not buy the land of the priests, because they received a regular allotment from Pharaoh and had food enough from the allotment Pharaoh gave them. That is why they did not sell their land. (23) Joseph said to the people, "Now that I have bought you and your land today for Pharaoh, here is seed for you so you can plant the ground. (24) But when the crop comes in, give a fifth of it to Pharaoh. The other four-fifths you may keep as seed for the fields and as food for yourselves and your households and your children."(25) "You have saved our lives," they said. "May we find favor in the eyes of our lord; we will be in bondage to Pharaoh." (26) So Joseph established it as a law concerning land in Egypt—still in force today—that a fifth of the produce belongs to Pharaoh. It was only the land of the priests that did not become Pharaoh's. (27) Now the Israelites settled in Egypt in the region of Goshen. They acquired property there and were fruitful and increased greatly in number. (28) Jacob lived in Egypt seventeen years, and the years of his life were a hundred and forty-seven. (29) When the time drew near for Israel to die, he called for his son Joseph and said to him, "If I have found favor in your eyes, put your hand under my thigh and promise that you will show me kindness and faithfulness. Do not bury me in Egypt, (30) but when I rest with my fathers, carry me out of Egypt and bury me where they are buried." "I will do as you say," he said. (31) "Swear to me," he said. Then Joseph swore to him, and Israel worshiped as he leaned on the top of his staff.

COMMENTARY. GENESIS CHAPTER 47

Joseph told his family to tell Pharaoh they were shepherds so that they could dwell in Goshen. This is what happened:

- Joseph presented five of his brothers to Pharaoh. Pharaoh was pleased to let them live in Goshen and requested that they tend his flocks also.
- Joseph subsequently presented his father to Pharaoh and Jacob blessed Pharaoh.

Read the conversation between Jacob and Pharaoh. Jacob appeared to be unhappy. He had been preoccupied with thoughts of his own death for many years:

- At least twenty years earlier he referred to his imminent death when he was misled about the death of Joseph.
- He referred to his imminent death again when expressing his concerns about losing Benjamin.

When Pharaoh asked Jacob his age, he replied that he had lived for one hundred and thirty difficult and evil years and his fathers had lived much longer. No one would disagree that Jacob had lived a hard life, but though reunited with Joseph and about to have a better life in Egypt, he spoke as though he was about to die. He actually lived for another seventeen years as we shall read later.

We do not know how old Abraham or Isaac were when they died, but Jacob was correct. Genesis records that Abraham and Isaac lived to a good age. Jacob made Joseph promise to bury him in Canaan.

Joseph continued to administer the food supply during the famine. He supplied Jacob's large family with food according to their number. Pharaoh had put Joseph in a position of trust. Joseph was honest and wise, and he did not take advantage of his position, or give the Egyptians cause for complaint by showing favouritism to his own family in the allocation of food.

When Pharaoh appointed Joseph to be in charge, the Egyptians officials were pleased. We now read the views of the ordinary Egyptians who acknowledged that Joseph had saved their lives. When they could not afford to buy grain, they willingly became Pharaoh's servants. Without having to pay, they received grain to eat and sow on condition that one fifth of all their future produce belonged to Pharaoh.

Before we learn the spiritual lessons that Joseph's latest strategy teach us, we must consider the priests' land, and the Egyptians' beliefs. Joseph lived surrounded by idolaters:

- The Egyptians believed that Pharaoh was a god.
- Egypt's wise men practiced magic and sorcery.
- Joseph's father-in-law was a priest of the sun god Ra.

The Egyptian priests had a special status. Pharaoh, not Joseph, ensured they had grain. They did not pay for it and Pharaoh did not obtain any produce from them.

Question: How did Joseph behave in a totally idolatrous environment when the priests received free of charge what the ordinary people had to buy?

Answer: Our view is that Joseph did not interfere in the traditions that Pharaoh and the people obeyed. But he:

- said that whatever he did, his God would enable him to do it successfully.
- referred to his God whether or not it offended his hearers.

Consider Joseph's first conversation with Pharaoh in the presence of Pharaoh's wise men who thought Pharaoh was a god. Joseph said his God would interpret Pharaoh's dreams.

Joseph made this confident statement before he knew Pharaoh's dreams, and after being told by Pharaoh that none of his wise men could tell him what his dreams meant. Pharaoh must have been extremely impressed with Joseph's confidence in his God.

Can you imagine what Pharaoh's wise men, who had failed him on this occasion, thought when they listened to Joseph? They heard a thirty-year old Hebrew slave, a prisoner, confidently state that his God could do what the Egyptian gods could not do. Pharaoh's wise men must have thought that only a foolish man would enter the Palace and claim his God could do what they, with their combined supernatural and demonic powers, could not do. But, no one present could deny the result. Consequently, they acknowledged that Joseph was the wisest man in Egypt. We ask an important question.

What action did Joseph take when asked to assist those whose religious views and practices offended his God?

Answer Part 1. Joseph did not:

- start an argument to prove that his God was the true God.
- cause any embarrassment to the wise men as to their failure to interpret the dreams.

Answer Part 2. Joseph:

- proved by what he said that his God had warned Pharaoh of the famine.
- did not need to refer to the Egyptians' gods or to the wise men's powers. It was obvious that they had failed Pharaoh in a matter that was of momentous importance to the survival of the Egyptians.

Although Joseph was married into the family of the priest of the sun god Ra, nothing indicates that he did other than live to please God. He knew that he had a task to do for God in Egypt that would take him at least fourteen years. Joseph impressed the Egyptians. Whenever they saw him, they were reminded that it was his God that had saved their lives.

We read that when the people could not afford to buy grain, Joseph supplied it to them free of charge, but on condition that they became Pharaoh's servants and gave one fifth of all their future grain to Pharaoh. We ask a question:

What three truths about God's Salvation come to mind when we read about Joseph?

Answer:

1. Joseph was the Egyptians' saviour. He saved the Egyptians from death. Without grain they would have starved to death.
2. Only those who went to Joseph obtained the grain they needed to live.
3. When the Egyptians could not pay, subject to a complete life change, the grain was free.

It might be that only those who are saved, we refer to them as believers in this book, will understand our, 'Answer.'

So, for the benefit of those who we pray will soon be saved, we explain the above three statements:

1. Only Jesus can save sinners from God's eternal judgment for their sins. We quote Romans 6:23. Paul was comparing the difference between, 'death,' and 'everlasting life.'

   Romans 6:23. GW. 'The payment for sin is death, but the gift that God freely gives is everlasting life found in Christ Jesus our Lord.'

   So that God could offer Hell-deserving sinners His eternal Salvation, Jesus was punished and died for our sins. He was buried, but He rose from death. He returned to Heaven and He is now seated on God's Throne.

   He is able to save sinners who repent and ask Him to be their Saviour. If you are not yet saved, if you repent and ask Jesus to be your Saviour, He can save you now.

2. Only Joseph could supply grain. It could not be obtained from any other person or from any other source

   - Jesus is the only Saviour.
   - Those who seek God's Salvation elsewhere, or try to obtain it in other ways, will remain unsaved.
   - God's Salvation is offered to everyone, but it is only those who are willing to repent of their sins and accept

Jesus as their Saviour, who receive it.

- Many are deceived by what their religion teaches. Many deceive themselves.

3. Joseph supplied free grain to the Egyptians when they could not pay for it. But, to obtain the free grain, they had to change their status and become Pharaoh's slaves.

The Egyptians ability to pay money for the grain ceased. They had to give their livestock to Joseph in exchange for grain. Eventually, to avoid starvation, they gave their land to Pharaoh and agreed to be his slaves.

Read Genesis 47:15-25. Note the Egyptians' plight as their financial position got worse. We quote five extracts using the GOD'S WORD translation:

1. Genesis 47:15. 'When the money in Egypt and Canaan was gone …'
2. Genesis 47:16. 'Joseph replied, "'If you don't have any more money, give me your livestock …"'
3. Genesis 47:20. 'Joseph bought all the land in Egypt for Pharaoh …'
4. Genesis 47:23. 'Joseph said to the people, "'Now that I have bought you and your land for Pharaoh …"'
5. Genesis 47:25. '"You have saved our lives,"' they said. '"Please, sir, we are willing to be Pharaoh's slaves."'

The Egyptians knew that they had nothing to pay for the grain. They also knew that they could not have grain on their own terms. They had to comply with Joseph's rules or starve.

The Egyptians had a realistic attitude to their inability to obtain grain that can only be contrasted with peoples' attitude today.

Many today believe fictions about God and Heaven, and think that Heaven will be their eternal home when they die. For instance, many believe that they should be in Heaven when they die because they have lived good lives. They believe that their good deeds should please God.

But, their belief must be wrong if it contradicts what The Bible teaches about God's Salvation and Heaven.

We are not surprised about the various fictions that people believe to be true because not many know what The Bible actually teaches about a holy God who detests our sin, God's Salvation, and Heaven. So, we list the truths that experience teaches us people do not know and we quote the verses that state the truths. We use the ERV Bible as the translators have made the text as simple as possible so that no one should be in doubt as to what The Bible teaches:

The First Truth: We Cannot Ignore Our Sin.

Unless we have God's gift of eternal life we shall suffer eternal death. We quote Romans 6:23. It was written to those in Rome who had eternal life as they had received God's Salvation.

We ask you to study this verse. Pay special attention to the word, 'but.' It separates two groups of people. They are called:

1. 'people.'

2. 'his people.'

As we were all born into the first group, called 'people,' ask yourself if you are still in that group, or if you belong to God.

Romans 6:23. ERV. When people sin, they earn what sin pays—death. But God gives his people a free gift—eternal life in Christ Jesus our Lord.

The Second Truth: We Cannot Earn God's Salvation.

Salvation is God's gift to those who repent and accept Jesus as their Saviour. Ephesians 2:8-9 was written to those in Ephesus who had received God's gift of Salvation:

Ephesians 2:8-9. ERV. 'God saved you by his grace when you believed. And you can't take credit for this; it is a gift from

God. Salvation is not a reward for the good things we have done, so none of us can boast about it.' Ephesians 2:8-9.

The Third Truth: Beware of False Church Teaching

Regrettably, many so-called Christian churches teach that we, must, 'do things,' to ensure our place in Heaven. Some of these, 'things,' require us to obey the church's own customs and comply with its non-biblical rituals. Such teaching is wrong because what we do cannot impress God.

So that readers know the truth, we quote Isaiah 64:6. Isaiah's words might surprise those who want to do good to earn their place in Heaven:

Isaiah 64:6. ERV. 'We are all dirty with sin. Even our good works are not pure. They are like bloodstained rags …'

The Fourth Truth: A Change of Lifestyle is Required

Only a change of lifestyles will prove that a person possesses God's Salvation. It will be obvious that they have received God's gift of eternal life and their sinful life is behind them. Jesus provides us with proof of this fourth truth and yet, so few seem to be aware of His words.

Jesus was teaching in The Temple when the Jewish chief priests and leaders spoke to Him. The crystal clear TLB translation of Jesus' condemnatory words to these hypocrites will be well worth the time you spend studying them.

Matthew 21:32. TLB. '"… John the Baptist told you to repent and turn to God, and you wouldn't, while very evil men and prostitutes did. And even when you saw this happening, you refused to repent, and so you couldn't believe."'

We need to carefully consider what Jesus accused these men of doing and why, despite their religious titles and their clothes so that they would be distinguished in public, it summed up their spiritual condition.

This is the background to Jesus' condemnatory words:

John the Baptist and Jesus preached and baptised those who repented. We know from The Gospels what they preached:

<u>JOHN THE BAPTIST: We have edited Matthew 3:1-8. ERV</u>.

'John .... began telling people a message from God. "Change your hearts and lives .... People came to John .... They confessed the bad things they had done, and John baptized them .... Many Pharisees and Sadducees came to where John was baptizing people. When John saw them, he said, "You are all snakes! Who warned you to run from God's judgment ...? Change your hearts! And show by the way you live that you have changed."' Matthew 3:1-8. ERV.

<u>JESUS: We have edited Mark 1:14-15. ERV.</u>

'After John was put in prison, Jesus .... told people the Good News from God. He said, "... Change your hearts and lives, and believe the Good News!"' Mark 1:14-15. ERV

The Jews were left in no doubt as to what God's message was. John the Baptist and Jesus preached a message that required people to repent and both mentioned that a change of heart and lifestyle was required:

- John the Baptist preached: "Change your hearts! show by the way you live that you have changed."
- Jesus preached: "Change your hearts and lives ..."

Note what John the Baptist said to the Pharisees and the Sadducees who thought that they were religious:

'"You are all snakes! Who warned you to run from God's judgment ...? Change your hearts! And show by the way you live that you have changed."'

John the Baptist preached a wonderful explanation of what repentance means. We have a visual means of testing whether or not a person has repented. This is required because we cannot see whether or not there have been spiritual changes in the hearts of those who say they have repented. If we see no changes in their lifestyles, we know that there has not been a change in their hearts. They have deceived themselves, and those who have believed them.

Only in Matthew 21:32 do we learn about the very evil men and prostitutes who believed John the Baptist's Gospel message. Their lifestyles changed. It proved that their hearts had also changed. The chief priests and the Jewish leaders knew about this amazing change in the lifestyles of those they once ostracised and regarded as sinners because they lived such shameless, sinful lives.

These so-called religious men also knew that this change of lifestyle was the result of these, 'outcasts,' believing John the Baptist's preaching. So, did these self-opinionated, pompous hypocrites also believe The Gospel so that their hearts and lives would also change? Jesus bluntly said that they, "refused to repent," and in consequence, "they couldn't believe."

Heaven will be the eternal home of believers. What they did before being saved we will never know because they have all been cleansed by Jesus' blood shed on the cross. Because Jesus rose from the dead, all believers are regarded by God as, righteous, 'right with Him.'

Consider these verses that support what we have written. These words, quoted from the ERV, in 1John 1:5-10, Romans 4:24-25, and Romans 5: 8-11 were written to believers in Rome and elsewhere. We can assure you that time spent considering what John, one of Jesus' disciples, and Paul wrote will be time well spent:

JOHN 1:5-10. ERV. 'We heard the true teaching from God. Now we tell it to you: God is light, and in him there is no darkness. So if we say that we share in life with God, but we continue living in darkness, we are liars, who don't follow the truth. We should live in the light, where God is. If we live in the light, we have fellowship with each other, and the blood sacrifice of Jesus, God's Son, washes away every sin and makes us clean. If we say that we have no sin, we are fooling ourselves, and the truth is not in us. But if we confess our sins, God will forgive us. We can trust God to do this. He always does what is right. He will make us clean from all the wrong things we have done. If we say that we have not sinned, we are saying that God is a liar and that we don't accept his true teaching.' John 1:5-10. ERV.

ROMANS 4:24-25. ERV. 'God will also accept us because we believe. We believe in the one who raised Jesus our Lord from death. Jesus was handed over to die for our sins, and he was raised from death to make us right with God.'

ROMANS 5:8-11. ERV. '... Christ died for us while we were still sinners, and by this God showed how much he loves us. We have been made right with God by the blood sacrifice of Christ. So through Christ we will surely be saved from God's anger. I mean that while we were God's enemies, he made friends with us through his Son's death. And the fact that we are now God's friends makes it even more certain that he will save us through his Son's life. And not only will we be saved, but we also rejoice right now in what God has done for us through our Lord Jesus Christ. It is because of Jesus that we are now God's friends.'

Regrettably, it seems that the vast majority love their sin and sinning and do not repent. Experience teaches that most categorically refuse to listen to The Gospel. Of the few that do hear it, the majority are not willing to respond and repent.

We read that you could depend upon Joseph. He was always faithful. God also wants us to know that we can trust Him. He always does what is right. We quote 1John 1:9. ERV. again:

'But if we confess our sins, God will forgive us. We can trust God to do this. He always does what is right. He will make us clean from all the wrong things we have done.'1John 1:9 ERV.

We can depend on God for eternal Salvation. God will do exactly what He says He will do. That is true whether it applies to God's blessings or God's judgment.

Do you recall what the Egyptians said to Joseph?

""You have saved our lives,"' Genesis 47:25.

Joseph saved them from starving to death. When you consider what Jesus did for each one of us:

- Do you recall a time when you repented of your sin and asked Jesus to save you?
- Do you now regularly thank Jesus for saving you from God's judgment for your sin?

We conclude the chapter by noting that Jacob and his family were saved from starvation in Canaan. God's Plan required that His people leave Canaan to live in Egypt. God used Joseph so that what He planned came to fruition.

Despite his shameful treatment, Joseph remained faithful to God. Joseph used God's gift to him to interpret dreams. He always said that his God had given him the interpretation. Joseph could do what others who did not know his God could not do. In a country of idolaters and those who performed magic and the like, everyone Joseph came into contact with knew that his God had given him unique abilities.

GENESIS CHAPTER 48

Some time later Joseph was told, "Your father is ill." So he took his two sons Manasseh and Ephraim along with him. (2) When Jacob was told, "Your son Joseph has come to you," Israel rallied his strength and sat up on the bed. (3) Jacob said to Joseph, "God Almighty appeared to me at Luz in the land of Canaan, and there he blessed me (4) and said to me, 'I am going to make you fruitful and increase your numbers. I will make you a community of peoples, and I will give this land as an everlasting possession to your descendants after you.' (5) "Now then, your two sons born to you in Egypt before I came to you here will be reckoned as mine; Ephraim and Manasseh will be mine, just as Reuben and Simeon are mine. (6) Any children born to you after them will be yours; in the territory they inherit they will be reckoned under the names of their brothers. (7) As I was returning from Paddan, to my sorrow Rachel died in the land of Canaan while we were still on the way, a little distance from Ephrath. So I buried her there beside the road to Ephrath" (that is, Bethlehem). (8) When Israel saw the sons of Joseph, he asked, "Who are these?" (9) "They are the sons God has given me here," Joseph said to his father. Then Israel said, "Bring them to me so I may bless them." (10) Now Israel's eyes were failing because of old age, and he could hardly see. So Joseph brought his sons close to him, and his father kissed them and embraced them. (11) Israel said to Joseph, "I never expected to see your face again, and now God has allowed me to see your children too." (12) Then Joseph removed them from Israel's knees and bowed down with his face to the ground. (13) And Joseph took both of them, Ephraim on his right toward Israel's left hand and Manasseh on his left toward Israel's right hand and brought them close to him. (14) But Israel reached out his right hand and put it on Ephraim's head, though he was the younger, and crossing his arms, he put his left hand on Manasseh's head, even though Manasseh was the firstborn. (15) Then he blessed Joseph and said, "May the God before whom my father's Abraham and Isaac walked faithfully, the God who has been my shepherd all my life to this day, (16) the Angel who has delivered me from all harm —may he bless these boys. May they be called by my name and the names of my father's Abraham and Isaac, and may they increase greatly on the earth." (17) When Joseph saw his father placing his right hand on Ephraim's head he was displeased; so he took hold of his father's hand to move it from Ephraim's head to Manasseh's head. (18) Joseph said to him, "No, my father,

this one is the firstborn; put your right hand on his head."
(19) But his father refused and said, "I know, my son, I know.
He too will become a people, and he too will become great.
Nevertheless, his younger brother will be greater than he, and
his descendants will become a group of nations." (20) He
blessed them that day and said, "In your name will Israel
pronounce this blessing: 'May God make you like Ephraim and
Manasseh.'" So he put Ephraim ahead of Manasseh.
(21) Then Israel said to Joseph, "I am about to die, but God
will be with you and take you back to the land of your fathers.
(22) And to you I give one more ridge of land than to your
brothers, the ridge I took from the Amorites with my sword and
my bow."

COMMENTARY. GENESIS CHAPTER 48

Jacob often said he was about to die, but on the occasion we are now considering, he was about to die. Joseph visited him with his sons, Manasseh and Ephraim.

Joseph bowed low to his father. Jacob mentioned the time when God appeared to him and confirmed the Covenant blessing on him. Jacob decided he would treat Joseph's sons as his own sons. This meant they would inherit equally with Jacob's existing sons, but not inherit from Joseph.

You can read the terms that Jacob imposed on Joseph and his sons. When Jacob blessed the boys he crossed his arms so that Ephraim, the youngest, was blessed with his right hand. This was not what Joseph expected. He had placed the boys at Jacob's knees with the older boy Manasseh at his right knee so that he could be blessed with Jacob's right hand. Joseph protested at Jacob's wish to bless the younger son but Jacob, with his God given knowledge of the future, made it clear that Ephraim would be head of a greater nation than Manasseh, although both nations would be significant in size.

Jacob informed Joseph that the family would return to

Canaan, a place that he called, 'The land of your fathers.' That was what God had promised Jacob before he travelled to Egypt. Jacob promised Joseph that he would inherit the choice land of Shekem, a valley and mountainside in Canaan. Joseph was Jacob's second youngest son and he had ten older brothers. Why did Jacob give Joseph the best land?

Genesis 48:22 has been variously translated. Unless otherwise stated, we quote from the NIV. We now quote this verses in two other translations, the MSG and the NirV:

MSG: "'As for me, I'm presenting you, as the first among your brothers, the ridge of land …'" Genesis 48:22. MSG.

NirV: "'But you, Joseph, are over your brothers. So I'm giving you the range of hills …'" Genesis 48:22. NirV.

Hence, Genesis 48:22 could mean that Shekem was:

- worth twice the share given to each of the other brothers.
- given to Joseph because he was superior to his brothers.

We read that Jacob had thought about Joseph's two dreams. Joseph's brothers had all bowed to Joseph. This gift to Joseph reflected the meaning of those dreams and the incredible events that had happened since.

We cannot leave this chapter without considering Jacob's statement that he had fought the Amorites for the land he was giving Joseph. There is no record of that conflict in Genesis, but this is not surprising for, as we have noted many times, years have passed between incidents without any information being given to us as to what happened in the meantime.

GENESIS CHAPTER 49

Then Jacob called for his sons and said: "Gather around so I can tell you what will happen to you in days to come. (2) "Assemble and listen, sons of Jacob; listen to your father Israel. (3) "Reuben, you are my firstborn, my might, the first sign of my strength, excelling in honor, excelling in power. (4) Turbulent as the waters, you will no longer excel, for you went up onto your father's bed, onto my couch and defiled it. (5) "Simeon and Levi are brothers— their swords are weapons of violence. (6) Let me not enter their council, let me not join their assembly, for they have killed men in their anger and hamstrung oxen as they pleased. (7) Cursed be their anger, so fierce, and their fury, so cruel! I will scatter them in Jacob and disperse them in Israel. (8) "Judah, your brothers will praise you; your hand will be on the neck of your enemies; your father's sons will bow down to you. (9) You are a lion's cub, Judah; you return from the prey, my son. Like a lion he crouches and lies down, like a lioness—who dares to rouse him? (10) The scepter will not depart from Judah, nor the ruler's staff from between his feet, until he to whom it belongs shall come and the obedience of the nations shall be his. (11) He will tether his donkey to a vine, his colt to the choicest branch; he will wash his garments in wine, his robes in the blood of grapes. (12) His eyes will be darker than wine, his teeth whiter than milk. (13) "Zebulun will live by the seashore and become a haven for ships; his border will extend toward Sidon. (14) "Issachar is a rawboned donkey lying down among the sheep pens. (15) When he sees how good is his resting place and how pleasant is his land, he will bend his shoulder to the burden and submit to forced labor. (16) "Dan will provide justice for his people as one of the tribes of Israel. (17) Dan will be a snake by the roadside, a viper along the path, that bites the horse's heels so that its rider tumbles backward. (18) "I look for your deliverance, LORD. (19) "Gad will be attacked by a band of raiders, but he will attack them at their heels. (20) "Asher's food will be rich; he will provide delicacies fit for a king. (21) "Naphtali is a doe set free that bears beautiful fawns. (22) "Joseph is a fruitful vine, a fruitful vine near a spring, whose branches climb over a wall. (23) With bitterness archers attacked him; they shot at him with hostility. () But his bow remained steady, his strong arms stayed limber, because of the hand of the Mighty One of Jacob, because of the Shepherd, the Rock of Israel, (25) because of your father's God, who helps you, because of the Almighty, who blesses you with blessings of the skies above, blessings of the deep springs below, blessings of the breast and womb. (26) Your father's blessings are greater than the blessings of the ancient mountains, than the bounty of the age-old hills. Let all these rest on the head of Joseph, on the brow of the prince among his brothers. (27) "Benjamin is a ravenous wolf; in the morning he devours the prey, in the evening he divides the plunder." (28) All these are the twelve tribes of Israel, and this is what their father said to them when he blessed them, giving each the blessing appropriate to him. (29) Then he gave them these instructions: "I am about to be gathered to my people. Bury me with my fathers in the cave in the field of Ephron the Hittite, (30) the cave in the field of Machpelah, near Mamre in Canaan, which Abraham bought along with the field as a burial place from Ephron the Hittite. (31) There Abraham and his wife Sarah were buried, there Isaac and his wife Rebekah were buried, and there I buried Leah. (32) The field and the cave in it were bought from the Hittites." (33) When Jacob had finished giving instructions to his sons, he drew his feet up into the bed, breathed his last and was gathered to his people.

COMMENTARY. GENESIS CHAPTER 49

We must consider in detail what Jacob said to his sons as he was dying. He wanted to tell each son about their particular future, and it was not good news for some of them.

There is a good reason for considering what Jacob said. He was an important man in, 'God's Plan,' to have, 'His special people,' that worshipped only Him in a world populated by idolaters. Of the fifty chapters in Genesis, twenty-five relate to Jacob. His birth is recorded in Genesis 25, his funeral in Genesis 50. His life story in Genesis, is longer than any other person, including Isaac, his father, and Abraham, his grandfather. God had a special relationship with Abraham, Isaac and Jacob. God spoke to them in different ways and told them of future events, and the future of their descendants. God promised that their descendants would have their own land, then called Canaan, now Israel. God assisted them and their descendants in amazing ways.

Jacob was the last of the first three heads of the Jewish Nation. Jacob referred to Canaan as, 'the land of your fathers.' God told Jacob the future of the Jewish Nation, and when Jacob was dying, he passed this information to his sons.

In Genesis 32 we read about Jacob's conversion. God changed his name to Israel because Jacob ceased to be a cheat. Jacob became one who could triumph with God.

Instead of putting his own selfish interests first, Jacob was willing to be obedient to God's Will. His sins were forgiven. He had a new start with God. This is still available today to anyone who will repent and receive Jesus as their Saviour.

Note that when Jacob spoke to his sons, he referred to himself by both His old and his new names. We ask two questions:

1. Was this to remind his unconverted sons that they could have the same new start with God he had experienced?
2. Was it to reinforce the fact that what he was about to announce was, 'God's Plan,' and that his God had changed a deceitful man into a man He could trust to do His Will?

Answers: Both names are so linked with his conversion that both explanations are possible.

Read what Jacob said to each son. We might not understand exactly what he meant, but his sons would know. Sometimes, he referred to the past before mentioning the future:

REUBEN: Genesis discloses his adultery. Although he was the eldest son, Jacob no longer regarded him as the firstborn.

He ceased to be the most honoured son and lost his right to inherit everything that belonged to his father.

SIMEON AND LEVI: In Genesis 34 we read that after Jacob's daughter Dinah was raped in the city of Shechem in Canaan, her brothers, Simeon and Levi, 'attacked the unsuspecting city, killing every male.' Jacob said to them, "You have brought trouble on me by making me obnoxious to the Canaanites and Perizzites, the people living in this land. We are few in number, and if they join forces against me and attack me, I and my household will be destroyed." Simeon and Levi received nothing from Jacob.

JUDAH: Genesis 38 records in some detail a sinful period in his life after he left Jacob's home and married a Canaanite wife, contrary to God's Covenant with His people. But, after the birth of Tamar's twins we know nothing about him or his lifestyle until Jacob's sons travelled to Egypt to buy grain.

When they went a second time, Judah guaranteed Benjamin's safety to Jacob. However, when Judah was speaking about Jacob to Joseph, he lied and said that Benjamin's brother was dead. Like his brothers, he had deceived Jacob when they sold Joseph to Midianite traders but pretended that he had died. In his blessing, Jacob praised Judah.

In view of Jacob's remarks to his first three sons, and what we read about Judah, it comes as a surprise to read what Jacob said about him. We can only wonder if Jacob knew something that is not disclosed in Genesis.

Jacob knew that it was possible for sinners to have a new start with God. He had taken advantage of God's desire to forgive and bless him when he was fleeing from Esau who had murderous intentions. Jacob had deceived their father, Isaac, and acquired the inheritance Esau considered should have been his. We can only assume that, like Jacob, Judah had completely changed from his sinful way of life, and because he repented, God had forgiven him. This assumption, and it is only an assumption, is based on what Jacob said about him:

- Judah's brothers would praise him and bow down to him. Jacob seemed pleased that this would happen. In view of his remarks to his first three sons, would he have wanted good things to happen to Judah if he was still living the sinful life mentioned in Genesis?
- Jacob looked into the future and said that Judah would rule until, 'Another,' came, because the sceptre was intended for, and would be His. The One that Jacob referred to as, 'Another,' we now know to be The Lord Jesus Christ.

The subject of, 'The Coming Ruler,' begins in Genesis and is developed in The Old Testament. Jacob knew that a King was coming who would rule over his descendants and all the nations, and He would come from Judah's descendants.

ZEBULUN AND ISSACHAR: We know nothing about these two sons, apart from the part they played in the crime against Joseph. Jacob foretold good things for both of them.

DAN: Jacob did not refer to his past. He was to be either a judge or one who provided justice. The remaining words said to him are difficult to understand because although they give the initial impression of being derogatory, they could mean that he would unseat wrongdoers in his pursuit of justice.

Jacob had spoken to seven of his sons at this stage. Before he continued, we read in Genesis 49:18 that he said:

"'I look for your deliverance, LORD.'"

Whether what Jacob had said caused him to be troubled we do not know. From a human viewpoint, and keeping in mind that apart from Joseph, we do not know Jacob's sons' histories, if carrying out, 'God's Plan,' depended on some of his sons, then the future of his descendants, who were to become a large nation, looked bleak. However, God had made promises to Jacob about the nation's future and He knew that God would always do what He had promised.

GAD, ASHER, AND NAPHTALI: What Jacob said to these three sons was short but approving.

JOSEPH: We know from the previous chapter that Jacob had spoken privately to him and his sons. Now, with all his sons present, Jacob disclosed his opinion of Joseph. Read the praise that Jacob reserved for Joseph. We must state that Jacob's words are variously translated. We have already quoted his words from the NIV, and now quote them from three other translations:

1. AMP Classic: '"the one separated from his brethren and is prince among them."'
2. Darby: '"him that was separated from his brethren."'
3. TLB. '"Joseph who was exiled from his brothers."'

Hence, Jacob's words could mean that:

- Joseph was once separated from his brothers.
- Joseph was once separated from his brothers and he is still separated from them because he is their head or prince.
- Joseph was separated from his brothers because he was now their head or prince.

BENJAMIN: Jacob spoke well of him.

Jacob died after giving instructions for his burial in Canaan. He referred to deceased family members being buried in the cave that Abraham bought to bury Sarah. Genesis does not refer to the deaths of Rebekah and Leah but Jacob stated that they were buried in the same cave. Some might think that their deaths ought to be mentioned in Genesis because they were Jacob's wives, but Genesis is not a, 'history book.'

Importantly, Genesis discloses:

- the beginning of, 'God's Plan of Salvation,' for sinners.
- the consequences that ensued when various people either disobeyed God or failed to trust Him.

We must be content that God has told us in Genesis all that we need to know to realise that if we are:

- unbelievers who need our sins to be forgiven, we must accept God's Offer of Salvation, or suffer God's eternal judgment for our sins.
- if we are believers, we need to pursue God's Will for our lives. This will save us from the spiritual consequences of following our own initiatives.

We are either believers or unbelievers. As there is no third option, we would be wise to ensure that we are believers.

GENESIS CHAPTER 50

Joseph threw himself on his father and wept over him and kissed him. (2) Then Joseph directed the physicians in his service to embalm his father Israel. So the physicians embalmed him, (3) taking a full forty days, for that was the time required for embalming. And the Egyptians mourned for him seventy days. (4) When the days of mourning had passed, Joseph said to Pharaoh's court, "If I have found favor in your eyes, speak to Pharaoh for me. Tell him, (5) 'My father made me swear an oath and said, "I am about to die; bury me in the tomb I dug for myself in the land of Canaan." Now let me go up and bury my father; then I will return.'" (6) Pharaoh said, "Go up and bury your father, as he made you swear to do." (7) So Joseph went up to bury his father. All Pharaoh's officials accompanied him—the dignitaries of his court and all the dignitaries of Egypt— (8) besides all the members of Joseph's household and his brothers and those belonging to his father's household. Only their children and their flocks and herds were left in Goshen. (9) Chariots and horsemen also went up with him. It was a very large company. (10) When they reached the threshing floor of Atad, near the Jordan, they lamented loudly and bitterly; and there Joseph observed a seven-day period of mourning for his father. (11) When the

Canaanites who lived there saw the mourning at the threshing floor of Atad, they said, "The Egyptians are holding a solemn ceremony of mourning." That is why that place near the Jordan is called Abel Mizraim. (12) So Jacob's sons did as he had commanded them: (13) They carried him to the land of Canaan and buried him in the cave in the field of Machpelah, near Mamre, which Abraham had bought along with the field as a burial place from Ephron the Hittite. (14) After burying his father, Joseph returned to Egypt, together with his brothers and all the others who had gone with him to bury his father. (15) When Joseph's brothers saw that their father was dead, they said, "What if Joseph holds a grudge against us and pays us back for all the wrongs we did to him?" (16) So they sent word to Joseph, saying, "Your father left these instructions before he died: (17 'This is what you are to say to Joseph: I ask you to forgive your brothers the sins and the wrongs they committed in treating you so badly.' Now please forgive the sins of the servants of the God of your father." When their message came to him, Joseph wept. (18) His brothers then came and threw themselves down before him. "We are your slaves," they said. (19) But Joseph said to them, "Don't be afraid. Am I in the place of God? (20) You intended to harm me, but God intended it for good to accomplish what is now being done, the saving of many lives. (21) So then, don't be afraid. I will provide for you and your children." And he reassured them and spoke kindly to them. (22) Joseph stayed in Egypt, along with all his father's family. He lived a hundred and ten years (23) and saw the third generation of Ephraim's children. Also the children of Makir son of Manasseh were placed at birth on Joseph's knees. (24) Then Joseph said to his brothers, "I am about to die. But God will surely come to your aid and take you up out of this land to the land he promised on oath to Abraham, Isaac and Jacob." (25) And Joseph made the Israelites swear an oath and said, "God will surely come to your aid, and then you must carry my bones up from this place." (26) So Joseph died at the age of a hundred and ten. And after they embalmed him, he was placed in a coffin in Egypt.

COMMENTARY. GENESIS CHAPTER 50

Jacob died seventeen years after he came to Egypt and twelve years after the famine ended. As we read this last chapter of Genesis, we sense the respect that the Egyptians still had for Joseph and his family.

Not only do Jacob's family mourn, there are seventy days of national mourning in Egypt. This is amazing when you consider that before Jacob lived in Egypt, the Egyptians hated the Hebrews. We read that Joseph's brothers had to eat at separate tables when they first came to Egypt to buy grain.

We have details of Jacob's funeral, and the involvement of the Hebrews, the Egyptians and the Canaanites. The impact on the local people caused them to change the name of the place to mark the occasion that they saw the Egyptians mourning.

In the last chapter we read that Jacob died. We now read that Israel was buried. We have sought to emphasise that, like Jacob, everyone can have, 'A New Start with God.' God's Salvation is available to all, but it can only be possessed by those who repent and accept Jesus as their Saviour.

Proof that we have repented and possess God's Salvation is our changed lifestyle:

- 'A New Start with God,' is a visible change.
- Our old sinful life stops when our new start with God starts.

We read about Jacob and his new start with God:

- His name at birth was Jacob, an awful name meaning cheat, but it reflected his character as he grew to manhood.
- Jacob was converted and God changed his name to Israel. It meant that he had triumphed with God. His new name

reflected his new life. Israel was his name when he was buried. His descendants became known as the Israelites and today, Canaan is called Israel.

While Jacob was alive, Joseph's brothers thought they were safe from punishment for their crimes against Joseph. We read of their fears now that Jacob has died, and Joseph is the head of the family and the second-in-command in Egypt.

The brothers reverted to their scheming, lying and deceitful ways and Joseph wept as he considered their actions. They appeared before him and bowed. In their initial message to him, they claimed they were God's servants. Joseph was not fooled or misled. He knew that his brothers would have written any lie if they thought it would save them from punishment.

Genesis 50 concludes by telling us that Joseph enjoyed his grandchildren and his great grandchildren, and he died when he was one hundred and ten years old.

Unlike Joseph, who was mortal like us, God is eternal:

- We read about God's Creation of the heavens and the Earth in the first verses of Genesis.
- Then we read that God made Adam and God used Adam's rib to make a woman.
- God has always desired a personal relationship with men and women, but their sin means that there is a gulf between a holy God and His sinful creatures.
- God sent Jesus came into the world to save sinners. Jesus had no sin, but when He was crucified, God made Him become sin so that in Him we could be right with God.
- God wants to be our Heavenly Father, but this is only possible if we repent. We must have our sins forgiven if we want an eternal relationship with God.

Sadly, experience teaches that few are willing to repent and accept Jesus as their Saviour and consequently, God cannot bestow His eternal Salvation on the majority of His creatures.

But, the good news of The Gospel is that God will forever bless those who do repent, accept Jesus as their Saviour, and receive His eternal Salvation.

God has given everyone a freewill. If you are travelling with the multitude on the broad road the leads to God's eternal punishment, choose now to be one of the few who leave it to enter through the narrow gate so that they can travel on the narrow road that leads to eternal life.

ABOUT THE AUTHOR

The author was born in Prestbury, Cheshire, UK, during World War II. He has since lived in Greater Manchester, UK.

His parents both read and respected the Bible. They accepted it as God's Word. From childhood, he attended the local Gospel Hall Sunday School. He was taught stories and truths from The Bible. His childhood abilities to read and memorise, discuss, argue and debate with those of senior years, have enabled him to investigate, analyse and evaluate for himself what he has read and been taught. These skills were also invaluable to him in his career as a litigation lawyer.

When only a boy, he realised that what The Bible taught about sin was true. He accepted God's offer of Salvation. That was over sixty-five ago, but he remains convinced today that:

- The Bible is God's Word.
- All have sinned against God and He requires all to repent.
- Jesus died to save sinners. God's Salvation is offered to all who will repent and accept Jesus as their Saviour.
- The Gospel is God's, Good News,' for sinners. It has the inherent ability to change the lives of those who believe it.
- The Bible tells us in simple and unambiguous language how we can have, and know we have, God's Salvation.

God's Salvation is available to you and to everyone. The following two verses should be carefully considered by those who do not possess God's Salvation:

1. John 14:6. ERV. Jesus answered, "I am the way, the truth, and the life. The only way to the Father is through me.
2. Acts 4:12. ERV. Peter said: "Jesus is the only one who can save people. His name is the only power in the world that has been given to save anyone. We must be saved through him."

ACKNOWLEDGEMENT

These translations of The Bible have assisted the author.

- GOD'S WORD
- The Amplified Bible Series of Bibles
- The Darby Bible
- The Easy Read Version
- The Good News Bible
- The King James or Authorised Version
- The Living Bible
- The New International Version Series of Bibles
- The New Living Translation
- The Weymouth New Testament

These translations of The Bible, and others, are available from www.e-sword.net. The author is grateful to e-sword and the various publishers for the use of The Bibles on the website.

OTHER BOOKS BY THE AUTHOR

YOU ALSO WERE INCLUDED - EPHESIANS

Dr Derek Stringer, who before he retired was the National Director of Good News Broadcasting Association (UK) writes,

'Harold Booth's profession was that of a Lawyer. Without knowing this it would probably become apparent as you read his commentary of Paul's Epistle to the Ephesians. I have often found that commentaries are rather dull. Sometimes they seem to focus on detail (much of it not immediately relevant) and to miss the sweep of the biblical book and lose its excitement. This commentary draws upon many years of study and reflection on the eternal riches of the Gospel. This is revealed with encouragement and guidance to reach for and grasp our full spiritual potential. It shows what Christ made possible by introducing life-changing principles leading to a truly blessed life. The style is analytical and comprehensive leaving the reader in no doubt that there is a difference between a believer in Christ and an unbeliever and the consequences. It is a challenging presentation of the message of salvation. Reading this book gives insights into the Word, ourselves, and the Lord.'

IS YOUR NAME IN THE BOOK OF LIFE?

The author believes that The Book of Life has become a forgotten truth and he desires to make it a primary truth again. This book sets out to help people understand that their names could be written in Heaven and why without God's Salvation, their eternal future is bleak.

This down to earth book is written in a clear and direct style. It does not duck difficult issues. It would be a very useful tool to those who wish to live wisely and well in this life because their eternal future in Heaven is assured. It will also be of value to those who want to share their Christian faith but struggle to present the Gospel. This book examines:

- How Jesus dealt with those who believed that their lives were good enough for God and who thought that they had no need to repent.
- How that The Gospel requires 'repentance toward God and faith in our Lord Jesus Christ.' What repentance means. What distinguishes those who repent and believe The Gospel from those who do not? The Answer is a visible change in lifestyle and a changed attitude to sin.
- God's love for sinners, hatred of sin, and eternal judgment for those who do not repent and accept Jesus as Saviour.

THE WORD FROM JOHN

JOHN'S GOSPEL CHAPTERS 1-4

Dr Derek Stringer writes: The Gospel of John is one of the

greatest books of all time. We owe so much to the insights of John in giving us a clearer picture of Jesus Christ. It is no small accomplishment to present time-honoured truth in a fresh way. But this is what Harold Booth accomplishes with distinction. With a lucid style, Harold takes us into the opening chapters. There are no cliché bromides here, but rather rigorous Biblical truth presented with eyes wide open to contemporary life and practical application. Read it because it is worth it.'

PAUL'S LETTER TO THE ROMANS

A VERSE-BY-VERSE COMMENTARY

Paul wrote the majority of the letters in The New Testament, but he wrote his letter to the Romans in a legal style. You must therefore expect Paul to introduce facts and evidence and argue the case for the truth he presented. Paul used legal words such as case, judge, judgment, defence, proof, evidence, sentence and witnesses.

Those who read The Bible soon realise that it God's Word, and not an ordinary book. Those who never read it are the ones who criticise it. Some unwisely think that it contains myth and stories suitable only for children. The letter to the Romans was written by a lawyer. It would persuade anyone prepared to read it that no one need lower their intellect to find God's Truth. But there is more.

Paul's letter was intended to deal with the fundamental doctrines of The Christian Faith. They were under attack. Even the truths of The Gospel and Salvation were being challenged. So, if you are a believer in The Lord Jesus Christ, you can expect to read wonderful truths as to why:

- Jesus and He alone is able to be your Saviour,
- God is able to forgive your sin that He detests, and give you the eternal blessings He has prepared for you.

Those not yet believers will discover in Romans why they need God's Salvation and why only The Gospel can deal with the problem of sin.

THE ACTS OF THE APOSTLES

THE ONE AND ONLY CHURCH

Who would have guessed that from the small group who followed Jesus, a worldwide Church would have emerged?

Although so diverse, its members are all cleansed by the precious blood that Jesus shed when He suffered and died at Calvary for the sins of the world. They are forgiven because they have believed The Gospel, the good news from God that Christ died for our sins, was buried but came back to life. They have their own story to tell as to how they were saved but when they were, they were built into The Christian Church. It began at Pentecost when The Holy Spirit indwelt those who were saved.

Down the centuries for two thousand years, those who are saved have preached The Gospel so it would not be easy today to name places where The Gospel is unknown. As technology develops, broadcasts will reach wider areas and as people hear the Gospel, accept The Lord Jesus Christ as their Saviour and are saved, The Church will continue to grow.

This book looks at the early days of The Church. Every event is considered and any changes that took place are studied to see if there are lessons to be learnt.

This book considers if The Church that began two thousand years ago is relevant today and if it will survive.

GOOD NEWS
BROADCASTING ASSOCIATION

Good News Broadcasting Association

Tom Ward, Director of GNBA, informs us that it is a Christian charity that has been teaching The Bible through radio for over 60 years.

Tom said:

- We create and distribute a number of different programmes to challenge and encourage believers while also trying to engage non-Christians who are exploring faith.
- We broadcast on local and national Christian stations in the UK as well as in Indonesia, the Philippines and the southern regions of Africa.
- We also broadcast on secular radio as well.
- To find out more about what we do or to listen to any of our programmes, our website is www.gnba.net
- If you would like to join our mailing list or contribute to our work, please:
    - email: info@gnba.net
    - write: Good News Broadcasting, Unit 27, Wilsons Park, Monsall Road, Manchester, M40 8WN